The Seventh
Rhode Island Infantry
in the Civil War

ALSO BY ROBERT GRANDCHAMP
AND FROM McFARLAND

Colonel Edward E. Cross, New Hampshire Fighting Fifth: A Civil War Biography (2013)

"Rhody Redlegs": A History of the Providence Marine Corps of Artillery and the 103d Field Artillery, Rhode Island Army National Guard, 1801–2010 (2012)

The Boys of Adams' Battery G: The Civil War Through the Eyes of a Union Light Artillery Unit (2009)

The Seventh Rhode Island Infantry in the Civil War

Robert Grandchamp

McFarland & Company, Inc., Publishers
Jefferson, North Carolina

The present work is a reprint of the illustrated case bound edition of The Seventh Rhode Island Infantry in the Civil War, *first published in 2008 by McFarland.*

LIBRARY OF CONGRESS CATALOGUING-IN-PUBLICATION DATA

Grandchamp, Robert.
The seventh Rhode Island Infantry in the Civil War /
Robert Grandchamp.
p. cm.
Includes bibliographical references and index.

ISBN 978-0-7864-9552-8 (softcover : acid free paper) ∞
ISBN 978-1-4766-0827-3 (ebook)

1. United States. Army. Rhode Island Infantry Regiment, 7th (1862–1865) 2. Rhode Island — History — Civil War, 1861–1865 — Regimental histories. 3. United States — History — Civil War, 1861–1865 — Regimental histories. 4. Soldiers — Rhode Island — Registers. 5. Rhode Island — History — Civil War, 1861–1865 — Registers. 6. United States — History — Civil War, 1861–1865 — Registers. 7. United States. Army. Rhode Island Infantry Regiment, 7th (1862–1865) — Pictorial works. I. Title.
E528.57th .G73   2014   973.7'45 — dc22   2007047434

BRITISH LIBRARY CATALOGUING DATA ARE AVAILABLE

© 2008 Robert Grandchamp. All rights reserved

No part of this book may be reproduced or transmitted in any form or by any means, electronic or mechanical, including photocopying or recording, or by any information storage and retrieval system, without permission in writing from the publisher.

On the cover: The Seventh Rhode Island
Infantry's hospital staff (top) and flag

Manufactured in the United States of America

*McFarland & Company, Inc., Publishers
Box 611, Jefferson, North Carolina 28640
www.mcfarlandpub.com*

To Ms. Horlbogen for inspiring
me to dream and Captain DiMaria
for showing me the way

Acknowledgments

This book is the end result of five years of research into the Seventh Rhode Island Volunteers during the Civil War and after. In the course of the research, I have traveled to follow the path of the Seventh from Providence to Vicksburg, Kentucky, and Virginia. That the Rhode Islanders came from the smallest state in the Union was extremely beneficial in conducting research. The historical repositories of Providence are nearby, making the task easy to accomplish. In a sense this book was written by the veterans of the Seventh Rhode Island; through their words, I was merely able to retell a long forgotten story that occurred throughout the country. In the course of my work, I have met hundreds of individuals and organizations that have provided material, without which this project would never have been possible.

The majority of the research was conducted at the Rhode Island Historical Society in Providence. To all of their staff, I am especially grateful for putting up with my weekly visits and nonstop requests for material. In addition, the staffs at the Public Library and the Hay Library at Brown University provided significant access and insight into the material in their collection. At the North Scituate Public Library, Ivy Brunelle patiently put up with my months of nagging and copied 100 letters of William O. Harrington.

Katie McDonald contributed immensely through her cover illustration; "Our Seventh Rhode Island Banner" is absolutely stunning in its re-creation of the Seventh's United States colors. I am not an artist, and Katie's work is superb. To her a great debt is owed for reading and listening to my rantings and producing sketches of the battle maps. A special mention of thanks is given to Kris VanDenBossche. Without Kris, this book probably would never have been written. In 1993, he produced two small volumes of edited letters written by Rhode Island soldiers in the Civil War, *Pleas Excuse All Bad Writing* and *Write Soon and Give Me All the News*. No historian can write about Rhode Island during the Civil War era without these two volumes; here for the first time are the words of Rhode Islanders directly from the past. They provided an unparalleled view into the Seventh and the effect of the war at home, particularly in southern Rhode Island and Kris's village of Ashaway. His contributions through providing images and research tips have been invaluable.

Craig Anthony, registrar of the Pettaquamscutt Historical Society in South Kingstown, was an excellent guide into the villages and history of South County from our first meeting three years ago. Craig gave me copies of many letters in the collection and allowed unprecedented access into the artifacts of the society, allowing me to handle the relics carried home from the Civil War. In addition, the Pettaquamscutt Historical Society graciously provided images for this book.

At the Paine House of the Western Rhode Island Historical Society Luane McDonald and Morgan Bergstrom were my constant companions as we "dug" through mountains of material trying to find those precious gems of history.

At my school, Rhode Island College, Dr. Marlene Lopes, Special Collections Librarian, provided guidance into her vast and excellent, but underused, department that was a mine of material always at my fingertips. In addition, special thanks are given to the professors of the History Department at Rhode Island College who taught me how to write history: Dr. J. Stanley Lemons, Dr. Robert Cvornyeck, and Dr. Ron Dufour.

The staffs at the Newport Historical Society, Foster Preservation Society, United States Army Military Historical Institute, and Pawtuxet Valley Historical Society all furnished excellent material from the Seventh Rhode Island in their collections. Phil Laino produced the beautiful maps that accent the volume. Thanks are given to the men of the Kentish Guards for providing some valuable information on Company H. Cherry Bamberg of the Rhode Island Genealogical Society provided information on her relatives in the Seventh. The small Greene Library is a gem in the "wilds" of western Coventry. The volunteers answered the many questions I had of the local community, which still appears as if the men of the Seventh left yesterday.

At the Rhode Island State Archives, Ken Carlson has been a guide during my visits for the past five years, patiently answering my many questions, and he provided information into the inner workings of the Adjutant General's office in Providence during the Civil War. In Hopkinton, at the Langworthy Public Library the volunteer staff was especially helpful and courteous as I investigated Peleg Peckham's ranting. David and Frank Rathbun both provided invaluable material on their ancestors in Company H. Shirley Arnold warmly welcomed me into her home and shared her "heap" of Knight material.

On the battlefields of Virginia, Maryland, and Mississippi, the staffs at Antietam National Battlefield, Fredericksburg and Spotsylvania National Military Park, Vicksburg, Petersburg and Richmond National Battlefields provided guidance and access to the invaluable park libraries and gave information on the ground where the Seventh fought and died. Also of importance was finding the specific locations where the Seventh performed their deadly work.

Another large thanks is given to the "officers and men" of the Columbia Rifles. Composed of volunteers from throughout the United States, these men have taught me what it was like to be a Federal soldier in the Civil War. Civil War reenactors are often portrayed as dressing up in fake wool uniforms to shoot blanks at each other and to consume alcohol. These men are different. Through hundreds of hours of research, they have made the Civil War come to life. With them, I have learned what the Federal soldier thought and went through during the Civil War. In the Rifles, I have experienced the fatigues of marching, the wonders of hardtack, and other minute details of the daily life of the common Union volunteer. Without the experience, I would never have been able to convey the experience of being in combat during the Civil War; although I have never been under fire, the movements and experience are as close as one can get without being injured. A special thanks is given to Caleb Horton, Kevin O'Beirne, Tom Craig, "Grumpy Dave" Towson, Pete Smith, and Bill Backus for their efforts.

My mother Patricia Townsend Grandchamp and grandmother; Joyce Knight Townsend gave me the initial spark into local history and supported me every step of the way.

During the course of research, I traveled to every town hall, library, and cemetery in Rhode Island. To those who assisted in this work: thank you.

Table of Contents

Acknowledgments	vii
Preface	1
1. The Seventh Rhode Island	3
2. Forming	6
3. Washington	18
4. To the Front	28
5. Fredericksburg	34
6. Falmouth	50
7. River of Death	63
8. Kentucky	80
9. Return to Virginia	89
10. "If it takes all summer"	106
11. Closing the Gap	128
12. Fort Hell	140
13. The Final Charge	149
14. Afterwards	156
Appendix I: Casualties of the Seventh Rhode Island	167
Appendix II: Roll of Honor	169
Appendix III: Enlistments by Town	177
Notes	179
Bibliography	187
Index	191

"The chances of war have called us to weep over the graves of so many noble comrades, those that remain are true as steel, as has been proven on many a hard-fought field."

— Lieutenant Colonel Percy Daniels,
Seventh Rhode Island Volunteers,
June 30, 1864

Preface

We often dream of discovery in our lives, whether it is a foreign land or a treasure that brings glimmer to the eyes. For a small group of people, the discovery occurs daily. They sift through thousands of old and faded pieces of paper, trying in vain to decipher handwriting until it brings a story from the past. The discovery for me occurred on a cold, January day in 2000. Climbing into the never-visited attic at my grandmother's house we pulled an old World War II ammunition trunk down and brought it to the kitchen table. After removing years of dust from the chest, we began to carefully pull the documents out of the box. Slowly it began to paint a picture of the Knight family of Scituate, Rhode Island. Birth certificates, old photographs, and letters began to emerge. At the bottom of the box was a faded leather book, titled "Genealogy of the Potter Family." Carefully opening up the pages of the book, printed in 1876, I began to realize my family history dated to the *Mayflower* and, as my grandmother would say, "The Knights were planted here." Toward the end of the book was a rather long faded piece of paper. I glanced over it quickly, taking mental note of the beauty in a poem clearly written with much thought and care. When reading the title, I quickly realized why it was written: In remembrance of a member of the Knight family who did not return from the Civil War, Alfred Sheldon Knight.

After visiting his grave, I had much more to learn. Spending a small sum of money, I quickly ordered Alfred's service records from the National Archives. Each day after school was spent poring over my growing file of material. From the records I learned that he had enlisted in the fall of 1862 to serve for three years as a member of the Seventh Rhode Island Volunteers and died of pneumonia at a place called Falmouth, Virginia. As soon as this information was received, I filled out an application and was accepted as a member of the local chapter of the Sons of Union Veterans. I was assigned to a "camp" named after a man who was a recurring figure in the small pieces of information I had discovered on the Seventh Rhode Island: Zenas Randall Bliss. All I knew of him was that he was a West Point trained officer and led the regiment into near annihilation at the Battle of Fredericksburg. Each May, I learned that the men of Bliss Camp traveled throughout northern Rhode Island to flag and repair the gravesites of Civil War veterans. On my first visits to the cemeteries a shocking and recurring fact kept on coming through. There were dozens of men from the Seventh who, like Alfred Knight, died in the service of their country. After more digging, I realized that although Rhode Island sent 24,000 men to the Civil War, they were all but forgotten even though they fought and contributed greatly in all but three major campaigns.

As I entered college and began the transition from someone interested in the past to a trained historian, I searched for any material I could find on Rhode Island in the Civil War. Despite my daily searching throughout the state, I could find only one book written on the Seventh, and the last tome produced on Rhode Island was published in 1985. It became necessary to go to historical libraries and archives to find material. If none of the secondary sources could provide information on the Seventh's story, the letters, journals, and photographs did. Soon I had a closet full of copies related to the Seventh Rhode Island.

When other families went to Florida or camping for their summer vacations, mine always went to Pennsylvania, where our country was founded and saved. During all of these visits we would always go to Gettysburg, site of the bloodiest struggle in American history. The Civil War was always an event that fascinated me, but now with a personal link to the conflict, I became engrossed in its study. During the trips to the battlefield, I would always pester the store owners throughout town, "Do you have anything pertaining to Rhode Island?" The answer was always no. The years of research I conducted, and the general fact that there were no books in the market on Rhode Island, led me to write this monograph.

During their three years in service, the Seventh traveled from Providence to Mississippi, Kentucky, and Virginia. Although history is generally conducted reading long forgotten manuscripts to discover what occurred, it became necessary during the research phase to travel the same route of the Seventh and walk in its path. From busy highways in Spotsylvania County, Virginia, to small back-country dirt roads in Kentucky, I have stood where the Seventh did, to gain a better appreciation of the history they made. From Woonsocket in the North to Block Island in the South, from Foster to Little Compton, I have searched throughout Rhode Island and the country uncovering everything that could be found on the Seventh and the men who composed it.

The result is the present work, which will fill this critical gap in Civil War literature. Although thousands of books have been published on the Civil War, only a small number have been written by Rhode Islanders, all of them by veterans of the conflict.

"In the following pages, the reader will find a plain unvarnished narrative, truthfully told, on the everyday life of the soldier, on the march, in the camp and in the field, written from the standpoint of the private soldier who was an active daily participant in the scenes and struggles." So wrote Nathan B. Lewis in 1902, and so it is with this volume. All quotations are taken directly from the letters of the veterans and have not been altered in any way. For historical accuracy, the many spelling errors have not been corrected. Through these simple pieces of paper from the past, the veterans continue to speak.

The Seventh was both similar to and different from the 2,000 regiments that served during the war. They had their share of incompetent officers and miscreants. But the overwhelming majority were composed of volunteers, who, despite all of the death and carnage around them, remained in their place, when they could have turned and run. It is my earnest hope that this volume will further the public's knowledge of the past about a small group of men who "showed them what Rhode Island can do."

1

The Seventh Rhode Island

When the Seventh Regiment was at my heels, I felt myself a match for anything the Confederacy could produce.
— *Lieutenant Colonel George E. Church, September 11, 1902*

It was December 30, 1898, when an old man awoke and dressed himself in a house near Washington, D.C. Slipping on a coat, perhaps he noticed the two stars resting on his shoulders. This man wore the uniform of his country for nearly fifty years; it took forty years to attain the stars of a major general in the U.S. Army. Today this general, a tall heavy-set man with a thinning white moustache, would meet with President William McKinley to receive the United States' highest honor for military bravery: the Medal of Honor. Perhaps in his mind he remembered that cold, dark day in 1862. At 12:20 P.M. on the thirteenth of December he led his regiment into "a perfect volcanoe of flame." Seven hours later the command left the field of battle, minus 220 members of the regiment who had charged into the very jaws of hell. This man was Zenas Randall Bliss. In 1862 he molded 1,000 young Rhode Islanders into a combat force destined to "prove itself on many a hard fought field."[1]

During the Civil War, the regiment was the basic building block of the army. Comprising men from the same state, it contained ten companies each recruited from the same community. Fifteen regiments served from Rhode Island during the Civil War. These men fought and bled on battlefields from Maryland to Florida and from Virginia to Texas. From Bull Run to Appomattox and from Red River to Antietam, the Rhode Islanders were there. The Seventh was the sixth of nine infantry regiments to be raised in Rhode Island. None of these regiments traveled farther or sustained a loss greater than that suffered by the Seventh. They left the state 1,000 strong; one year later only 100 were left. When the Seventh was mustered out of service, they sustained an 80 percent casualty rate. The war had a dramatic impact on those who fought in it. Some rose to great prominence because of their actions while others came home to die of unspeakable diseases caused by unsanitary conditions. The events of this regiment tell a greater tale than just one of loss. It is a story of human survival, political injustice, and valor on the fields of Virginia, Kentucky, and Mississippi.[2]

The Seventh Rhode Island was raised following the desperate call for men to support the Union cause; the last of the three years' volunteers. Throughout the summer of 1862 they gath-

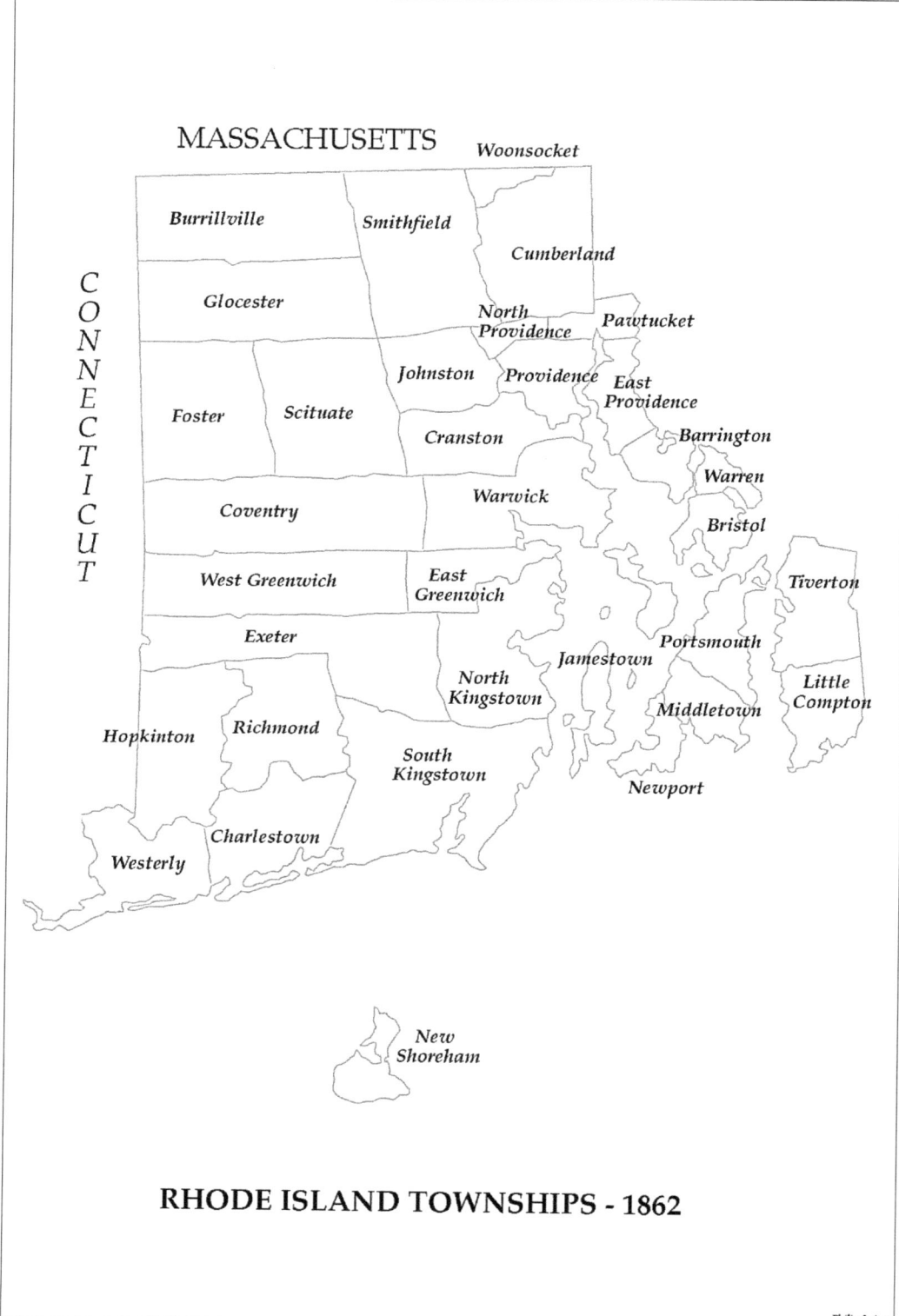

RHODE ISLAND TOWNSHIPS - 1862

ered in the capital of Providence, training and waiting for their time to come. On July 1, following the defeat of Union forces on the Virginia Peninsula, President Abraham Lincoln issued a call for 300,000 men to preserve the Union. From Woonsocket in the North to Westerly in the South, Rhode Islanders by the hundreds answered the call. The ten companies that composed the Seventh were raised from throughout the state. Arriving in Washington at the height of the national emergency they joined the Army of the Potomac. Here the Seventh Rhode Island was assigned to the Ninth Corps. These men traveled farther and saw more of the American continent than any other group of Federal soldiers. With their corps, they fought on from the bitter defeat at Fredericksburg to suffer from illness and privation in the swamps of Mississippi, and they experienced the horrors of combat on grand levels during the Overland Campaign.[3]

Millions of men served during the Civil War. Today they are often lumped together as "the common soldier." The truth is there was no common soldier. Each man brought to the unit his own story and life. Together through three years of war they banded together to form Rhode Island's Seventh Regiment, which in its time was considered to be an uncommon regiment; when other units broke and ran, the Seventh remained. One chronicler of the regiment recorded: "They were above the average in all that goes to make an ideal command — fearless, courageous, and determined."

The history of the Seventh Rhode Island is more than a narrative of combat and Civil War battles. It is a human interest story that transcends time; indeed, one can still experience the costs of the conflict in every small graveyard in Rhode Island. In 1903, William P. Hopkins, who served as a drummer in the regiment, set about to record the deeds of the Seventh Rhode Island for posterity. His resulting tome is considered by many to be among the finest of the hundreds of postwar regimental histories. Yet much history remains to be told. In 1939, Elisha Watson drew his last breath and with his passing went the last survivor of the regiment and the final living connection to the history accomplished by the Seventh. Since 1636, Rhode Island has had a proud historical legacy. Unfortunately few of her citizens know the contributions of this group of young men who left their homes in the fall of 1862 to preserve the country. None of these men could have imagined what the next three years of their lives bring. After the last musket was fired and the carnage had ended, many felt as though their sacrifice would always be remembered. Except for short sentences in scattered historical texts, the history of this regiment is largely forgotten. For 100 years, the story of the Seventh Rhode Island Volunteers has been lost to the ravages of time — until now.[4]

2

Forming

No better material was ever gathered than that composing it.
— Julia Emily Babbitt, 1890

The second summer of the Civil War arrived in the smallest state in the United States. For a year, Rhode Islanders were fighting in the war for the preservation of the Union. They were mostly young, between fifteen and thirty. Many found work as farmers, jewelers, mill workers, and fishermen. They came from villages with names such as Ashaway, Wilbur Hollow, and Woonsocket. They were all volunteers, compelled to enlist to prevent the further destruction of their country. The majority were native born while others came from Canada, England, and Ireland. In 1861 and the early months of 1862, they watched as their friends and neighbors returned home, some dead or maimed for life from places they had never heard of: Bull Run, Fort Pulaski, Hilton Head, New Berne, and Fort Macon. At each battle, Rhode Islanders contributed. At the start of the new year, 6,000 men were under arms in Virginia, North Carolina, South Carolina, and Georgia: Still more Rhode Islanders were needed.[1]

On May 22, 1862, Governor William Sprague issued General Orders Number Twenty-Seven for the recruiting of the Seventh Regiment of

Welcome B. Sayles supported the suffrage movement of Thomas W. Dorr in 1842.

Infantry to be raised in Rhode Island. On this day, Captain Chester T. Turner of the governor's staff opened up the first recruiting office in Providence. In the process Sprague began the complicated process of selecting the regimental officers and agents to travel throughout the communities of Rhode Island to enlist men in the regiment. During the Civil War, many of the initial appointments of officers went to those with political connections to the governor or had recruited the prerequisite number of men for a commission. Of the Seventh's original officers, only three captains and ten of the lieutenants had seen any service; few being in combat. This was a larger amount than any other Rhode Island regiment. When the First Rhode Island took the field, all of the officers were perfect amateurs. As the officer casualties began to mount, the

Governor William Sprague activated the Seventh Regiment.

veteran sergeants were promoted, thus creating a solid regimental structure.[2]

The first to be awarded was the lieutenant colonelcy. This was given to Welcome B. Sayles of Providence. He was fifty years old and possessed no prior military training. He was a powerful Democrat who owned and printed the *Providence Post*. In 1848, he lost his bid for Congress. Sayles was a supporter of the universal suffrage movement of Thomas Wilson Dorr in 1842. In an armed rebellion, Dorr attempted to expand the electorate in Rhode Island by giving the right to vote to those whom did not own property. Sayles supported the cause and served as Dorr's secretary of state for several weeks. The rebellion failed and Dorr was captured. Sayles went into hiding for three years while the situation calmed down, maintaining a secret correspondence with Dorr, who was convicted of treason and sent to prison. In addition to working as a printer, Sayles was also the Providence postmaster and was known throughout New England for his stamp-making abilities. His position insured Democratic Party support of the regiment. The new lieutenant colonel moved his headquarters to southern Providence and opened a camp for regimental headquarters.[3]

The Seventh was only created for several days when an emergency in Virginia disrupted the recruiting efforts. By May 25, Thomas J. Jackson and the Confederate army in the Shenandoah Valley had defeated every Federal force in their wake and were advancing in strength down the Shenandoah Valley in what was thought to be an attack upon Washington, D.C. At midnight on May 26, Governor Sprague received a communication from Secretary of War Edward Stanton to raise troops immediately to serve for three months in the defense of Washington. The next day, Sprague issued orders for the raising of the Ninth and Tenth Rhode Island Regiments, in addition to a battery of light artillery. The Ninth was composed of the militia companies in the state, including the Westerly Rifles, Natick Guards, and Pawtucket Light Infantry. Some of these men were veterans of the First Battle of Bull Run and all of the militia companies had contributed men to the other Rhode Island regiments. The Tenth was recruited almost entirely from Providence and was known as the National Guard. On May 28, the regiments left Rhode Island for Washington. Garrisoning the lines north of the city, the regiments set about to establish a camp and learn the military movements. Although nearly all of the men were trained in the use of their weapons, they did not possess military discipline, and the majority of its members were under twenty; many of the new soldiers in the Tenth were high school or Brown University students.[4]

Governor Sprague began the daunting task of finding a commander for the Seventh. The position had to be awarded to a man who was competent in military skills, and was politically neutral to all parties. Rhode Island was a small state with few skilled military leaders. The only West Pointers and Regular Army veterans were already engaged in the service, promoted, or dead. Ambrose Burnside, originally the colonel of the First Rhode Island, was now a major general, Frank Wheaton was the colonel of the Second Rhode Island, and John Stanton Slocum was dead, killed leading his men during the early stages of First Bull Run. The leaders of the Rhode Island Militia, like other senior officers, were already serving at the front; Isaac P. Rodman was now a general and William H. P. Steere a battle-hardened veteran led the Fourth Rhode Island. There was one remaining officer who fit all of the prerequisites. He was quiet, politically indifferent, and a native

A quiet West Point graduate, Colonel Zenas R. Bliss led the Seventh Rhode Island. Courtesy of the USAMHI.

Rhode Islander, an almost unassuming man with a black moustache. Militarily, he was a West Point graduate, a captain in the Regular Army, and saw nearly seven years of service in Texas. Most importantly he was available immediately to take command. This man was Zenas Randall Bliss.[5]

Bliss was born at Johnston, Rhode Island, in 1835. In 1850 he won an appointment to West Point, graduating near the bottom of his class in 1854. The following year he was commissioned a second lieutenant and was assigned to the Eighth United States Infantry, then stationed in Texas. Bliss settled into the service and was constantly engaged in skirmishes against the Comanche tribe in western Texas. He was promoted to first lieutenant in 1860. When Texas seceded from the Union in early 1861, General Daniel Twiggs, in command of the United States forces in the state, surrendered his command to the Texas government. At this time, the Eighth Infantry was garrisoned, ironically, at Fort Bliss, near the Mexican border. The Eighth attempted to reach the Texas coast to take a transport to the north. However, the aged commander, Lieutenant Colonel Isaac Reeve, led the regiment in an attempt to recapture San Antonio. Before leaving Fort Bliss, he had allowed each man to carry only ten rounds of ammunition. Discovering he was surrounded, Reeve dispatched Bliss to investigate the Texan defenses. Upon hearing Bliss's findings that the Texans were heavily armed and prepared for battle, Reeve surrendered without firing a shot. Bliss and his command were detained in Texas until February 1862, when he was transferred to a slave prison in Richmond, Virginia. While in captivity, he was promoted to captain. By March, all of the men had been exchanged. Bliss was among the last, being traded for a Confederate naval officer in late April. Upon his release, Captain Bliss proceeded immediately to Rhode Island.[6]

Bliss arrived in Rhode Island in mid May and returned to Johnston to be with his dying father. When the Tenth Rhode Island was raised, Governor Sprague immediately tendered the command, which was promptly accepted. Colonel Bliss remained in Rhode Island for several days to attend the funeral of his father. Upon his arrival at Camp Frieze, the regimental headquarters, Colonel Bliss began the process of transforming the young men into soldiers. He published a list of fourteen orders to guide the men. They were simple, mundane tasks that were vital for one to become a good soldier, such as how to properly salute an officer, how to appear, and the preparation of food. In less then a month the Tenth became well disciplined and ready for the front. However, the entire brigade remained in the Washington defenses. During their three months of service, the regiment's greatest achievement was the capture of a small Confederate cannon near Tennallytown, Maryland. In late June, Bliss and the Tenth finally received a major.[7]

Jacob Babbitt was a fifty-three-year-old banker from Bristol. Like Sayles, Babbitt was a lifelong Democrat, having attended several national conventions and served in the Rhode Island General Assembly. At the 1860 Democratic National Convention, he became disenchanted with the party and with Southerners. Prior to leaving the convention, Babbitt wrote that he "counted life not too dear a price to pay" if secession occurred. He was active in Bristol affairs, founding a new church, cemetery, yacht club, and fire company in the town. Babbitt was not just a politician; since 1833, he served as a major in the Rhode Island Militia. The position was a political appointment, but one Babbitt was well suited for. In 1826 he graduated from Norwich University, a private military college in Vermont. Babbitt was known for his ability to drill and was well liked by the men. He refused to accept any rank higher than major and went to Washington to take his place in the Tenth.[8]

The field officers of the Seventh consisted of a colonel, lieutenant colonel, major, adjutant, and an enlisted sergeant major. The adjutant was Charles Page; his duties were to maintain the regimental paperwork and to ensure the commander's orders were carried out. The medical staff consisted of a surgeon with the rank of major, two assistant surgeons ranking as lieutenants, a hospital steward, and several nurses detailed for the task. Supporting them was a chaplain, regimental quartermaster, quartermaster sergeant, and a drum major, in charge of the field musicians.

The Seventh was fortunate to have a competent medical staff to treat the stricken soldiers. James Harris was appointed as the surgeon and was well tasked for the duty. He was a Brown graduate and had received his medical training in New York. After his training, he volunteered as a surgeon during the Crimean War, learning firsthand the horrors of battlefield surgery. Returning to Rhode Island he was commissioned as the assistant surgeon of the First Rhode Island. At Bull Run he remained with his patients and was captured rather than abandon them. After being paroled he worked at Portsmouth Grove, a military hospital near Newport, before accepting the position of surgeon in the Seventh. Albert G. Sprague served as the first assistant surgeon. William Gaylord served for several months in 1862, but was replaced in early 1863 by Charles G. Corey. All of the Seventh's medical officers were older men who had spent years in the medical profession. Harris Howard was commissioned as the chaplain of the regiment. Originally named Harris Howard Tinker, he had dropped the last part of the name. He was an Episcopal minister by training and also worked in the hospital in preaching to the men. Some in the regiment complained that Howard always carted around enough baggage "to fill two mule carts." The hospital steward was Stephen F. Peckham, a chemist from Providence; his duties were to dispense the medicine and supervise the nurses and other hospital staff. Peckham was a Quaker by birth, one not used to joining the service. "I had no military ambition," he wrote. With these medical officers, the men of the Seventh would be well cared for.[9]

Jacob Babbitt refused any rank higher than major during the war.

With the regimental staff commissioned, the line officers

Surgeon James Harris (seated, center) served in the Crimean War and was captured at Bull Run instead of leaving his patients. Library of Congress.

began the process of recruiting agents to help them in their task of traveling throughout Rhode Island to enlist men; there was a bounty of three dollars to be awarded for each recruit raised. The initial volunteers for the regiment were those who lived in Providence and traveled the short distance from home to join. On June 1, William H. Barstow, a mason from Providence, was walking to work when he met a friend. The friend commented to Barstow, "let's enlist." One hour later, Barstow found himself a member of Company A. On July 1, 1862, following a series of bitter defeats on the Virginia Peninsula, President Abraham Lincoln issued a call for 300,000 men to serve for three years. Rhode Island was tasked with the raising of the Seventh, a regiment of cavalry, and a battery of light artillery. In addition, recruits continued to be collected for the Second Battalion of the Fifth Rhode Island Infantry. Governor Sprague began to issue quotas to the towns for their number of recruits, based on the town population. Calling for the 300,000 recruits was the spark that led men to enlist. There was a very real threat that the United States would be destroyed forever. Speaking at a ceremony in 1895, Augustus Woodbury, a veteran of the First Rhode Island, spoke as to why the Rhode Island soldier enlisted. He said: "It was from an overmastering sense of duty; it was from the impulse of the purest patriotism that this unparallel act proceeded."[10]

Scituate was typical of the towns of Rhode Island. It was a thriving industrial center, located seven miles west of Providence along the banks of the Ponagansett and Pawtuxet Rivers. Since the 1830s mills had cropped up along the rivers, and the town transformed from

The village of Ashland in southern Scituate was typical of the mill villages that the volunteers left from in the summer of 1862. Ashland was home to several men in Company K.

a quiet farming community to an economic center with large mills producing wool and cotton fabrics. Scituate's quota was sixty men. Unable to raise the number by the end of July, Scituate offered a bounty of 400 dollars to all who enlisted before August 18; by that date, Scituate's complement was full. In neighboring Foster, a rural community of dairy farmers and tradesmen, the money was direly needed. The railroad had recently arrived in nearby Greene and the farmers took their products to be carried to Providence, severely cutting into the small profits they earned. The farmers had long suffered from economic hardship and many took the opportunity to enlist in the Seventh. The quota was for twenty men; twenty-four natives of the town volunteered while others came from northern Rhode Island to enlist with their friends.[11]

Hopkinton was both similar to and different from Scituate and Foster. Composed of both farms and mill villages, the long, narrow strip of land that made up the town was incorporated in 1757. After the Industrial Revolution began, the citizens of Hopkinton were quick to establish mills along the Ashaway and Wood Rivers. Early settlers had brought a faith unique to this area. The Seventh-Day Baptists believed in holding their Sabbath on the Saturday, rather than Sunday. As such, entire villages shut down to honor the day, and the believers had two days of rest, as the mills remained closed on Sunday. In 1858, an academy was established in Ashaway offering various courses to the students. The majority of the older students enlisted in the fall of 1861 in the Fourth Rhode Island. Now in the summer of 1862, the remaining students of military age left to fight with the Seventh. Partially encouraging them was Joseph W. Morton, their principal and preacher who served as one of their officers.[12]

In each of the Rhode Island towns, the communities did their utmost to recruit. In late July and into August, the line officers began to travel throughout Rhode Island to enlist men. Though the towns did offer the large bounties, these men were all volunteers, not the conscripts who deserted by the thousands later in the war. The large bounties were needed to secure the finances of the families while they were at war; the private's pay was only thirteen dollars per month. In addition, the Seventh was their last opportunity to see something of the world, outside of their farms and small communities. Perhaps some of them who had thoughts of joining for the adventure of the fight read a letter Lieutenant Governor Samuel G. Arnold wrote in 1861 to the *Providence Journal*. Arnold wrote, "It is no holiday sport for which you have volunteered. A firm resolve on your part to submit to the most rigid discipline, without regard to personal comfort. Any one who hesitates to endure every hardship, to obey without question every order, to think of himself as part of the corps. Need not apply." The core of Providence men that were at the encampment in the summer of 1862 were transferred throughout the companies to bring each one up to 100 men. Though the recruiting of the companies in the same communities enabled the men to retain a semblance of home while they were campaigning, it also had a severe flaw; if one particular company suffered heavy casualties it could prove disastrous for the town.[13]

By the end of August, 800 men had assembled at the encampment, named Camp Bliss; recruits continued to pour in each day. On August 6, Colonel Bliss returned to Rhode Island to take command of the Seventh. After arrival at Camp Bliss, each man was assigned to a tent and after a thorough medical examination was issued a uniform. The first Rhode Islanders left for the front wearing an odd uniform of a pull-over blue shirt, gray trousers and a high felt hat. The Seventh was issued the standard uniform of the U.S. Army. It consisted of a pair of black leather shoes, sky-blue trousers, rough wool shirt, and a forage cap. The dress coat contained nine buttons, and was piped in a light blue cording, the color of the infantry. The uniforms were manufactured in Providence; a highlight of the Seventh's coats was an extra high collar, which extended to near the chin and caused much aggravation. The officers of the regiment wore similar uniforms, but of a higher grade fabric. In addition, the men were issued winter overcoats, wool and rubber blankets, and knapsacks, all equipment that was thought necessary to provide comfort in the field. Perhaps the most important piece of equipment issued was a simple tarred cotton bag known as the haversack. The bag hung on the right shoulder and carried food, along with cooking implements. Upon the issuing of the uniforms, many of the men went to the photograph studios on Westminster Street to have their image taken. Stephen Peckham was somewhat distressed upon his arrival at Camp Bliss on August 15: "I went down to Camp Bliss and found a regiment of men and their officers who generally speaking knew no more of military affairs than myself."[14]

Upon his return to Rhode Island, Colonel Bliss started a strict training regimen that would help transform his men into soldiers. The men were awakened at five each morning, followed by breakfast. Company drill was held from 9:00 to noon, when they broke for lunch. The battalion drill was held for three hours in the afternoon. Here each company came together to maneuver as one body under Colonel Bliss's command. Following supper and two roll calls, held between dress parade, the men finally retired to their tents with the sounding of taps at 9:30 at night.[15]

With the enlistments of the Ninth and Tenth Rhode Island set to expire on August 26, the War Department offered an incentive to the veterans. If they enlisted for three years in the Seventh, they would be discharged immediately to spend the remaining terms of their service at home before joining their new regiment. Major Babbitt talked to each man and encouraged him to do his duty in his country's hour of need. Upon learning that Babbitt would be their major again, seventy veterans of the Ninth and Tenth enlisted in the Seventh.[16]

With the regiment completed, Colonel Bliss and his officers again began the process of turning the volunteers into soldiers. Though a stickler for discipline, Colonel Bliss instilled a great sense of pride in his regiment. One soldier commented, "Perhaps the fact that the colonel of the regiment was a graduate of West Point and a captain in the Regular Army at the commencement of the war, contributed much to the high degree of discipline and soldierly bearing of the regiment." In only a few months he transformed 1,000 young Rhode Islanders into a combat force ready to become "a match for anything the Confederacy could produce." Steward Peckham was impressed with his first views of the colonel, claiming "He took excellent care of his men." On September 3, Colonel Bliss allowed the regiment twenty-four hours leave to visit their families or to complete their business before leaving for the front. Many of the men rushed to their homes to bid farewell to their loved ones; for some, it was the last time they would ever be seen. By September 4, all of the men had arrived at Camp Bliss. On this day, the officers of the regiment received their commissions and the noncommissioned officers were issued their warrants. Many of the sergeants were veterans of the Regular Army or the earlier Rhode Island regiments; one of them, Samuel F. Simpson, had served in the Mexican War with Thomas "Stonewall" Jackson. First Sergeant William H. Barstow was married at Camp Bliss by the regimental chaplain, Harris Howard. On the next day, all of the men returned and the regiment made plans for the front. On September 5, 1862, Robert E. Lee and the Army of Northern Virginia invaded the North and the Seventh received orders to leave immediately for Washington.[17]

The Seventh was composed of ten companies, each recruited in a separate Rhode Island community. Each was commanded by a captain, who had a first and second lieutenant to assist him. A first sergeant took care of the company paperwork while four sergeants helped to maintain the line during battle and to directly supervise the privates. The corporal was the leader among the men, supervising small details and serving as the living embodiment of the soldier in being clean, disciplined, and well drilled. Eight were assigned to each company, spread out in the front rank. Each company also had a wagoner to take care of the company baggage and two musicians, a fifer and drummer. The remainder of the company was composed of sixty to eighty privates, who were the cogs of the regiment that ensured the tasks were completed.

Company A of the Seventh Rhode Island was recruited from southwestern Rhode Island. The majority of its members were from the towns of Richmond and Hopkinton. Peleg Peckham was a carpenter from Charlestown who enlisted in the regiment and became the fourth sergeant. Tryphena Cundall was a widow, living in the village of Ashaway in Hopkinton. Cundall's son Edward was a member of the Westerly Rifles, then serving with the Ninth Rhode Island. In early August, Edward wrote to his brother Isaac not to enlist. He stated that Isaac would be unable to survive the rigors of the soldier's life. Isaac Cundall enlisted on August 5. Three brothers-in-law arrived from the village of Rockville: Abel B. Kenyon, Isaac Saunders, and Weeden Burdick. Their captain was Lewis Leavens, who owned and operated a mill in Rockville. Company A recruited above its required numbers and so ten men, including Kenyon, were transferred from Company A to Company K to complete its organization.[18]

Company B was recruited from Providence and contained some of the reenlisted veterans of the Tenth, in addition to those who had enlisted earlier in the summer. The men of Company B also had the most varied employment records of the men of the Seventh. First Sergeant Darius I. Cole was a veteran of five years in the Regular Army, having seen service in Utah with the Tenth United States. From its inception, Company B suffered from desertion.[19]

Companies C and D were both recruited from among the farmers and mill workers of northwestern Rhode Island. Company C primarily came from Glocester. Emor Young, a farmer from West Glocester left his wife and two sons to join the regiment. Alfred Sheldon Knight was a twenty-nine-year-old farmer who lived on his father's farm in southern Scituate. His physical description was typical of the Seventh volunteer. Knight stood five feet and ten inches, had hazel eyes and black hair. The Knight family was among the earliest settlers of Scituate and were respected members of their community. Knight was the seventh of fourteen children, all of whom were still alive. Although his family was wealthy, Knight was among those who felt an overwhelming sense of duty to enlist in the Seventh. Company D recruited from Burrillville and northern Rhode Island. Charles and William Hopkins were both musicians before enlisting, and joined as drummers. Prior to being commissioned into Company H as a lieutenant, George B. Inman had established a drill company in Pascoag, which met every week to train the local men in military discipline.[20]

In Company E marched men from northeastern Rhode Island, under the command of Captain Thomas F. Tobey. Tobey was previously the adjutant of the Tenth Rhode Island, and had escaped an overbearing father who did not permit him to enlist. Tobey was also good friends with John Hay, Abraham Lincoln's private secretary; both men had attended Brown University together. The first lieutenant was twenty-one-year-old Percy Daniels, described as "immature" by one Seventh soldier. Among the enlisted men was a French immigrant, Augustus Joyeaux, a veteran of the French army who had fought in Africa with the Zouaves. Joyeaux was known for his singing abilities. In addition, a large proportion of the men in Company E were of French-Canadian descent.[21]

Company F hailed from North Kingstown and Exeter. The commander was Captain Lyman Bennett, a veteran officer, who had served during the Harpers Ferry incident of 1859. In addition Bennett was known to Colonel Bliss, the two having served together in Texas. Corporal Nathan B. Lewis was a school teacher in addition to working at the post office in the rural village of Arcadia. Colonel Bliss noticed his skills by appointing him regimental postmaster. Captain Rowland G. Rodman recruited Company G from among the men remaining in South Kingstown; in 1861 the Narragansett Guards, the local militia company, formed Company E of the Second Rhode Island. These men became the first Federal forces engaged upon the field at the Battle of Bull Run. The majority of Captain Rod-

This unidentified private served in Company A. Courtesy of Kris VanDenBossche.

man's men were carders, spinners, and weavers who were employed in the Rodman family mills. The Rodman mills were beginning to feel the economic loss from the war; they had primarily produced cheap cotton cloth with which to make slave clothing. Unable to trade with the South, the mills were on the verge of being closed as they struggled to find a new market. Jared and John Potter were twin brothers and laborers from Richmond when they enlisted. Another member of Company G was Sergeant John K. Hull, an experienced school teacher at age twenty-one who abandoned his fifty dollar a month salary to gain seventeen dollars as a sergeant in the Seventh.[22]

The men of Company H styled themselves the Kentish Guards, a militia company in active service since the Revolutionary War, which saw men such as Nathanael Greene and James Mitchell Varnum upon its rolls. Composed of men from East Greenwich and Warwick, the company was commanded by Captain James Remington, a student from Warwick. He graduated as the valedictorian at Brown and gave the address in his captain's uniform, worn underneath his cap and gown. Remington was well known for his writing abilities and maintained records on many accounts. Company I was recruited in Bristol and Newport Counties. Peleg Jones left a lucrative career as a carpenter, in addition to his wife, two children, and mother. Many of the members of Company I were sailors or involved in the sea trades.[23]

Company K of the Seventh Rhode Island was recruited from Coventry, Foster, and Scituate. Like the majority of their comrades, many of the men in Company K were farmers or mill workers. One of the members was William O. Harrington, a thirty-two-year-old dairy farmer living in the small village of Moosup Valley in Foster. He left his wife Eunice and three children to join his friend George Potter in the regiment. As he left Rhode Island, Harrington's wife gave birth to his third son; Eunice Harrington would not name the infant until William decided upon a name. John F. Austin worked as a carder at the Ashland Manufacturing Company. Only twenty-one, Austin left his new bride Emily to join with his friend John Studley. From the time he left Scituate, Austin missed his wife immensely. Even the small hamlet of Hopkins Hollow, located in southwestern Coventry, consisting of a Baptist church, cemetery, and a dozen dairy farms, contributed four men to Company K. Captain George N. Durfee, the eighteen-year-old commander of the company, owed his position to his father, a former congressman. The men in this company left behind a close-knit community that would suffer severely in the years ahead.[24]

The Seventh Rhode Island Volunteers were mustered into United States service on September 6. On this day, the regiment drew their weaponry. The Seventh, like most other Rhode Island units, was armed with the .577-caliber Enfield rifle-musket, made in Britain. The Enfield was four and one half feet tall, and with a fixed bayonet was nearly as tall as some of the men in the regiment. The weapons were captured off the Massachusetts coast by the U.S. Navy from a Confederate blockade-runner and were forwarded to Rhode Island. In addition, the men were issued waist belts and cartridge boxes. The cartridge box was normally slung from the shoulder by a wide leather sling to support the weight of forty lead cartridges. The Seventh wore their box on the belt, along with a bayonet and a cap pouch, containing percussion caps to fire the musket. The belt buckles were a rather large, plain brass shield with the initials "US" upon them. On September 9, the men were paid the initial state bounties. In a tense moment, Major Jabez Knight called a volunteer forward to collect his thirty dollar state bonus. The clerk said that the man had already been called, which the soldier denied. Knight said, "I would rather lose thirty dollars then allow a soldier to." He later discovered that the clerk was wrong and all of the men received the state bounty. In order for the men to receive the town bounties, they had to send back a monthly certificate signed by an officer claiming that they were still in the service.[25]

On the morning of September 10, Colonel Bliss issued orders for the regiment to assemble and gather their possessions; the Seventh was leaving immediately. At noon, the men put on their equipment and assembled in a line four abreast and the men marched by companies to the Mashapaug Station. Unlike every other Rhode Island regiment which left for the front, the governor did not address them, the regiment did not parade, and, worst of all, no colors were presented to the Seventh. At 3:30, the Seventh Rhode Island was aboard the train of the Stonington Railroad taking them to Groton, Connecticut. Here they boarded the steamer *Commonwealth*. As the regiment departed, they suffered their first casualty. Private Isaac B. Manchester fell into the water and went into shock; he was discharged from the service but died in December from the injury. As the men sailed down Long Island Sound toward New York, the Rhode Islanders could only wonder what the next three years of their life would bring. For the Seventh Rhode Island, the journey had only just begun.[26]

An orphan from Woonsocket, Percy Daniels served as the first lieutenant of Company E. Courtesy of Kris VanDenBossche.

3

Washington

Yesterday thare were 15 thousand of us drilling together, I am on seacish soil.
— *Private Alfred Sheldon Knight, September 21, 1862*

The journey of the Seventh Rhode Island to Washington began after their departure onboard the *Commonwealth* on September 10. At New York, the regiment again boarded a steamer for South Amboy, New Jersey. Here the regiment again boarded a train, which delivered the Seventh to Philadelphia. As the Rhode Islanders marched into the city, the men broke into singing the new song, "We are coming Father Abraham, Three hundred thousand more." The tune was popular with the volunteers of the late summer of 1862 as they rushed into Maryland and Kentucky to stop the first Confederate invasion of the North. In Philadelphia, the Seventh was entertained at the Union Volunteer Saloon and Cooper Saloon. These were volunteer agencies that provided for the comforts of the soldiers as they left for the front. The regiment was able to partake of several types of food and received some stationary to write home. The Seventh left Providence with 960 men, and they were evenly divided between the two saloons.[1]

Leaving Philadelphia, the Seventh boarded one more train to Baltimore. Peleg Jones was surprised to see a brigade of Federal soldiers patrolling the tracks north of the city. Here the only incident of the journey occurred. Drummer William Hopkins fell from the top of the car and suffered some head trauma. In Baltimore, William O. Harrington met his brother Josiah, serving as a surgeon in the Eighteenth Connecticut. Before the war, Josiah Harrington attended medical school at Yale and moved to the nearby town of Sterling, Connecticut. Instead of enlisting in a Rhode Island unit, Lieutenant Harrington was commissioned into the Connecticut regiment. Though he never saw his brother again, the two maintained a correspondence through their letters. Baltimore was in a heightened state of alert, due to the Army of Northern Virginia's presence in western Maryland, but unlike the earlier riots of 1861, no violence occurred. In Baltimore, several members of Company D raised two dollars and sixty cents. The money was used to purchase a small American flag. After switching engines, the regiment finally arrived in Washington near midnight on September 13.[2]

Colonel Bliss left the regiment in command of Lieutenant Colonel Sayles while he traveled to the War Department for orders. One of his first actions was to order stationery with the

Seventh name and the U.S. Capitol upon it. These sheets were made available for the enlisted men to purchase through the regiment. The first impression registered by Corporal John F. Austin was to the nearly completed Capitol building looming in the distance. "We are campt at the capitol hill in sight of the capitol of Washington City the capitol is one of the handsomes buildings that i have ever saw." Upon viewing the hundreds of guns and forts ringing the city, Private Jones wrote, "Wash can never be taken." Some of the men arrived in Washington ill, among them Private Knight, whom "dronk too much water."[3]

Colonel Bliss returned with his orders to take the regiment across the river to Arlington Heights to continue with their training. Before moving, Colonel Bliss conducted one of the important tasks in the early history of the Seventh. As the officers were all commissioned on the same day, their seniority needed to be designated. The seniority of the captains also represented the designation of their company in line. The position of honor was thought to be on the right flank, with the second highest honor being on the left flank of the battalion. These companies were called flank companies and were often thrown forward as skirmishers or into other points of danger. Instead of assigning the companies in line, Colonel Bliss decided to use lots to designate the placement. Captain George E. Church, a civil engineer from Providence, drew the position of honor; his Company C was positioned on the right flank. Even when a captain left his company, the command remained in the place originally designated. From left to right, the ten companies of the Seventh were placed as B, A, D, H, E, I, F, K, G, C. During combat, the lieutenant colonel commanded the right five companies while the major commanded the left companies.[4]

During the late summer of 1862, Washington was full of Federal soldiers as they prepared to leave for the front as soon as they were trained. On September 15, the Confederates captured the Harpers Ferry garrison. On September 16, George B. McClellan and the Army of the Potomac prepared to engage the Army of Northern Virginia on the fields west of Antietam Creek, some sixty miles from Washington. The men listened to the cannonading in the distance, and could only imagine the horrors that accompanied it. On this day, Lieutenant Colonel Sayles received orders to take the first battalion of the Seventh and prepare to march. They crossed the Potomac into Alexandria, Virginia, and camped for the night. Private Knight wrote, "I am on seacish soil." The Battle of Antietam was fought on September 17, 1862. Despite 12,000 Union casualties, the battle was a clear Federal victory; Lee was defeated and turned back to Virginia. The battle had a large personal consequence for Captain Rowland G. Rodman in command of Company G. His brother, Brigadier General Isaac Peace Rodman, was mortally wounded as he attempted to rally his shattered division. The general was carried to a house in Hagerstown, Maryland. Colonel Bliss granted Captain Rodman a desperate leave of absence as he rushed to Hagerstown to console his family and be with his brother in his dying moments. General Rodman's body was returned to Rhode Island where he was buried in one of the most impressive funerals Rhode Island had ever seen. The captain returned to his company in October. On September 18, the first battalion was joined by Major Babbitt and the second battalion as the entire regiment moved to a new camp at Arlington Heights.[5]

The Seventh was assigned to Gabriel Paul's Brigade of Silas Casey's Division. Like the men under his command, Casey was a native Rhode Islander, West Point graduate, and a Mexican War veteran. In 1854, he translated a French drill manual. The tactics used by the U.S. Army at the time were little changed from those used during the American Revolution. Casey presented a much simpler manual that was easy for both volunteer officers and soldiers to learn. He split the manual into three parts. The first was called *School of the Soldier*, and it contained lessons for individual soldiers on the use of their rifle-musket, including over ten different ways to position the weapon and how to fire it. The second book, *School of the Company*, taught individual companies to maneuver on the field with movements such as "Company on the right by file into line" and how to establish a formation of skirmishers; the men formed a loose formation and fought in teams of two, using cover to engage the enemy. The company fought in a two-rank formation when advancing in line of battle. This line was broken down into a tight column of fours for quick maneuver on roads. *School of the Battalion* was the name of the third book. This book drew on the previously learned tactics to create new ones for the entire battalion to move as one on the field. The tactics that were studied included one known as "By companies into line." In this movement, each company of the battalion deployed from a column into a line of battle; the maneuver was often accomplished under fire. A testament to a regiments training was how quickly they could come onto the line and begin firing. The regimental officers and sergeants studied every night to learn the tactics and to properly teach them to the men. The Enfield rifle-musket required nine steps to load, including biting off a paper cartridge, ramming the ball down the barrel, and placing a percussion cap on the cone to fire the weapon. In a rather comical affair, one lieutenant gave the command, "Load in nine times, load." He then told the men to attempt the movement, as he did not know how to accomplish it.[6]

General Silas Casey was a native Rhode Islander who trained the volunteers rushing into Washington. Courtesy of the Library of Congress.

General Casey established Camp Casey to train the volunteers flooding into Washington. Using his tactics, Casey transformed the untrained volunteers into soldiers. Most of the regiments encamped near the Seventh were commanded by volunteer colonels who were not as schooled in the drill as Colonel Bliss. On September 19, the Seventh turned out for drill, but was returned to their quarters because they did not have any colors. Colonel Bliss secured Company D's flag. Sergeant Frederic Weigand nailed it to a rake handle and the small banner served as the regiment's colors. The men drilled constantly, preparing for service at the front. On one occasion, they remained at "present arms" for an hour. One soldier commented, "it is the hardest work I ever did." Colonel Bliss inspected the regiment almost constantly to

Opposite: A page from Casey's tactics, as learned by the Seventh.

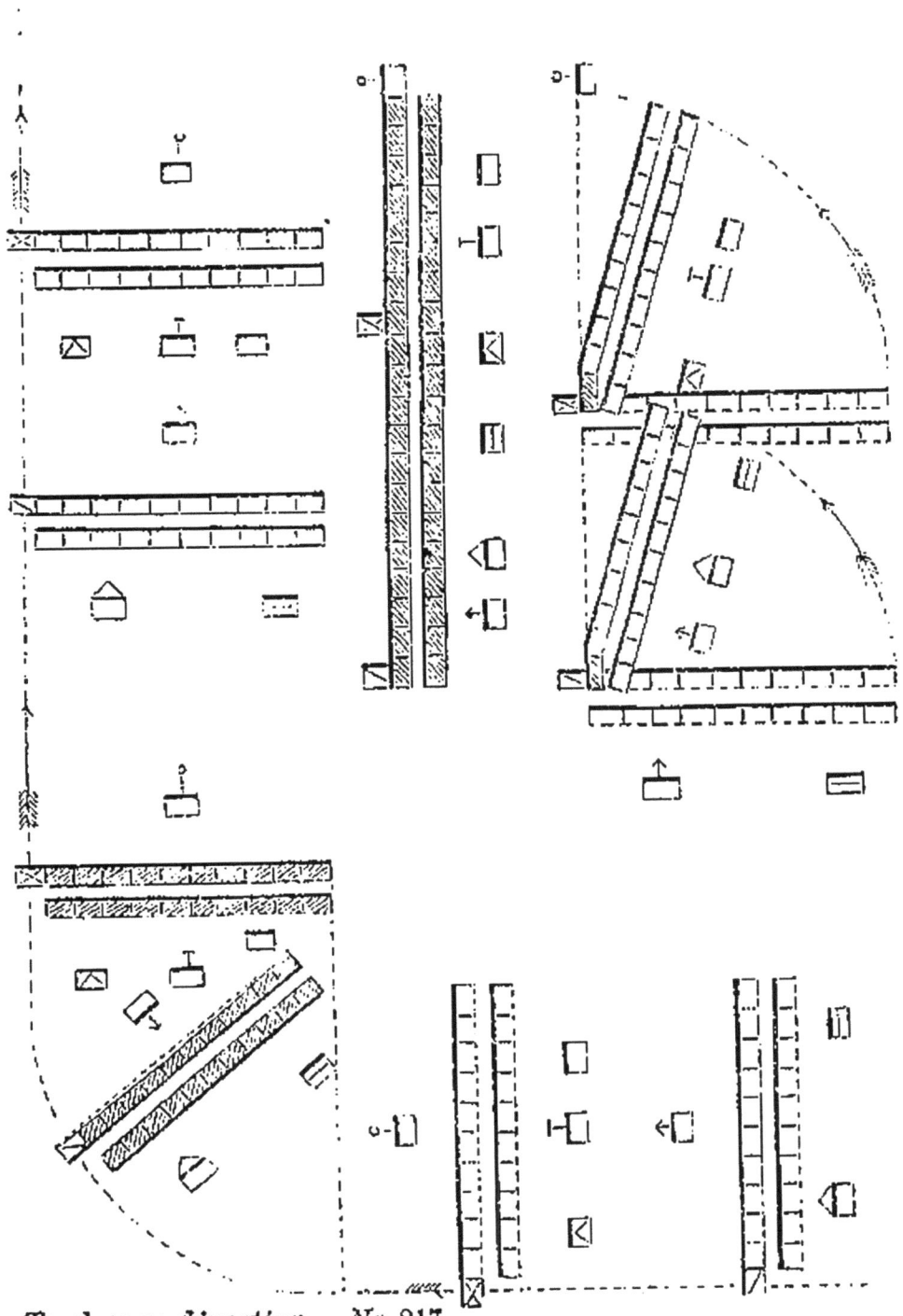

Left into line wheel.—No. 213.

To change direction.—No. 217.

To march in Column.—No. 202.

insure that the men performed to his orders. The time the regiment spent at Camp Casey was spent finishing the training that began in Providence; the Seventh learned how to become a regiment, but it had to wait for its baptism under fire. Sergeant John Hull wrote, "I suppose we shall not go into action unless we are forced into it, until we are drilled more."[7]

Colonel Bliss learned many valuable lessons during his training at West Point. Although he knew tactics and military theory, perhaps the most important lesson taught to him was that men were to be respected and, in return, they would show respect. These men were volunteers, not professional soldiers. Oftentimes the volunteers needed to be told why a certain maneuver was being called for or to what purpose polishing their boots served. Bliss was a patient man, who was liked by his officers and men. Like many of his contemporaries, Colonel Bliss was fond of whiskey. Stephen Peckham claimed that he only drank it at night, when all the tasks were accomplished, while remaining in "control." Bliss gave valuable lessons to his line officers, the majority of whom had never been in combat before. He taught these leaders that a commission from the governor did not make one an officer. His answer was "respect and obedience," which had to be given and earned. In several weeks at Camp Casey, the Seventh Rhode Island came together as a regiment. Through discipline and countless hours of drill the Rhode Islanders learned how to become soldiers while the officers learned their tasks. Like all units though, they awaited the ultimate test to see if the training had any effect.[8]

While the regiment was encamped at Arlington Heights, the men took note of their new surroundings and wrote home about them. All enjoyed their initial time at Washington, taking in the sights and watching President Lincoln as he reviewed the army. Battery E of the First Rhode Island Light Artillery was camped outside of the city, and many of the western Rhode Island soldiers took the opportunity to visit friends in the battery. While at Camp Casey, many of the men in the regiment saw blacks for the first time. These men brought eggs and baked goods to sell to the men of the Seventh, who used what little funds they had to help supplement their diets. Some of the officers of the regiment took the "contrabands" in their charge and used them as servants, paying them minimally for the services they rendered. Despite being in Washington for two weeks, some among the regiment were already ill. The only water available was located a mile from camp and was described as "poor." The water, coupled with the rations issued to the men, contributed greatly to the spread of disease. The rations of the Federal soldier were designed to simply keep the soldiers alive and often provided no nutrients. At Camp Casey, the food consisted of uncooked bacon, potatoes, white bread, and coffee. In later years, this was considered high fare for the enlisted men, but it was enjoyed by those eating it. In only a few short weeks, the men regretted the change in their diet as they moved into the field to experience hardtack for the first time. Typhoid and dysentery spread quickly. On September 26, Private Edwin Allen reported to his friend Edwin Greene in Hopkinton that Greene's brother Charles was ill from drinking the water. Also on this night, the band of the Eleventh New Hampshire serenaded Colonel Bliss. Lieutenant Colonel Sayles gave one of the fiery political orations for which he was known. As usual, Colonel Bliss did not speak, simply listening to the speech. Some thought they would remain in Washington all winter; however, as with most camp rumors, it proved to be false.[9]

On September 29, Colonel Bliss received orders to have his command ready for immediate service at the front. Many in the regiment wrote home to notify their families of the movement. Corporal Austin wrote, "we are ordered to march but we do not know wheare." Others believed they would be joining the Army of the Potomac, encamped in western Maryland. Colonel Bliss ordered the Seventh to leave their knapsacks behind, taking only rolled up blankets. The knapsacks followed the regiment on another train. The Seventh marched to the depot of the Baltimore and Ohio Railroad and prepared to take the train for the field. However, the train did not arrive until the next morning, forcing the men to spend a chilly night sleeping in the street. The morning of September 30, the regiment boarded an old, wornout locomotive to Baltimore. On October 1, the Seventh arrived in Frederick, Maryland; here the regiment remained for two days. At Frederick, several members of the regiment were sent to the hospital, deathly ill with typhoid fever. Sergeant Hull took the opportunity to explore the battlefield near South Mountain. On September 14, Federal troops had forced the Confederates from the passes of the Catoctin Mountains. He commented, "It was a sight to behold, the dead bodies were lying between the rocks." Captain Tobey and Company E became upset when the company was assigned to guard Chaplain Howard's baggage; the chaplain continued to reduce his load until he could fit it all on his person or horse. Also at Frederick, the Seventh was issued its first ammunition; sixty rounds of .58-caliber conical balls for use with their Enfields. On October 2, one of the strangest incidents to occur in the regiment happened. First Sergeant Henry Roberts was recognized by an officer of the Fifth Connecticut. Major George E. Rice told Colonel Bliss that the sergeant was in fact Corporal Edward Root. Root had deserted from the Fifth to avoid prosecution for a crime he did not commit. He traveled to Providence and enlisted in the Seventh. Roberts was discharged from the Seventh and returned to the Fifth Connecticut as Edward Root; he served honorably throughout the rest of the war.[10]

On October 3, the Seventh prepared to leave Frederick for Pleasant Valley, located south of Sharpsburg, Maryland. McClellan had brought the Army of the Potomac to this location following the Battle of Antietam. Lincoln pleaded with "Little Mac" to advance and finish his victory by defeating Lee. McClellan claimed his forces needed rest and could not be moved. On the third, the Seventh boarded flat cars to take them to Harpers Ferry. Taking all of their personal belongings and two days rations of hardtack, the train brought the regiment the short distance to the ferry. After a march, the Seventh camped near Sandy Hook, Maryland. Here Colonel Bliss set off to again find orders for his regiment. While at Sandy Hook, several members of the regiment began their search for additional rations. Although foraging was forbidden by army regulations, few commanders took any notice of the act. Corporal Austin and several men of Company K found some potatoes and fried them up to make "a good breakfast." In addition, the citizens sold the men peaches and biscuits for twenty-five cents per meal. The Seventh established their camp 200 feet above the Potomac River, overlooking the town of Harpers Ferry. From the heights above the town, the Rhode Islanders could look into the Shenandoah Valley and view the Allegheny Mountains in the distance. Stephen Peckham remembered, "The seane has longed in my memory ever since." On the fifth, two of the privates who had been sent to the hospital in Frederick died of typhoid fever. They included Private Charles Baker Greene of Company A. During the Civil War, it was the responsibility of the company commander to notify the next of kin of the soldier's death, in addition to forwarding home his personal effects. Private Edwin R. Allen wrote to Greene's family, "Charley is gone, it is sad to think that he was called far from home." On October 6, the regiment received a visit from President Lincoln as he reviewed the Army of the Potomac, while Colonel Bliss returned with the orders. The regiment marched the short distance to Pleasant Valley to join the Army of the Potomac. Colonel Bliss was to attach his command to the Ninth Corps.[11]

Major General Ambrose Burnside commanded the Ninth Corps. Burnside was a native of Indiana and an 1847 West Point graduate. Serving on the western frontier for several years, he came to Fort Adams, located in Newport Harbor. Here Burnside married into a prominent

Bristol family and began experimenting with a breech-loading cavalry carbine. Burnside resigned in 1853 and moved to nearby Bristol to build a factory to construct the weapon, named the Burnside. After the U.S. Army failed to purchase the firearm, Burnside became penniless and searched for work, eventually becoming a railroad executive under his old friend George B. McClellan. With the outbreak of the Civil War, Governor William Sprague tendered him the command of the First Rhode Island Infantry. Rushing to Washington on April 20, 1861, Burnside's men were among the first into the city and were known for their "businesslike" appearance. Commanding a brigade at Bull Run, his men performed credibly, becoming the first Federal infantry engaged on the field near Matthew's Hill. He was commissioned a brigadier general on August 6, 1861, and soon set in motion a plan to win the North Carolina coastline back for the Union. McClellan gave him command of a division of his choice and many of Burnside's men were from New England and included the Fourth and Fifth Rhode Island Regiments. Landing at Roanoke Island in February, the division performed well. By April, the city of New Berne and Fort Macon were in Federal hands and Burnside was commissioned a major general for his actions. He was given command of a corps, from the forces in North Carolina and South Carolina. Marching north in August, they fought at Second Bull Run, South Mountain, and Antietam.[12]

A farmer from Hopkinton, Private Charles B. Greene was the first death the Seventh suffered in the field. Courtesy of Kris VanDenBossche.

Burnside assigned the Seventh to the First Brigade, Second Division of his corps. The Second Division was commanded by Samuel Sturgis, recently given a field command, after serving in the Washington defenses. Brigadier General James Nagle, a veteran from Pennsylvania commanded the First Brigade. His brigade consisted of the Sixth and Ninth New Hampshire, Forty-Eighth Pennsylvania, and Second Maryland. The Sixth and Forty-Eighth had fought in North Carolina, while all of the regiments, except the Ninth, had suffered severe losses at Second Bull Run. The Ninth New Hampshire was transferred to make up for these losses in early September. Still more men were lost at South Mountain and during the storming of the Rohrbach Bridge at Antietam. The Seventh Rhode Island was assigned to the brigade because of the additional losses. In addition, the Eleventh New Hampshire and Thirty-Fifth Massachusetts were joined to the Second Brigade.[13] As the men began to adapt to life in the field, some in the regiment began to grumble about the lack of supplies; Sergeant Hull watched as his shoes wore down each day. Finally on October 16, each man was given an additional pair of shoes. In addition the men waited for the paymaster to visit them once more. Those given a town bounty were required to send a certificate home each month, signed by an officer attesting that they were still in the service. William O. Harrington mailed one every week to his wife Eunice, who failed to receive them. Corporal Austin continued to miss his wife, while wanting to fight a battle "to force the thing to a close." The men also engaged in their first opportunities at picket duty. Each night, the men assembled in a guard under the command of an officer and marched one to three miles from camp. Here each private was assigned to a certain "beat" under

A Rhode Islander by adoption, Major General Ambrose Burnside commanded the Ninth Corps.

the command of a corporal. When the sentinel heard an approaching sound he was to call out for the person to advance and report if he was a friend or foe. If a friend, the person was allowed to pass, if it was an enemy, the soldier fired his weapon and called out the guard. One night, Major Babbitt was inspecting the lines when he fell into a hole, yelling out, "The Devil." The picket gave the standard reply, "Advance the Devil and Give the Countersign."[14]

The knapsacks finally arrived, and the men were able to live in some comfort; though they wrote home continuously asking for warm clothing and food items. In the village of Moosup Valley, the local women pitched in to send a box to William O. Harrington and George Potter. On October 17, the regiment was issued shelter tents. These were small tents based upon a French design. Each man carried a half of the tent and buttoned the two sides together to make a suitable shelter. Although it would not offer protection in a severe storm, it helped to shelter the soldiers from the elements and reduced the baggage train; only field officers were allowed tentage. The soldiers did not carry candlesticks; instead, they used their bayonet shank to hold the candle. One night, Private William C. Durfee was reading by this manner when his open candle destroyed the tent and badly singed his hair. The veterans in the other regiments visited the Seventh to teach them how to set up the tents and to tell them stories of soldiering.[15]

The Seventh was only at Pleasant Valley for a week and a half when death again struck the regiment. On October 18, Private George W. Gardiner died of pneumonia; he was followed on the 19th by Gideon F. Collins, whom died of typhoid fever, which he contracted at Washington. Both men were from Company A and resided in Hopkinton. These were the first two deaths in the regimental hospital, and severely shook the men as they came to see the realities of soldiering. The men of Company A decided on a military funeral for October 20. The procession started as the band of the Ninth New Hampshire played "The Shining Shore." Eighteen members of Company A marched with reversed arms as a symbol of mourning, followed by the remains of Collins and Gardiner, the remainder of Company A, and the entire regiment. Chaplain Howard read from the book of Jacob as Company A fired three volleys over the graves of their comrades. Corporal Charles P. Nye, a neighbor of the men, proclaimed, "it was the solomens sene I ever witness." During the first month in the field, 100 men were ill, while 800 were available for duty. Many men in the Seventh wrote home about the illness in the regiment and to tell their families that they were still well. Charles Frank Colvin, a farmer from Scituate, remarked, "at presant thare is diferent kinds of sickness but mane sickness is homesickness." As for Colvin's health, "I hav had the best helth since I left home." From her home in Hopkinton, Tryphena Cundall maintained communication with her son Isaac, serving in Company A. He was among those ill with typhoid. The Cundalls were fervent Seventh-Day Baptists, and Tryphena wrote in her diary constantly praying for the safety of her son.[16]

As the Seventh settled into the regulations and regimens of army life, the men continued to learn the life of a soldier, evident through the letters home. Some enjoyed the trials of being a soldier. Although it was a hard life, many were used to such conditions on their farms. Captain James Remington wrote, "if I had not expected such a hard life, I would not have enlisted." The captain also commented that he knew of the danger of his profession, but was ready to accomplish the task. In Company K, Private Albert A. Winsor camped with his friend and neighbor Enos Farrow; both men were from Foster. He described his life as "tip top," and was fond of the food. Many in the regiment gained weight on the rations they were eating. In addition, the men experienced one of the least enjoyable parts of being a soldier—lice began to infect the regiment, causing a large amount of discomfort. Hugh McInnes, a fellow Rhode Islander serving in the Ninth Corps, wrote home about the Seventh's introduction to army life. "The boys look very well at presant but they think that the liveing is poor but if the 4th Reg got what they get we would think that we was liveing high but they will see it themselves."[17]

The weather continued to be pleasant, although the nights were cooler. A hurricane hit on October 26, destroying some of the equipment. The men continued to acquire warmer clothing from home, in addition to the much appreciated overcoats issued in Providence. With little to accomplish while McClellan planned his next move, some of the men repaired their clothing and washed it in Antietam Creek. Many of the married men in the regiment did not know the skills performed so often by their wives. Sergeant Hull learned how to darn socks and asked his sister, "Does it hurt woolen shirts to boil them?" Corporal Austin was used to having Emily accomplish all of the domestic tasks at their home in Ashland. He learned how to make pancakes and repair his clothing, while directing his wife to watch her spending and not to work in the mills. The enlisted men were pleased at the appearance of their commander and liked the way he dressed, "an old black hat an blouse." In addition many finally met friends in other units whom they had not seen for a year.[18]

The Fourth Rhode Island was camped near the Seventh. Raised in the fall of 1861, the Fourth fought in the North Carolina Campaign. In August 1862 they were transferred to the Army of the Potomac as they pursued Lee into Maryland. The regiment was heavily engaged at Antietam, losing half their strength in a forty-acre field of corn against A. P. Hill's veterans. The Fourth was in a ragged condition, in comparison to their brothers in the Seventh, who were fully equipped. George H. Allen described their condition as being, "A woolen blanket and a piece of shelter tent twisted together and thrown over our shoulders; haversack loaded with a dozen hardtack and a small piece of 'salt horse'; little bag of coffee and sugar mixed together; all sorts of hats and caps; little to eat but plenty of ammunition, dirty, ragged, and with a full assortment of grayback. But we were veteran soldiers." The veterans of the Fourth enjoyed the "many pleasant hours" that were spent talking to their comrades from home.[19]

Enlisting in the Seventh on a moment's notice, First Sergeant William H. Barstow was wounded at Bethesda Church.

On October 27, after waiting at Pleasant Valley for six weeks, McClellan finally issued orders for the Army of the Potomac to advance. The cry was again "On to Richmond" as the Federal forces began their next campaign. The Seventh prepared to use their two months of training. Through countless hours of drill, the men learned to move as one uniformed body, while forming the core values of being a soldier: obedience, preparedness, and being ever dutiful in ones actions. As the long roll beat that morning, the enlisted men gathered what little possessions they owned and packed them in their knapsacks as the Seventh fell into line. At one o'clock in the afternoon the regiment assembled and marched out of Maryland into Virginia. With rations in their haversacks, sixty rounds of ammunition and Enfields on their shoulders, the Seventh Rhode Island Volunteers started a march south for what many hoped would be a battle to "whip" the Confederates into defeat.[20]

4

To the Front

All I know is that the prospect is that there will be a bloody battle before long.
— Private Emor Young, November 25, 1862

Major General George Brighton McClellan commanded one of the largest armies ever to see active field service in North America. After waiting at Pleasant Valley for six weeks while his forces gathered, he formulated plans to finally capture Richmond and end the war by Christmas. The 12,000 casualties suffered at Antietam were replaced by twenty new, full strength regiments that brought the Army of the Potomac to 100,000 men, against Lee's 50,000. In the spring and summer of 1862, McClellan attempted to capture Richmond by traveling up the Virginia Peninsula and take Richmond by the flank but the attacks had been defeated. Now, after the Battle of Antietam, he attempted a second campaign.[1]

On his current expedition, he had a much different plan; during a meeting with President Lincoln in early October, the commander in chief suggested that McClellan take a different route south. Marching straight out on the roads leading south from Harpers Ferry, the Army of the Potomac hoped to draw Lee out of the Shenandoah into battle on the plains west of Manassas. If they did not succeed in this, the army would march south, through Fredericksburg, into Spotsylvania County to resupply on the York River and then cross the James River and capture Richmond. As usual, McClellan had a case of the "slows." Captain James Remington was fearful of the results of the winter campaign. He noted in a letter to his father that the mud would slow their progress. He also wanted to see Richmond firsthand, "I should like to gain sight at least of Richmond and its fortifications before winter." On October 31, the men were finally mustered for their pay, but no paymaster arrived; at the end of each two-month cycle the company officers had to report back to the War Department a listing of their men and who was to be paid each amount.[2]

The Seventh Rhode Island actively took part in the campaign, but was frustrated by the slow pace of the advance; on October 29 and 30, the regiment only marched five miles each day. In addition, on the twenty-ninth, Colonel Bliss finally addressed a serious issue that was facing the regiment. He issued an order for all commanders of companies to "immediately produce a listing of those absent and by whose authority." In every Civil War regiment, desertion was a major issue, especially in the later stages as the "bounty jumpers" practiced their trade in great numbers. The Seventh resembled many other regiments in that it suffered from some desertion; indeed, it was normal attrition that weeded out the shirkers and left behind a solid core of soldiers. Between September 10 and December 15, forty soldiers deserted, the majority of whom were non-native Rhode Islanders who enlisted from Providence. During their entire term of service, the regiment lost only sixty-six men to desertion; the remaining men all deserted after being sent to the hospital and leaving for oftentimes inadequate medical care. McClellan took a terribly slow approach in this latest campaign. By November 1, the Army of the Potomac had only advanced seventeen miles into Virginia.[3]

Lincoln looked at McClellan's command as little more then his personal bodyguard. Although he knew how to create and effectively discipline a group of men into soldiers, McClellan was not a field commander. Faced with little choice, Lincoln decided to remove the beloved Little Mac from his command. Many in Washington feared that the soldiers, loyal to McClellan, would follow him in a move on the capital reminiscent of Julius Caesar. To accomplish the hazardous mission, Lincoln dispatched Brigadier General Putnam Buckingham south with two envelopes; the first relieved McClellan of command and the other carried orders for the new commander of the Army of the Potomac. On November 9, Lincoln formally relieved McClellan of command and replaced him with Major General Ambrose Everett Burnside. Burnside had twice declined command of the Army of the Potomac, claiming he was not up to the challenge of leading such a large body of men. Upon being told that if he did not assume the command, General Joseph Hooker, Burnside's rival would, he consented. The Rhode Islanders were pleased with the selection of their new commander. Captain Remington commented: "There is nothing that could suit me better. Certainly Rhode Island, the home of Burnside cannot be disappointed with the honor." In addition Remington, like many soldiers, hoped the war would be decided in one last battle.[4]

While the politics of command were being argued in the field and in the halls of Washington, the Seventh continued marching south into enemy territory. The men complained of their aching backs, caused by the weight of the knapsacks. Many threw away small trinkets from home and army-issued articles that were deemed unnecessary. As they advanced, the Confederate cavalry was constantly to be seen as they probed the Federal defenses. At midnight, on November 4, Corporal Austin was on picket when Major Babbitt rode up to him informing Austin the Confederates were approaching. In an instant the regimental drummers began beating the long roll; Colonel Bliss began yelling, "Seize your muskets and fall into line," as the men shrugged out of their blankets, loaded their Enfields, and waited. The Seventh waited for several hours without hearing any additional firing. They then returned to their blankets and prepared to move. The next day, the Seventh arrived in Upperville, a small town near Manassas Gap.[5]

From Upperville, the Army of the Potomac turned south toward Warrenton. Burnside finally pushed the Ninth Corps to march between fifteen to twenty miles per day. The Seventh enjoyed the opportunities to forage the hostile countryside. One night Private Harrington could not sleep; finding several other Company K soldiers, the men soon discovered a farm, where they "got one sheep and ducks and turkeys and 3 chickens." Although forbidden, many officers accepted bribes of food from their men in exchange for not reporting the activity. On November 8, the army arrived near Waterloo and began to follow the Rappahannock River. Several of the men were keen to observe their first real contact with black slaves. Drummer William P. Hopkins noted the peculiarities of their small cabins; they were of irregular construction. He was most surprised when the mother called her two sons; both were named Abraham Lincoln. Even more interesting was the names of the other family members, including George Washington, Andrew Jackson, and Fred Douglass. The mother yelled at her children that "Them Yankees will carry you off and eat you." Colonel Bliss discovered an intelligent boy named Robert and adopted him as his servant.⁶

The date November 10 represented a first in the history of the Seventh. On this day, the regiment suffered its first combat casualty. Private John Seamens of Company H was captured by members of the "rebel cavalry," as he was attempting to reach the regiment after straggling. Upon his release, Seamens was sent to Camp Parole in Maryland to await his formal exchange. In a letter to Captain Remington, he wrote, "I regret much being taken prisoner." Seamens was later discharged on account of illness. Captain Remington also experienced some of the distractions that went with his profession. Phebe Briggs, a destitute from "east greenwitch" was abandoned by her husband George, a private in Remington's company. She had lost two children and her husband and pleaded with Remington to help her secure her husband's bounty. By 1865, Briggs had not only abandoned his wife, but the Seventh; he deserted while ill in New York. Furthermore, the officers began the tedious process of understanding the "red tape" of army life, filling out thirty different forms to five different departments in Washington.⁷

The illness that the men had contracted around Washington and Pleasant Valley continued to plague the Seventh. Many were sent ill to the hospital, and in the most severe cases, they were evacuated to Washington. The men were primarily facing typhoid fever, a waterborne illness, transmitted through contaminated food and water. After several weeks, spots appeared on the chest, before the man's bowels began to fail; it was a terrible way to die. With little medicine available other than quinine and whiskey, the medical officers of the Seventh could do little to prevent the spread of the disease. In addition, chronic dysentery left many with poor appetites. Sergeant John Hull was among the ill; the month of campaigning had left him with a large boil and rheumatism on his left side. The rheumatism was caused by lying on the cold, damp ground with only a rubber blanket as a shield against the elements; for over three-quarters of a century after the war, the Federal government awarded millions in pensions for the ailment.⁸

In Hopkinton, the town was reeling from the loss of three of its sons; Charles B. Greene's body was returned home and buried in the family plot near Westerly. In Ashaway, Tryphena Cundall received the news on November 3 that Isaac was ill with the disease, indeed many in Company A were. His closest comrade, Sergeant John K. Tower of Company A, wrote to Tryphena informing her of Isaac's condition. She did not know where Isaac was nor had she heard about his condition. Cundall received spotty reports from Sergeant Tower and Horace Wells. By November 12, she had written several letters, including one to Captain Lewis Leav-

Captain James Remington of Warwick commanded Company H. Courtesy of the USAMHI.

4. To the Front

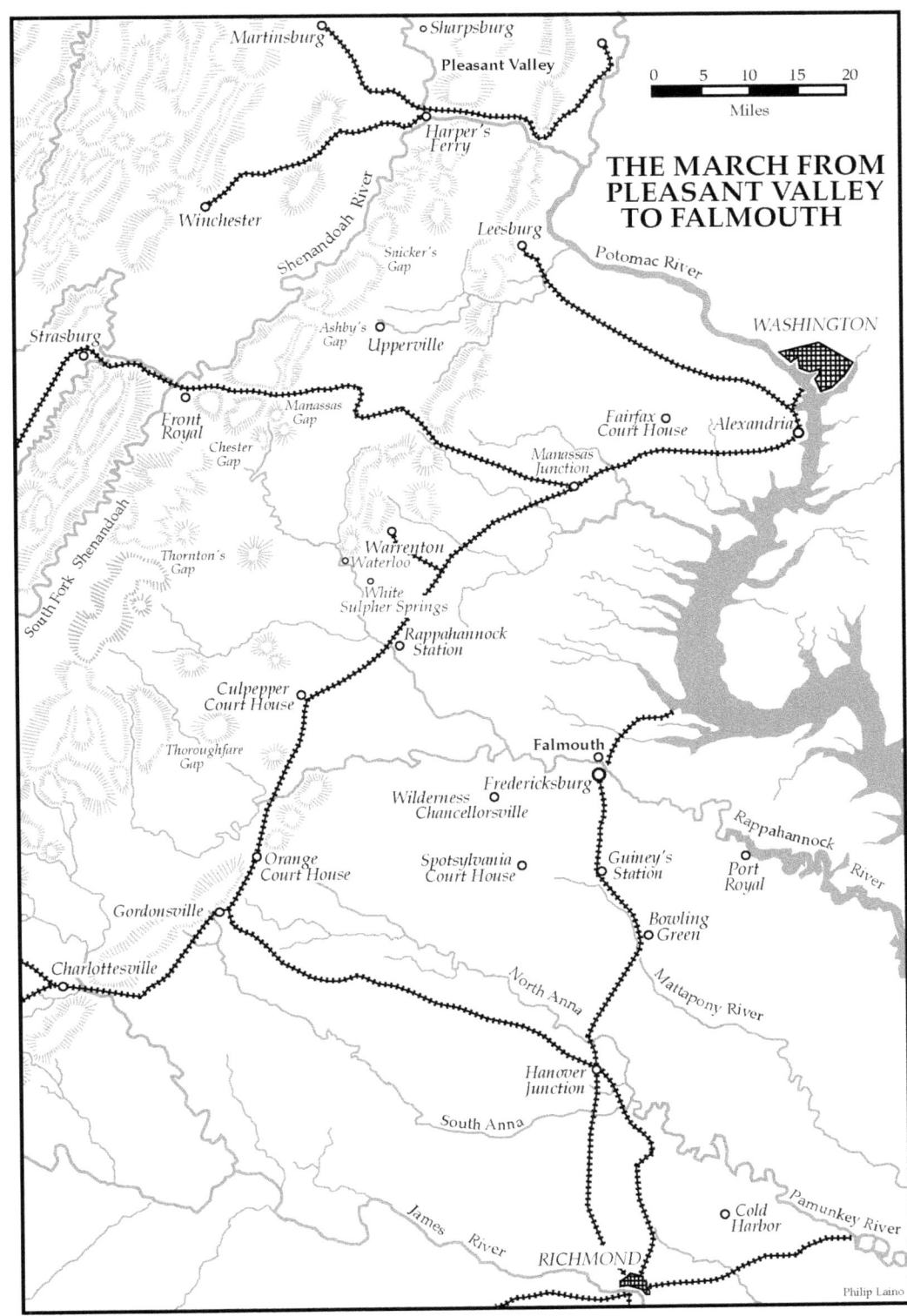

ens of Company A, but received no response. "Oh Savior, interpose to put an end to this dreadful war," was her diary entry one day. On November 22, Sergeant Tower wrote that Isaac was looking "badly." Wanting to look out for her son, Tryphena dispatched Edward Cundall to find and care for his brother. Despite being severely ill, Isaac continued to follow the regiment in an ambulance. Horace Greenman, another Company A soldier had "already seen enough of this war." Some of the ill were line officers; already two lieutenants had resigned and several more were following the regiment in the ambulances. In Virginia, the Seventh was issued rations and assigned to guard the wagon train of the Ninth Corps along with the Thirty-Fifth Massachusetts; for the Seventh action was soon to come.[9]

On November 11, Burnside rested the army as he took over his new command. Colonel Bliss used the time to erect a target 200 yards from the camp. Each man was then allowed to fire three rounds at the target. This was the first time many of the men had ever fired a weapon, and "the excitement was great," wrote one member of the regiment. On November 12, the Seventh arrived at White Sulphur Springs, near Warrenton, Virginia. Here they were detached for picket duty near a ford on the river. On the 14th, Captain Thomas H. Carr took his Company I to the ford to complete the task. In the evening, members of J.E.B. Stuart's cavalry were viewed in the vicinity. Early the next morning Captain George E. Church, together with Companies C and D arrived at the ford. Captain Church took command, and threw his companies forward near two small hills on the opposite bank of the river. The men were deployed in a skirmish line, with five paces between each man, allowing each to use the ground for cover. After dividing some rations, the Confederate artillery opened up on the Rhode Islanders. Corporal John F. Austin recalled, "I could her the shells as they went whising over my head." Soon Stuart's cavalry approached, dismounted, and started to fire at the Seventh. The Confederate artillery hit near the Ninth Corps baggage train, killing two men. Two 20-pound Parrott rifles of Roemer's New York battery opened fire, driving the Confederate artillery off the field. The Confederates pushed Company C off the hill, and across the bridge as Company D valiantly attempted to hold their position before they too were repulsed. Captain Carr led Company I into action as the three compa-

Private William Barber of Hopkinton served in the Seventh's hospital detachment during the war. *Courtesy of Kris VanDenBossche.*

nies worked together to hold their position. The Seventh held their ground, as they fired the Enfields with effect, which "probably occasioned some loss of life." The defense was successful, the wagon trains were saved; the Rhode Islanders suffered no casualties, except for some of the men's equipment; several haversacks and other straps were shot to shreds by the severe artillery fire. The Seventh took note of their first taste of battle and the experience of hearing the shells explode around them.[10]

After fully assuming command, Burnside drove his army hard to the south. It was getting late in the season and the roads of Virginia turned to a quagmire of mud. Sergeant Hull became a "drowned rat" in the rain as the army closed in on Lee. Burnside ordered the men to carry their rations, as they marched ever deeper south; rations were cut to eight hardtack per day. The hard cracker was a peculiarity of the soldier's diet; it was four inches square and made of flour and salt. The chief purpose of the cracker was to keep the soldiers alive; however, many invented interesting dishes to eat the often moldy, inedible product. The crackers often arrived from the factory full of weevils, allowing the men to toss them into their coffee to rid the cracker of the pest. The one government ration that the men of the Federal army felt that they could not live without were the ample rations of coffee and sugar; even in the worst of weather, a cup of the liquid could give the men energy to carry on. Captain Remington particularly enjoyed cooking his own meat, coffee and crackers, "it makes about the best marching ration that can be enjoyed." Although the men had complained about the hardtack at Pleasant Valley, they now devoured it. In addition, they spent what little money that was available on cheese and other products from the regimental sutler. Furthermore, many wrote home requesting funds and other to help them survive the elements. Despite the poor weather and worsening conditions in their food supplies the men began to again think of the pending battle.[11]

Burnside realized that his army was too large for him to effectively command the massive force. In order to facilitate easier command and control over the vast columns of men marching south, Burnside established three "Grand Divisions" of two corps each. The Right Grand Division composed the Second and Ninth Corps under Edwin Sumner. Joseph Hooker commanded the Center Grand Division, comprising the Third and Fifth Corps, while the First and Sixth Corps comprised the Left Grand Division under William Franklin. The force was so large that the troops had to march on separate roads. The weather started to turn again as the roads became quagmires, yet the men pushed farther south. On November 22, the Rhode Islanders were among the first to reach their objective: Falmouth. Directly across the river was the city of Fredericksburg, standing in the path to Richmond. Burnside's campaign from northern Virginia had been successful; Lee had not even moved his army. In the ranks of the Seventh, the men began to feel a sense of foreboding, that only they as New Englanders could recognize; it was the calm that preceded the storm. Private Emor Young wrote, "All I know is that the prospect is that there will be a bloody battle before long." As they looked across the river into Fredericksburg they could only imagine what would happen next; the only Confederates in the city were a small brigade. Although the river rose and fell daily, it could have been easily forded. Burnside ordered pontoons from Washington, which would allow the Army of the Potomac to cross without getting wet. Corporal Austin was eager to cross the Rappahannock; "the 7 rhodes islands boys will recive them and give them a warm welcome." Like his predecessor, Ambrose Burnside decided to wait.[12]

5

Fredericksburg

We marched onto the field through a murderous fire of shot and shell but we did not flinch.
— Private William O. Harrington, December 16, 1862

After arriving in Falmouth, the men of the Seventh Rhode Island could only predict what would happen next. Burnside set his artillery along Stafford Heights and set about covering the approaches to the city as Confederate reinforcements continued to travel each day into Fredericksburg. On November 24, Private Joseph J. Kenyon became the latest Company A soldier to perish; the fourth since the company left Hopkinton. On the twentieth he appeared at the regimental hospital complaining he was ill. Hospital steward Peckham found nothing wrong with him, except he was homesick. Kenyon died unexpectedly on the twenty-fourth of what proved to be typhoid. Peckham and his small staff laid out beds consisting of leaves and branches covered with blankets. The hospital steward complained that some of his nurses, especially those from Company A, were too young to be working in the hospital. One of them, Henry Godfrey was returned to the company. Each night, one company of the regiment went out in the cold to perform the vital task of picket duty along the Rappahannock. For Thanksgiving, all one member of the regiment could find were some turnips. In Company K, Private Harrington thought the Seventh would establish winter quarters along the river. Others heard a camp rumor that Colonel Bliss and the Seventh had been ordered back to the defenses of Washington, "it is talked that Col Bliss has been offered the duty of garding the city this winter if we take it if that is so we shall have an easy job."[1]

The supply trains finally caught up with the regiment at Falmouth and the men spent what little money they had to improve their diet. On December 2, Corporal John F. Austin carried on a long-held Rhode Island tradition — he purchased a pint of corn meal for five cents and made Johnny Cakes, a dish that all Rhode Islanders relished. Some of the men in the Seventh turned their attention to home; by December 7, William O. Harrington had finally decided to name his son either Waty or Bill.[2]

On December 8, Colonel Bliss issued orders for the Seventh to begin to prepare winter quarters, although many of the men had begun to do so in November. The encampment was given the title of Camp Mud, due to the red, claylike soil of Virginia that abounded in the area. The enlisted men drew axes and shovels from the quartermaster department and began clearing the land on which to build the encampment. This consisted of clearing the earth down to three feet, and building up walls made of logs, chinked together with mud. They often held two to four men, who built bunks and decorated the huts to their liking. Many also gave them flamboyant names such as the "Olneyville Retreat" or "Pine Cottage." Fireplaces were made of old barrels and stones, while the shelter tents were used for the roof. Such furnishings provided the men with comfortable quarters to shelter them from the elements. Each company was assigned a specific area, and the men camped as if they were in line of battle. The regiment had not been supplied since leaving Providence and many of the men were in poor condition. Surgeon Harris established a regimental hospital, consisting of a large tent to treat his patients. In addition he built a cemetery nearby. Many in the regiment were ill with the dysentery and typhoid they had contracted at the Pleasant Valley encampment.[3]

As the Army of the Potomac continued to wait for Burnside to make a move, or for the pontoon bridges to arrive, Robert E. Lee continued to move the Army of Northern Virginia into the Fredericksburg area. His lines stretched along many miles of front, yet Lee knew that the main assault would take place in front of Fredericksburg. In the rear of the city of Fredericksburg there lay a series of hills and swamps. The Army of Northern Virginia had prepared a daunting position for the Army of the Potomac to attack. It stretched for over five miles and was defensible at every turn. The main defense lines lay across Prospect Hill, which Thomas J. Jackson and his Second Corps defended. The line stretched to Marye's Heights, which was held by James Longstreet and his First Corps. On the Heights, Longstreet positioned two battalions of artillery, totaling twenty-four guns under Colonel E. Porter Alexander including among them the famed Washington Artillery of Louisiana. The artillery built defensive redoubts to shield the guns from the expected Fed-

A farmer from Hopkinton, Joseph J. Kenyon died of typhoid fever. Courtesy of the USAMHI.

The Washington Artillery on Marye's Heights had a clear field of fire that killed many Rhode Islanders. *Battles and Leaders of the Civil War.*

eral onslaught. Near the right of the Confederate line atop the hill, Lieutenant Galbraith of the First Company, Washington Artillery, posted his 10-pound Parrott rifle. In front of his position lay the Telegraph Road, which skirted the base of Marye's Heights. Years of use had eroded the road so it was now three feet below the base of the hill. It was reinforced in front by a four-foot high stone wall, allowing for a perfect defensive fire. Into this road, Longstreet placed a Georgia brigade under Brigadier General Thomas R. R. Cobb. Cobb's Georgians were mostly armed with .69-caliber smoothbore muskets, instead of rifles. These weapons fired a large round ball, in addition to three smaller pieces of buckshot. The resulting fire could produce the effect of four muskets. Separating Marye's Heights and the city of Fredericksburg was a half-mile wide plain that the Federals would have to cross in order to reach the hill. The Confederates had built their lines so that it could be covered from all angles and units could be maneuvered along the line as needed. Colonel Alexander said in reference to his defenses and the attackers, "Scarcely a chicken could live upon that field when we open up upon it." Unfortunately his prophecy would soon come true.[4]

As the days passed, the soldiers of the Seventh Rhode Island grew more restless. They had not been paid since leaving Rhode Island and many failed to receive their mail from home. The regiment had developed ferocious appetites and often ate anything that could be found, including cheese, hardtack, and "salt junk." In addition some of the men meditated on their coming fate. Private William Coman was an apple farmer from Glocester before the war. He enlisted as the wagoner of Company C. One morning he reported to Captain George E. Church stating that he felt it would be safer as a private in the ranks then working with his mule team. Captain Church consented and Coman took his place in the ranks. Major Jacob Babbitt, whom had given up the comforts of home at his advanced age to join the Seventh Rhode Island, turned his attention one night to his family. In a letter written on December 10, he wrote, "Know this, if I fall it shall be in defense of our beloved Constitution."[5]

On the morning of December 11, the pontoon bridges finally arrived from Washington as Burnside called for engineers to build three bridges across the Rappahannock. Brigadier General William Barksdale and his Mississippians, who were holding the city proper, picked off the engineers as they built the bridges. Burnside then ordered the artillery under Rhode

5. Fredericksburg

This simple stone wall shielded Confederate infantrymen below Marye's Heights, making the position almost impossible to carry. Courtesy of the Library of Congress.

Island colonel Charles Tompkins to bombard the city. The bombardment accomplished nothing; the Mississippians soon reappeared and continued the fight. A brigade of the Second Corps was then dispatched to drive them out, thus accomplishing the first bridgehead landing in American military history, including the first ever large-scale urban combat fought in the Civil War.[6]

On this day, the Seventh Rhode Island made preparations for the coming battle. Three days of rations of hardtack, salt pork, and coffee were issued by Lieutenant John R. Stanhope, the regimental quartermaster, in addition to sixty rounds of ammunition per man. Burnside planned to defeat the Army of Northern Virginia and to advance straight to Richmond. In order to do so the men left behind their knapsacks and carried only their blankets and shelter tents rolled on their backs. Due to the cold weather, the men would wear their over-

George E. Church was given a battlefield promotion at Fredericksburg.

coats. Thirty men remained behind at Camp Mud under the care of Steward Peckham. The regimental surgeons crossed with the Seventh, and prepared for what many knew would be gruesome work ahead.[7]

In addition, the brigade welcomed the arrival of the Twelfth Rhode Island, fresh from the defenses of Washington. The Twelfth was raised from the same areas as the Seventh, except these men were only serving for nine months rather than for three years. In Company E of the Twelfth marched the firemen of Major Babbitt's company; they styled themselves the King Phillip Rifles. The Twelfth nearly mutinied in Providence; in order to prevent desertion the regiment would not be paid the state bounty until they were in Washington. After a riot, Battery H of the Rhode Island Light Artillery deployed with their guns on the fringes of the camp and threatened to open fire; the bounty was finally paid, but in Washington. The regiment left Rhode Island in late October and occupied the same ground at Camp Casey as the Seventh. After performing picket duty in the lines around Washington, they were dispatched to join the Army of the Potomac. Through his political connections, Lieutenant Colonel Welcome B. Sayles was able to secure the attachment of the Twelfth to Nagle's Brigade.[8]

Burnside had run out of options; the Army of Northern Virginia now blocked his way to Richmond. In order to advance he would have to crush Lee at Fredericksburg. With no options, he ordered a frontal attack on Fredericksburg for December 13. The Seventh awoke early on the morning of December 12, and prepared to cross the river into Fredericksburg. Following a breakfast of hardtack, salt pork, and coffee Colonel Bliss allowed a gill of whiskey issued to each man. At 9:30 the regiment marched to the middle pontoon bridge and crossed the river. As they crossed the bridge the band of the Twelfth New Hampshire struck up the tune "Bully for You," but it was silenced by several shots from the Confederate artillery upon Marye's Heights. Colonel Bliss moved the Seventh onto Caroline Street and ordered them into a tobacco barn for the night. In revenge for the devastating losses that some of the Federal regiments had taken at the hands of the Confederates, the men who wore the blue pillaged Fredericksburg — the first sacking of an American city since the War of 1812.[9]

Some members of the Seventh captured a large quantity of tobacco and clay pipes. Other members of the regiment took some casks of mackerel and molasses; the result was a feast amidst the pillaging and looting. Tom, the black servant of Captain Lewis Leavens of Company A, attempted to carry a piano out of the city, but was turned back by the provost guard. Corporal William R. Northrup discovered a library and took a copy of *Pilgrim's Progress*. Brigadier General Marsena Patrick and his provost guard attempted to stop the looting, but little could be done. The company officers and enlisted men spent a chilly night in the barn, with only their blankets and overcoats to protect them from the December cold. That night Colonel Bliss shared one of the few beds in the city with Lieutenant Colonel Sayles, Major Babbitt, and Adjutant Charles Page.[10]

The next morning the Seventh was awake early, eating a cold breakfast and preparing for the attack. Colonel Bliss gave his watch and personal effects to Major Harris in the event he fell. At 11:30 the Second Division of the Ninth Corps moved to the western edge of Fredericksburg and lined up in column on Frederick Street. Ferrero's Second Brigade was first, followed by the First Brigade. Nagle positioned his brigade with the Sixth New Hampshire in front, followed by the Seventh Rhode Island, Second Maryland, Twelfth Rhode Island, and Ninth New Hampshire. The Forty-Eighth Pennsylvania was held in reserve.[11]

The First Battle of Fredericksburg began on December 13, 1862, when the First and Third Corps attacked Jackson's lines at Prospect Hill. They succeeded in breaching the line, but were repulsed when Major General William Franklin refused to send reinforcements to their aid. Burnside now began to concentrate all of his forces against the stone wall and Marye's

5. Fredericksburg

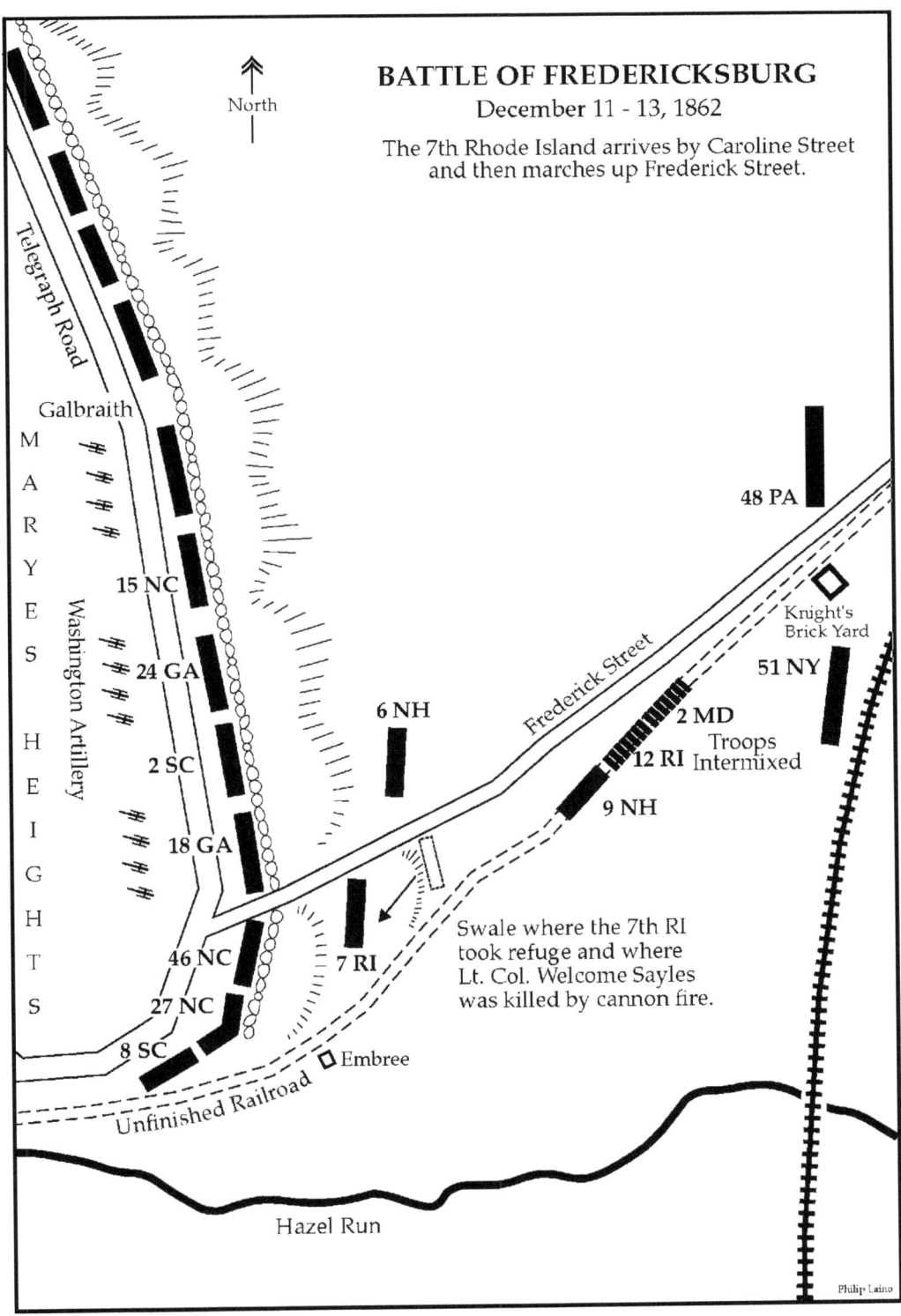

Heights. His initial attack began as the Third Division of the Second Corps made their charge up the slope toward Marye's Heights. They were repulsed by the artillery and Cobb's Georgians. This was followed by the charge of Major General Winfield Scott Hancock's First Division, Second Corps. The veterans almost reached their objective; members of the Fifth New Hampshire died within paces of the wall. Soon Hancock and his division were spent.[12]

Major General Edwin Sumner then planned for his third wave. This time he would send two divisions at the same time to attack the Telegraph Road. Major General Oliver Otis Howard's Second Division, Second Corps, would attack from the right, while Brigadier General Samuel Sturgis's Second Division, Ninth Corps, would attack from the left across the plain to Marye's Heights. At 12:00 Sturgis gave directions to the commanders in his division with a simple order, "advance to the front." Ferrero's Brigade of Sturgis's Division made their assault, keeping abreast of Howard's Division. As the Seventh was waiting to be ordered forward, Second Lieutenant Edward T. Allen rushed from Camp Mud to join Company G. Allen was severely ill with typhoid, and had just returned from a furlough in Rhode Island. Despite being ordered to remain behind, he took his place as a file closer; behind the two ranks of riflemen making sure they stayed in place and giving orders to the men. At 12:20 Sturgis gave the order to Nagle's Brigade — they were going in to support Ferrero.[13]

The Seventh Rhode Island loaded their muskets while Colonel Bliss strapped on his saber and revolver. He was a fairly large man, weighing 260 pounds, and found it difficult to lie down with his gear on. In order to make himself less conspicuous upon the field, Bliss traded his dark blue overcoat for an enlisted man's sky blue coat. Lieutenant Colonel Sayles contented himself with a flask of whiskey. Colonel Bliss counted the men in his regiment as they marched by him; there were 570 line officers and enlisted men in the ranks this day. As the regiment prepared to leave the city and advance forward, the first shell from Marye's Heights struck the regiment. It landed in Company F, killing Private Nicholas W. Matthewson and wounding Private Calvin R. Matthewson: they were brothers. As the Seventh Rhode Island cleared the city, Nagle's Brigade deployed from a column formation into line of battle and continued to march forward.[14]

Another shell exploded near Company K, wounding Corporal Austin in the neck and John Studley in the leg. Austin recalled: "I was wounded when we first went on the field, Studley was wounded through the knee and i left him at the hospital." Austin was evacuated almost immediately to Washington. In order to avoid crossing Hazel Run, Nagle sent his regiments forward into a railroad cut. This launched them into the heaviest concentration of Confederate fire. As the regiments advanced farther onto the battleground, Nagle lost control of his brigade as the regimental commanders took command and pressed forward.[15]

After clearing Knight's Brickyard, the Seventh began to receive the Confederate fire in earnest. Lieutenant Colonel Charlton Mitchell of the Fifty-First New York watched as Colonel Bliss ordered the double quick. The men threw the Enfields onto their shoulders and ran as fast as they could while trying to maintain their ranks. These men were Rhode Islanders, used to harsh weather conditions such as blizzards and Nor'easters. They had never experienced a storm such as this; it was a storm of steel and lead that knocked men out of the ranks for every step the regiment advanced. One Federal soldier remembered the bombardment. "The heavens were lurid with a fiery flame; crash on crash; benumbing the hearing and almost bewildering the senses."[16]

Nagle's Brigade advanced to the railroad cut of the Richmond, Fredericksburg, and Potomac Railroad. This was a deep cut, with walls fifteen feet high. The left wing of Nagle's Brigade simply froze in its position as the fire from the Washington Artillery slammed into the ranks of the Ninth New Hampshire and Twelfth Rhode Island; the majority of the 130

The railroad cut presented a major problem to the left wing of Nagle's brigade. *Battles and Leaders of the Civil War.*

casualties suffered by the Twelfth occurred as the shells landed in the cut. One lieutenant, Richard A. Briggs, climbed to the top of the embankment before being "riddled with bullets." In the confusion of the battle, the Twelfth changed positions with the Second Maryland in the line so they were now on the left of the Seventh. The Ninth New Hampshire and Second Maryland remained in their positions; they could neither advance nor retreat. Major Cyrus Dyer, in command of the left wing of the Twelfth, was severely wounded by a shell as he approached the railroad cut. William Coman's safety in the ranks disappeared, as did he — shot down by a missile from the Washington Artillery. The Seventh Rhode Island and Sixth New Hampshire climbed out of the steep walls of the cut and continued to advance forward into a fire that was becoming murderous.[17]

Three hundred yards from the Telegraph Road, the Seventh came to a slight depression in the ground that provided some cover. Michael Kerr was severely

Lieutenant Winthrop A. Moore escorted the remains of Lieutenant Colonel Sayles to Providence.

wounded, causing a "ragged hole" in his head. Private Abel B. Kenyon recalled, "I can tell you the canon balls and rifle balls come thick and fast when we was going on to the field but we went up in good line though we had to walk over many dead and wounded men." In addition, Kenyon recalled shells exploding within twelve feet, killing Henry S. Cole, a dairy farmer from Foster; Cole's body was never recovered.[18]

As the men advanced into the swale, Lieutenant Colonel Sayles crawled to within twenty feet of Colonel Bliss. In an instant, a Parrott shell from Marye's Heights struck the colonel in the chest. Sayles evaporated as pieces of his body flew over members of the regiment. Colonel Bliss's right side was covered with blood and pieces of Sayles's lungs. For the Seventh Rhode Island it was the moment of truth. Colonel Bliss wiped the blood away and yelled out, "let them have it." The enlisted men crawled to the front of the swale and began to fire against the Confederates in the sunken road. Lieutenant George Wilbur was shot through the thigh, while George Potter went down with a wound to the shoulder. Sergeant Peleg Peckham distinguished himself as a courier, running back to Nagle with communications from Colonel Bliss. Captain Theodore Winn's tin shoulder strap was shot away from his shoulder. Across the river, Stephen Peckham could hear the sounds of the battle around him. He saw four Rhode Islanders carry the badly wounded Lieutenant Wilbur to his position; he was clutching Sayles's sword. The lieutenant told the hospital steward that he had last seen the Seventh advancing "into a most destructive fire."[19]

The Seventh could not hit any of the Confederates in the Telegraph Road, except those running down Marye's Heights or poking their heads above the works. General Cobb was mortally wounded by a Union artillery shell, which hit his position. Private John Bradbury had half his foot shot away. Private Charles T. Greene of Company I was the son of Lieutenant Thomas Greene. Private Greene had enlisted without his father's permission into the company; now his father watched in horror as the young man received a terrible wound. With Union forces approaching closer to the wall, Longstreet sent two more brigades into the road; the Seventh was now facing fire from the Twenty-Seventh and Forty-Sixth North Carolina. Private Harris C. Wright of Burrillville was killed by a shot to the head. Colonel Bliss secured his musket and went to the front of the swale to join the men on the firing line in order to encourage them to hold their position. His actions earned him a brevet majority in the Regular Army and in 1898 the Medal of Honor.[20]

As the Seventh was exchanging fire in the swale, other Rhode Islanders were making history as well. In order to relieve pressure on his corps, Major General Darius Couch ordered a battery into action. Upon being told that it would not survive, he said "well it can die there." On the right of the battlefield, Captain John G. Hazard led Battery B, First Rhode Island Light Artillery, into a position 150 yards from the wall. Battery B did some damage to the Confederates running into the sunken road, but was sustaining terrible losses. The battery remained there for a half hour before losing sixteen men, three of them mortally wounded, as well as a large number of horses.[21]

After remaining in the swale for thirty minutes, Colonel Bliss again gave the command to advance. The Seventh rose up and continued forward. As they left the swale, First Sergeant Charles H. Kellen, a teacher from Willimantic, Connecticut, was shot through the leg. He was evacuated to Washington but did not survive the amputation. At the age of seventeen years, he was posthumously promoted to the rank of second lieutenant. Sergeant Major Joseph Manchester had his right arm blown off by a shell. As the regiment neared the stone wall, the fire was becoming more intense. Private Hartford Alexander became lost and immediately went back into action, fighting with the Fifty-First New York. Above the roar of the battle, the only audible sounds were the yelling of the company officers to "close up," be steady, and to "guide forward on the colors." Fifty years after the battle, Daniel Ballou could still recall the "harsh cries of command" of the officers as they advanced closer to the stone wall.[22] Captain James Remington went down, shot through the jaw, and made his way to the rear, yielding his company to Second Lieutenant Ethan Jenks. Sergeant Charles K. Knowles was shot in the leg and bled to death on the field. Corporal Alonzo Jenks lost his hand; he survived and served throughout the war, rising to the rank of first sergeant. William O. Harrington remembered, "we marched onto the field through a murderous fire of shot and shell but we did not flinch." Another member of the regiment said, "the rifle balls sounded just like a swarm of bees huming around the hive."[23]

Sergeant Major Joseph Manchester lost an arm at Fredericksburg, but returned to the service and rose to the rank of major. Courtesy of the USAMHI.

The Seventh approached the stone wall as two fences blocked their path. The first was cleared with no problem. As Colonel Bliss was running alongside his men, they were being shot down all around him. The second fence required the Seventh to stop and tear it down. A shell exploded in front of Colonel Bliss, knocking a hole in the fence and wounding three men in front of him. The colonel described it as "a perfect volcanoe of flame." Adjutant Charles Page was struck in the head by a piece of case shot, tearing an eye from its socket. After the war, Page was fond of showing people the bullet that caused the damage. Private Knight of Company C remembered, "The balls and shells fell like hale around us." In an ironic twist, Captain Rowland Rodman of Company G was hit in the same location as his brother, who was wounded at Antietam; the captain survived. Corporal Joseph Marcoux, a young French-Canadian immigrant, was mortally wounded in the neck, his blood spraying onto the U.S. flag.[24]

Near the Embree House, fifty yards from the Telegraph Road, the Seventh Rhode Island halted for the second time. The regiment could advance no further as they were receiving point-blank fire from the Confederates in the road. From behind the stone wall, Lafayette McLaws' Confederates were pouring a continuous fire into the ranks of the Federal soldiers. One New Hampshire soldier remembered it as "sheeted damnation in a terrible manner." The Seventh was one of the few regiments to get close to the wall without losing its regimental formation. They found a three-foot high ridge and laid down behind it to escape the fire. The Rhode Islanders continued to fire their Enfields, but to little effect. The sixty rounds

First Sergeant Charles H. Kellen was posthumously promoted to lieutenant for gallantry at Fredericksburg.

each man had carried were running low as the men began to rifle the boxes of the wounded and dying men lying next to them. When the ammunition was expended, Colonel Bliss ordered the men to fix bayonets and lie down in the mud to escape the fire. Color Sergeant Frederic Weigand advanced forward several more paces with his banner, placing it in the front of the Seventh; it was hit by sixteen bullets and nearly ripped in half by a shell. The Seventh's banner became the farthest advanced Ninth Corps flag. Weigand's actions earned him a lieutenant's commission.[25]

Near sundown, Colonel Bliss decided to make one more attempt to capture the Telegraph Road. He then discovered that the Seventh was receiving fire from its rear. General Andrew Humphreys had led his Pennsylvania Division of the Fifth Corps into action. The men of the One Hundred and Twenty-Seventh Pennsylvania did not see the Seventh Rhode Island in their front and were firing over their heads. Colonel Bliss sent Major Babbitt to tell them to stop the firing. The major rose to his feet to pass along the order, but as his letter had predicted, he was shot in the chest. The final sortie never occurred. The entire regimental staff of the Seventh was dead or wounded; Colonel Bliss had several narrow escapes, being hit by spent bullets.[26]

Drummer William Hopkins of Company D remembered that the time seemed to pass very quickly. In total darkness, Colonel Bliss cautiously evacuated the Seventh from the slight rise back to the swale. At 7:30 that night an aide from Sturgis ordered them off the field as the Third Division of the Ninth Corps, including the Fourth Rhode Island, moved up to relieve the Second Division. The Fourth Rhode Island advanced into the darkness near the railroad cut. Lieutenant Colonel Joseph B. Curtis ignored the order to abandon his horse and advance on foot. As he rode in the rear of the Fourth, the colonel was struck in the head by a piece of case shot; ironically he was the regiment's only fatality. As the Seventh passed the Fifty-First New York, Colonel Mitchell yelled out, "Three cheers for the Seventh Rhode Island." The Confederates again opened fire as the Rhode Islanders fell back. Private William Rathbun, one of three brothers in Company H, attempted to drag the wounded Oliver Dowd, when a shell took off his left leg. The wound "never caused any problem," allowing Rathbun to maintain a normal life after his discharge. Private William J. Pollock was killed at the side of his brother as the Seventh finally left the field.[27]

Second Lieutenant George Stone returned to the field to recover the bodies of several members of the regiment. Unable to light a candle, he found Lieutenant Colonel Sayles by passing his arm directly through the colonel's chest, and he noticed the prominent whiskey flask hanging from his neck. The colonel's remains were placed in a rubber blanket and brought back to the city where Chaplain Howard looked at the body. Only Sayles's upper torso remained intact, but he could be identified by the silver leaves upon his shoulders. A private removed his flask and kept it. Colonel Bliss dispatched Lieutenant Winthrop Moore the honorable duty of escorting Sayles remains home. The remains of both Lieutenant Colonel Curtis and Sayles were transported to Providence where they lay in state at the Rhode Island State House. There were still those in Providence who never forgave Sayles for his participation in the Dorr Rebellion, especially members of the Republican Party. The *Providence Evening Press* reported, "Let his glorious death make his peace with those who disrupted him in life." Lieutenant Colonel Welcome B. Sayles would finally receive his peace under a small marble monument in Providence.[28]

Major Jacob Babbitt was mortally wounded trying to complete a critical mission at Fredericksburg.

First Lieutenant George Inman, on detached duty to the Ninth Corps ambulance train, hurried along to deliver the wounded to the surgeons. A forty-minute march to Caroline Street brought the Seventh back to its barn. Here the company sergeants gave the customary roll call after a battle to determine the number of men lost on this day; only 350 answered the call. As the regiment assembled, the enlisted men began cheering their colonel for the performance he had just shown in the battle. With a heavy heart and tears in his eyes, Colonel Bliss looked at his decimated regiment. Never one to say many words, Bliss could only tell his Rhode Islanders, "You have covered yourselves with mud and glory."[29]

Major James Harris commandeered a church as he and the other surgeons began to treat the wounded. Colonel Bliss visited the men and found Major Babbitt tucked into the pulpit of the church. He seemed to be in good spirits and hoped to return to duty soon. He was evacuated to Washington, but his wound became infected. Major Jacob Babbitt died on December 23, 1862. Colonel Bliss then returned to his bed, recalling, "I was pretty well tired." In the night, the Seventh again was called and after drawing ammunition they went on picket duty. On the morning of December 14, Ambrose Burnside planned to personally lead the Ninth Corps in yet another assault upon Marye's Heights. Luckily for the men of the Seventh, another attack never materialized. On the night of December 15, the Army of the Potomac evacuated Fredericksburg and returned to Falmouth. The Seventh was one of the last regiments to cross the river. Private Knight remembered that they left in a great hurry; it was believed Jackson and his men were going to launch an assault against the retreating Federals.[30]

The toll of battle was heavy for the Seventh Rhode Island. Three commissioned officers and forty-one enlisted men were dead or mortally wounded. Some of the wounded would not succumb until months after the battle; Private Alpheus Salisbury was the last, dying on July 4, 1863. Eight officers and 128 men were wounded. A further forty were classified as missing. Some of these men were killed or wounded, while others were simply lost. Among them was Private Knight of Company C. Originally classified as killed in action, Knight was one of the twenty men who returned to Camp Mud in the days after the battle. Ten men took the opportunity to desert during the battle. In total, the Seventh Rhode Island Volunteers suffered 220 casualties or 40 percent of the regimental strength, the highest ever taken by a Rhode Island regiment in a single battle. The overwhelming majority of the casualties occurred in the right wing of the battalion, victims of Lieutenant Galbraith's Parrott rifles. One private wrote, "There was a great many that went to there long home that day. Our Regt got badly cut up."[31]

Hardest hit was South Kingstown's Company G with nine killed and twelve wounded. Foster and Scituate's Company K lost four dead and nine wounded. Corporal Nathan B. Lewis of Company F recalled, "There were 48 in our company engaged in the fighting of these 16 were killed or wounded." Most companies mustered fifty men and the majority had 30 to 40 percent of their men killed or wounded. Corporal Austin survived the initial battle wound and was transported to

As the Seventh left the field at Fredericksburg, Private William Rathbun (right) gave his left leg to save Private Oliver Dowd. Both men were from Company H.

Portsmouth Grove Hospital, in Portsmouth, Rhode Island, along with 200 other wounded Rhode Islanders. Here Austin suffered back pain and stomach disorders, along with almost catching smallpox. He was finally discharged in March and returned to Scituate.[32]

The Seventh Rhode Island was nearly destroyed at the Battle of Fredericksburg. For the smallest state in the Union, the casualties suffered on this day were appalling: Nearly 400 Rhode Islanders were killed, wounded, or missing. Within one five-mile radius of Foster, Glocester, and Scituate seven men were dead. The youngest was Albert A. Winsor of Foster, at nineteen. Some families never knew what became of their husbands, brothers, and sons. William Coman's widow searched forty years for any information on what became of her husband. She eventually erected a small memorial stone in the family cemetery, located in Coman's apple orchard. Others, such as Jedediah Greene and Olney D. Williams, were never seen again. In the Sixth Principal and Free Will Baptist churches of western Rhode Island and among Seventh-Day faithful in the southern part of the state, ministers held service for loved ones killed in the horrors of the battle. Many would be laid to rest in small family plots in the meadows and forests of their native state. After the war, some members of the Seventh Rhode Island finally reached Marye's Heights, being buried in the National Cemetery at Fredericksburg. After lying in state, Lieutenant Colonel Sayles was buried with military and Masonic honors at Swan Point Cemetery in Providence. He was interned near Colonel John S. Slocum and Brigadier General Charles T. James. Major Jacob Babbitt was buried on January 1, 1863, in Bristol. Governor Sprague, many members of the Rhode Island Militia, and the entire town attended the service. The old warrior was laid to rest in the new Juniper Hill Cemetery. Ironically Major Babbitt helped to found the cemetery before the war. Nearly fifty members of the regiment were incapacitated by their battle wounds and were discharged from the service. Others were transferred to the Veterans Reserve Corps, a unit of disabled soldiers that was used to guard prisoners and perform light duty in the rear, allowing the soldiers in those areas to report to the front.[33] Captain Leavens best summed up the Seventh's loss, "Scarce a man but had lost a friend or relative."

After charging up Marye's Heights, Private Thomas Colley deserted and returned to Providence. Courtesy of Cherry Bamberg.

The Seventh received their baptism by fire in one of the deadliest battles of the Civil War. Despite being under a murderous fire, the regiment had performed extremely well for their first test of combat. They were mentioned by their corps, division, and brigade commanders for their bravery in the face of a determined foe. Brigadier General James Nagle wrote, "Too much praise cannot be given to the Seventh Rhode Island Volunteers." In 1869, Chaplain Augustus Woodbury of Burnside's staff recorded: "They stood at their posts with the

Left: Private Jesse Barber was one of nine men to die in Company G at Fredericksburg. Courtesy of Kris VanDenBossche. *Right:* Private John P. Lane was wounded at Fredericksburg and was discharged from the service.

steadiness of veterans; they advanced with the enthusiasm of genuine soldiers, they won the encomiums of all who witnessed their valor on this, their first day of battle." After the battle, as Colonel Bliss compiled his official report for posterity, he could have no higher compliments for his Rhode Islanders. He wrote: "They remained under a heavy fire without flinching, and of the long list of killed and wounded are stronger proofs then words of mine that the regiment has done its duty."[34]

As the men again settled down into their camp at Falmouth, they began to take stock of what had just happened to them. Many wrote home immediately to tell their families they survived or to convey the fates of their dead or wounded comrades. Private Harrington wrote a letter home every day for a week describing the battle to his family. He wrote, "I shall never forget the scenes of the firs Battle." Even in his recalling of the battle, Harrington continued to help his wife direct some affairs on the farm, telling her to sell the new colt for additional income. Tryphena Cundall's son Isaac was spared the battle, as he remained ill with typhoid. In her diary entry for December 19, she wrote: "My heart aches for the loved ones, many very many have fallen to rise no more but to be huddled in the grave of a battlefield. Many more will die of wounds received on the 13th of December at Fredericksburg Virginia and many more will linger out a life maimed crippled and suffering. What can I write, how can I express my feeling, it is in vain to try."[35] Several of the enlisted men were critical of Burnside's performance at Fredericksburg. Although he was beloved by the soldiers of the Ninth Corps, Burnside was despised by most Federal enlisted men. The general had performed creditably in North Carolina, Virginia and Antietam but was always remembered for his defeat at Fredericksburg. In the Seventh there was a universal feeling of never wanting to see another battle again and of belief that Colonel Bliss had nobly led his regiment. Private Harrington wrote in yet another letter to his wife Eunice that "I can see nothing in the battle accept a failer or a defeat." In another letter to his brother Josiah, Harrington claimed, "the most of our officers ware half drunk and some more than that when we marched onto the field but most off them got sober before they left." Lieutenant Harrington replied that his brother should not write such comments about his officers. Almost 13,000 Federal soldiers were killed, wounded, or missing and not a single inch of ground was gained. Recovering from his wounds at home in Warwick, Captain James Remington wrote a scathing letter to his friend Harry about the battle. He stated: "I do not know what your opinion of the late Battle of Fredericksburg may be; as for myself, I consider it to be the most fruitless massacre of the entire war." With the memory of the Battle of Fredericksburg still fresh in their minds, the Seventh Rhode Island Volunteers settled in for what they hoped would be a quiet winter at Falmouth, Virginia.[36]

6

Falmouth

Thare is a good many sick here.
— *Corporal Charles F. Colvin,*
January 18, 1863

At the end of 1862, the morale of the United States had fallen nearly to where it stood in July 1862; following yet another defeat the citizens of the North wished that the war would finally come to an end. In the Peninsula Campaign, the Union army had advanced it seemed so near to Richmond that the city should have fallen into Union hands. With the freshness of victory still being felt after South Mountain and Antietam, many hoped the war would be over by Christmas. Fredericksburg had changed all of that; 13,000 Federal soldiers became casualties during the fruitless assaults upon Marye's Heights and, despite the high casualties, no ground was captured. In Rhode Island, seventy-four families mourned the loss of family members killed at Fredericksburg. For such a small state, the losses were unimaginable. Near Falmouth, Virginia, the survivors of the Seventh Rhode Island returned to Camp Mud and the brutalities of winter. Of the 570 men who crossed the Rappahannock, 150 never returned to the regiment, creating voids that were never filled.[1]

Colonel Bliss was faced with perhaps the largest dilemma of all; every member of his staff was either dead or severely wounded. Sergeant Major Manchester returned to the regiment, but was quickly promoted to lieutenant and joined the division staff. First Lieutenant John Sullivan of Company K was promoted to adjutant; he was well tuned to the position having served as a sergeant-major in the Regular Army. The promotion was passed, allowing Sullivan to collect the additional $10 per month the adjutant's position granted. The lieutenant colonelcy and majority were harder to fill. As senior captain, twenty-nine-year-old George E. Church was commissioned to replace Sayles. Church was a civil engineer by trade, and before the war had surveyed in Argentina, fighting the natives in several bloody encounters. The position of major proved more difficult to fill. Captain Rodman was the second captain, but his wounds proved to be too severe to return to the regiment, and he resigned his commission. By the end of January, Captains Gilbert Durfee, Lewis Leavens, Lyman Bennett, James Remington, and Thomas Carr had resigned their commissions as well. The next senior officer was Captain Thomas Tobey of Company E. Tobey had served with Bliss in the Tenth Rhode

The Seventh received this flag at the Falmouth encampment and carried it until 1865.

Island and as a Brown graduate was well suited to dealing with the paperwork the majority entailed.[2]

The subaltern ranks were also particularly hit hard at Fredericksburg; eight resigned and returned to Rhode Island. This opened up seven captaincies and eighteen lieutenant positions to be filled; many would not be completed until March. Although Colonel Bliss and Governor Sprague issued commissions and warrants to the men of the regiment, the Seventh was never as fully officered as it was when the regiment left Rhode Island. With such a large number of officer ranks to fill, Colonel Bliss promoted the sergeants and enlisted men who had shown leadership potential at Fredericksburg. The highest amount was awarded to Company D, which saw four of its enlisted men raised to the rank of second lieutenant. With scores of noncommissioned officers incapacitated, many warrants were issued. From first sergeant to eighth corporal, a large number of men sewed on the stripes of a sergeant or corporal, among them Sergeant Hull, who was promoted to the rank of first sergeant of Company G.[3]

The weather continued to worsen, changing from rain to snow every day. On December 16, the Seventh returned to Camp Mud and repaired their small huts. Private John Malone froze to death during the night; his remains were added to the Seventh's growing cemetery. By December 18, many of the men had developed severe colds on account of the weather. On this day, Lieutenant Thomas Greene gathered together what was left of Company G to go out on picket near the Rappahannock. His company mustered thirty men; fully half of those that had crossed the river were gone. In the hospitals around Washington and Falmouth, sick and wounded Rhode Islanders continued to be treated. In Hopkinton, Tryphena Cundall finally learned that her son was feeling better; Isaac recovered from typhoid and was ordered to report back to Company A. For Christmas the entire regiment was assigned to picket duty along the river. On December 28 — "a fine day" — Lieutenant Moore returned from Rhode Island with fifty-five pairs of mittens for Company E. On December 31, Colonel Bliss was given command of Nagle's Brigade, while Burnside tendered his resignation to President Lincoln. The resignation of Burnside was denied, while the men of the Seventh Rhode Island struggled to survive near Falmouth, Virginia, waiting for 1863.[4]

January 1, 1863, was another rainy day in Virginia, as the regiment again turned out for picket duty. The task was vital, as the Confederates were directly across the river, and within earshot. The first day of the new year also brought the Emancipation Proclamation into effect. From now on, the war would be not just about fighting to preserve the Union but also about battling to free the slaves. Many in the regiment disapproved of the new cause; some even lost faith in their commander in chief. The recently promoted lieutenant Peleg Peckham wrote, "In his philanthropic sympathy for the external nigger he had left all the poor cusses still in bondage." The Emancipation Proclamation only freed slaves in states rebelling against the United States. However, in most areas, it was impossible for the Union forces to free

First Lieutenant William H. Johnston was promoted from the ranks and served with the Seventh through every campaign. Courtesy of the USAMHI.

the slaves, as they were not operating in the area. Those who were freed were detained as "contraband of war" and employed as laborers and in other menial tasks. Lieutenant Peckham referred to the freemen as "black rascals." In a dark letter to Captain David R. Kenyon, Peckham voiced his hope that a revolution would be held "at once & Old Abe will be hurled from his seat." Like many, he hoped for "Little Mac" to return and take command of the Union army. On the reverse side of Lieutenant Peckham's views could be found those of Private Isaac Cundall, raised from an early age to be an abolitionist. Before the war, the Cundall family had operated a stop on the Underground Railroad from their small house in Ashaway. Under the cover of night the slaves were dressed in women's clothes and hidden in the cellar until they were smuggled to the next stop, before reaching freedom in Canada. It was Isaac Cundall's views of the Civil War as a morale crusade to end slavery that prompted him to join the Seventh Rhode Island.[5]

Taken in Kentucky in 1863, this image shows from the left, Private Henry Wilson, Private John P. Jones, and Sergeant Franklin Gonsolve.

By January 4, the weather had calmed so much that the Seventh could hold its first parade and inspection since the Battle of Fredericksburg. Private Henry Winsemann wore size twelve shoes. Before the inspection, he had failed to polish the rear of the boots, which were caked in a layer of yellow Virginia mud. Upon being chastised by the inspecting officer, he said, "A good soldier never looks behind." Only six officers were present at the parade. During the Ninth Corps review on the sixth, the Seventh finally received a U.S. flag, courtesy of the ladies of Providence. The flag was regulation size, with the words "7th R. Island Vols." inscribed upon its center. In addition to "Fredericksburg," written on the top stripe; there was room for many further honors. The small flag used by the Seventh at Fredericksburg was also carried and was called the "Fredericksburg Flag." During a review of the regiment, General Edwin Sumner, the second in command of the Army of the Potomac, proudly showed off the Seventh, saying "they fought like buggers" at Fredericksburg. Sergeant Hull claimed that they only fought so well because it was safer to go forward, instead of retreating. In addition, Hull finally received several shirts and socks from his sister in South

Kingstown. The mail did not always arrive at Falmouth, leading many to wonder where the items sent from home had gone. On December 21, Private Alfred S. Knight wrote to his sister requesting "to wooling under sheets and a pare of buckin gloves." Knight received the items on January 12, but then requested $5.00 in "govirment money." Like most in the regiment, Knight continued to write that he was in good health; the news was given so as not to worry those at home.[6]

January 9 represented an important day in this winter of 1863. On this day, the commissions of the officers were finally received from Governor Sprague; all commissions dated to January 7. During dress parade, the officer assignments were given, as the new officers reported to their respective companies. One promotion did not come to the Seventh, namely, that of Colonel Bliss to brigadier general. General Sumner submitted his name to President Lincoln, who then forwarded it to the Senate; however, no action was taken on the nomination, despite the high remarks Bliss had received for his leadership. Not all of the men were happy about their promotion. First Lieutenant Edward T. Allen of Company G was assigned to the command of Company A. Allen was timid by nature, and felt that he was not up to command of a company yet. Despite his misgivings, and his request to be transferred to a company commanded by a captain, Allen took command of the company. The men were pleased to receive a neighbor and well-known man to command them. With no other officers in Company C, Second Lieutenant James N. Potter was promoted to captain of his company. Along with his displeasures of army life, Lieutenant Peleg Peckham was very unhappy with his promotion, "I am no more sastified with 2nd Lt than I was Sergeant, now I want to be a 1st Lt." Peckham was assigned to Company E, commanded by Percy Daniels; he was displeased due to the "high livers" of his new mess. The officers were required to purchase their own rations from Lieutenant Stanhope for one dollar per day. Peckham was accustomed to cooking "flap jacks" as a sergeant and was unused to the mess system. The promotion did bring one small benefit — soft bread instead of hardtack. Furthermore, some of the officers were displeased about the time that it had taken for Governor Sprague to issue the commissions; they lost seniority when the governor did not send the commissions to the regiment in time.[7]

In addition, on January 9, the Seventh finally received something that was lacking in the regiment. Other than the regimental name of the Seventh Rhode Island, there was no distinguishing mark to show they were Rhode Islanders. The answer finally arrived. It came in the form of a gift from the ladies of Newport. The article was a large, dark blue banner, with gold fringe. Painted in the middle of the flag was a large silver, fouled anchor: the symbol of Rhode Island. Above the anchor were the words of the founder of the state, Roger Williams. The phrase was also the motto of the first state to offer religious freedom: "In Te Domine Speramus." Translated the simple words meant "In God We Hope." Even from a distance, the flag produced a powerful message that these men were Rhode Islanders.[8]

The enlisted men protected themselves as best they could in the small huts at Camp Mud. The ground froze and thawed with every storm, creating a miserable environment. Private Emor Young used his skills as a baker to get out of picket duty. Young complained that "the work is nasty and smoky but I do not have any guard duty to do these cold nights." William O. Harrington was glad to welcome George Potter back to the regiment. Potter had received a slight shoulder wound and, upon recovering from it, he was promoted to corporal to replace John F. Austin. Harrington and Potter went to the forest near the encampment one day. After chopping some wood, they and two other Company K soldiers built "a cabin and it is very comfort able." The forest near the Ninth Corps encampment continued to disappear as the men replaced the shelter tent tops with a sturdier roof of logs. For some in the regiment, the

The Seventh built small huts similar to these to keep out of the elements at Camp Mud.

encampment was starting to take on the appearance of the Valley Forge encampment their grandfathers had survived some ninety years earlier.[9]

The paymaster continued to elude the Seventh; despite the fact that all of the other regiments in the brigade, including the Twelfth Rhode Island, were paid off. The Fourth Rhode Island nearly mutinied after being told they would only receive four months of pay. In addition, thirty-six dollars would be deducted for the first set of government-issued clothing, as the men had already drawn a set before leaving Rhode Island. The men were famous for their rioting; in August 1862, the Fourth rioted after their lieutenant colonel was passed over for promotion. They eventually settled the pay account by being told the regiment was not to be paid for six more months if they did not accept the pay now. Some men were surprised to receive a pittance for their six months of service; one poor private received two three-cent postage stamps. In the Seventh the men were also starting to feel the crunch. Those who had received a town bounty continued to see to it that the amount was paid to their wives and families. However, despite being in the field five months and completing numerous pay roles, none of the men were paid. Corporal Charles F. Colvin commented, "thay hant paid us and that makes the boys mad." Colvin contemplated thoughts about deserting if he was not paid. He wrote that the Seventh "did not come here to bee punished to free the niges." The dissatisfaction was felt at all levels of the Seventh. The pay was desperately needed. Lieutenant Peckham felt he should leave the Army of the Potomac; however, as a carpenter, the service represented one of the few ways he could advance himself socially.[10]

Disease continued to infect the Seventh as if a plague had descended upon Falmouth. The only water to drink and cook with came from the already polluted Rappahannock while many of the latrines were placed near the huts; the combination was ripe for the spread of typhoid and other waterborne diseases. In addition, the cold weather had produced cases of pneumonia, in addition to infecting every member of the regiment with the common cold. The men were almost starving, as the supply trains failed to reach Falmouth, often delivering moldy and spoiled hard bread. The fortunate men who received boxes from home often sold some of the contents to their destitute comrades. Corporal Potter and Private Harrington scrapped some funds together to purchase "ham, sausage, butter, fried cakes & dried apples." Harrington gave specific directions for his wife to include items in the box she was planning to send to Falmouth. In Hopkinton, Tryphena Cundall found it impossible to mail anything as the express company was not accepting packages for Burnside's army. Major James Harris and his medical team worked hard in their tent to treat the ill, yet hardly anything could be accomplished. On January 12, 343 men were present for duty, while 126 were sick in the hospital. The number continued to climb each day; on January 18 three men a day were leaving the regiment on account of illness. In the entire army, three to eight men died every day, while men deserted by the score. It was perhaps the lowest point of morale for the Union soldier during the Civil War.[11]

In even the worst weather, Colonel Bliss continued to hold reviews and inspections every day. The men spent much of the time in their huts while one company of the regiment was always on picket duty; each company rotated every twenty-four hours along the Rappahannock. In their huts the men remembered the Battle of Fredericksburg, waiting while Burnside planned his next move. With the rain pelting their log homes daily, even the Rhode Islanders began to complain about why they were sitting at Falmouth rather than in Richmond. First Sergeant Hull wrote that General Henry Halleck, the Federal army commander in Washington, "ought to be presented with a leather medal for forgetting the pontoon bridges." Patriotic songs, such as the "Battle Cry of Freedom," "Battle Hymn of the Republic," and "The Girl I Left behind Me" encouraged the men to remain at their posts, while many died and deserted around them.

Despite the suffering around them, the citizens of Rhode Island listened to the calls for help. A schooner was chartered to bring fresh supplies and other items of comfort to the Seventh. Those who had family in the regiment rushed to mail the packages in time. In Hopkinton, Tryphena Cundall learned that her son had recovered from typhoid and was back with Company A. Isaac desperately wanted to come home, and was willing to give up his bounty. Many in the Seventh wanted to, "the Regiment would be glad to give theirs if they could but return to their homes and do it honorable," wrote Isaac Cundall.[12]

While the Seventh struggled to stay alive, Burnside began his second campaign. He would advance up the Rappahannock and march around Lee's flank on the road to Richmond. The Second Division of the Ninth Corps was held in reserve; although the men still had to continue the menial task of performing picket. He issued orders for the Army of the Potomac to commence marching on January 21. The rain began on the twentieth; however this rain was unlike any the men had seen at Camp Mud, their huts became flooded, while the camp was turned into "one vast quagmire." Private Harrington continued to direct the affairs on his farm, hoping his wife would take up farming in the spring. In addition he wrote, "We are having a regular old northe easter to day it began to rain last night." The Fourth Rhode

Island received their orders and began to march out of their camp up the Rappahannock. The rain became so intense that some feigned illness and erected their shelter tents rather then continue marching. Private George Allen commented, "Virginia mud had this peculiarity; that when wet it assumes a paste like consistency, and sticks to the feet like glue." The order was rescinded, and the Fourth returned to camp. Several of the French Canadians in the regiment decided they were tired of army life, and returned to Rhode Island by walking out of camp in civilian clothes; the morale was so broken that the officers did not even care. Rumors flew through the army that entire battalions were being sucked up by the mud. Artillery pieces became stuck in the mud-clay mixture, as horses and mules died along the road. It was the darkest time for the Army of the Potomac. By the end of the first day, the army had only advanced four miles from Falmouth.[13]

After surviving a severe wound at Fredericksburg and battling disease at Falmouth, Private Elisha Kenyon Crandall was discharged and returned to Richmond. Courtesy of the Town of Richmond.

The rain continued for two more days as the Seventh received orders to join in the advance. Hundreds of Union soldiers became separated from their commands and struggled to find their place in line. In a letter to his brother, Sergeant Hull claimed it would be a good plan for the women of Rhode Island "to be making soldiers for we shall need them before the rebellion is crushed." Upon learning her son was stuck in the mud, Tryphena Cundall wrote in her diary, "oh the horrors of war." By January 22, William Hopkins noted that the mud was waist deep while at Camp Mud the mud was a foot deep. Each morning the men had to "bail" the water out of their huts as they attempted to survive in the freezing conditions and many could not even attempt to light a fire; indeed, the situation was nearly as bad as, if not worse than, Valley Forge. Federal soldiers were dying each day with no end in sight. Even in the despair of the campaign, the men of the Seventh still felt it was their duty to be fighting against the rebellion. Martha Young, the wife of Private Emor Young, had written her husband to stay away from the danger in the next battle. Young replied that he did not enlist to keep out of the fight. He felt it was his duty to remain at Falmouth. In addition, Young wrote that his children would never be disgraced by their father's actions in battle. On January 24, the rain stopped and the Seventh spent another day on the picket line. The rain then commenced again on January 26, changing to knee deep snow by the end of the month.[14]

For some in the regiment, the rain and picket duty had become too much. Private Alfred Sheldon Knight was admitted to the regimental hospital on January 27. Major Harris diagnosed him with pneumonia; there was nothing that could be done. Harris tried to make

Knight comfortable as he awaited the end. As his son was dying in a crowded hospital tent in Falmouth, Virginia, William Warren Knight wrote to Alfred telling him of the events on the Tunk Hill Farm in Scituate; all of the family was fine, except for his mother, Elizabeth, who had a minor cold. In Scituate, the citizens heard many rumors of the march, "One Day we hear that it has crossed the Rappahannock and the next day it is contradicted." Scituate was growing weary of the conflict; three men were killed at Fredericksburg while four had already died of illness near Falmouth. By the time the army left Falmouth, six more Scituate soldiers were dead; nearly all of them from the Seventh. Private Knight's condition continued to worsen until he died on the afternoon of January 31. His cousin, Almon Knight wrote, "When last we saw him on his cheek, the glow of health was bright. The stamp of manhood on his brow, And in his eye Hope's Light. He went from us with noble thoughts, with high and holy aim. With fond hope whispering in his heart, that he'd come home again." Knight's remains were forwarded to Scituate where he was buried on the Tunk Hill Farm five days after what should have been his thirtieth birthday. His personal effects, consisting only of what he had requested from his sister, were also sent home.[15]

Detached to Ninth Corps Headquarters, First Lieutenant George B. Inman resigned at Falmouth.

The Army of the Potomac returned to Falmouth on the twenty-fifth. On January 26, Burnside tendered his resignation again to President Lincoln; this time it was accepted. The people of the North had grown weary of the war, and many wanted to negotiate a peace with the Confederacy. Although he had commanded only for two months, Burnside had destroyed the army at Fredericksburg. Lincoln replaced Burnside with Major General Joseph Hooker. Hooker was a native of Massachusetts, West Point graduate, and a Mexican War veteran. He had performed well on the Peninsula and at Antietam. Now he attempted to reorganize the shattered army. His first act was to win the hearts and minds of the soldiers. On February 4, ten enlisted men in each regiment were allowed a furlough of ten days at home. February 6 brought a welcome change in the diet of the regiment; Hooker allowed a loaf of soft bread issued to each man. Some of the Seventh impaled the loaves on their bayonets and in their excitement paraded around with the bread. As February began, some in the regiment heard a camp rumor that was about to become true. Sergeant Hull believed the Army of the Potomac would be broken up and the various corps sent to different places. He also wanted to return to teaching, instead of remaining at Falmouth. In an attempt to remove some of the men from the camp, a dozen men were allowed to transfer to the understrength artillery batteries; several men in the Seventh were assigned to Battery D, First Rhode Island Light Artillery. The veterans who had survived Burnside's second expedition termed it the "Mud March." The wet, muddy weather had a severe effect on the Seventh. By February 2, only 283 men were available for duty. Since the regiment left Rhode Island, 400 men were ill or recovering from wounds. On February 1, tragedy again struck the Brown family of Exeter. On October 5, 1862 Private Joshua Brown was the third soldier to perish in the regiment, due to typhoid. On February 1, his brother Albert died of pneumonia near Falmouth; both men were returned home and buried together in the family plot in North Kingstown.[16]

The change in diet boosted the morale of the regiment as they struggled to regain their health. Some soldiers, like William O. Harrington and Charles F. Colvin, continued to gain weight as they ate the poor food. In Company K, Charles P. Nye had gained twenty-nine pounds since leaving Rhode Island, and he commented that "soldiering agrees with me first rate." For many in the regiment, there were only two paths to follow; either they died or were

This encampment at Brandy Station in the winter of 1864 was similar to that of the Ninth Corps at Falmouth. Library of Congress.

discharged, or they lived and thrived. It was a process of natural selection, even though some of the best men left the regiment, the soldiers who remained were veterans that could face almost any challenge posed to them. With Burnside gone, Orlando B. Willcox was appointed to the command of the Ninth Corps. Nagle returned to command of the brigade while Colonel Bliss returned to his Rhode Islanders. The men welcomed the change. Lieutenant Colonel Church had become known as a stricter disciplinarian than Colonel Bliss and was disliked by many in the regiment, particularly the men of Company A. As the weather continued to improve, the camp rumors proved to be true.[17]

On February 8, Adjutant Sullivan read orders for the Seventh to prepare to leave Camp Mud the next morning. As with every move, the men wrote home to tell their families that they were leaving. The orders were issued to the entire Ninth Corps; some felt as though they were being punished because Burnside had led the corps. The orders did not specify where the regiment was headed; some thought North Carolina, or the West. Sergeant Hull was happy to be leaving, "I don't care where we go, we cannot go to a place worse than this." On February 9, the men awoke early to tear down their huts and remove the shelter tents from the roofs of their huts. They piled the old, discarded equipment into large heaps; in one hour the Seventh was ready to march. In their two months at Falmouth, the regiment lost 50 percent of its strength, while seventy men died at the Battle of Fredericksburg and from illness at Camp Mud; indeed many left the regiment for good, some to suffer for the rest of their lives with the disease contracted. All of the sick were sent to the hospitals around Washington. Upon recovery they were transferred back to the regiment, giving a constant trickle of men leaving and arriving. Drummer Hopkins could best sum up the feelings of the men, "Good bye Rappahannock." At noon, the Seventh Rhode Island boarded a train to Acquia Creek. They then embarked upon the steamer *Georgia* to Fortress Monroe.[18]

The Ninth Corps was transferred to the Virginia Peninsula in an attempt to open up a second front against Richmond. The new camp had an immediate impact on the Seventh; the sickness seemed to dissipate. On February 13, William O. Harrington reported that he was eating soft bread, fresh beef, rice and beans. He wrote, "A good deal better fellings prevails amoungst our men." Isaac Cundall claimed that if the Seventh remained at Falmouth another six months the entire regiment would have died. As the regiment arrived on the Peninsula, the ever-conniving Lieutenant Peckham wrote that he would show his loyalty to President Lincoln if he received a commission as a major in one of the black regiments then forming. Despite being in the field only six months, three-quarters of the regiment was discharged, sick, or dead; eighty men had perished since the Seventh left Rhode Island, nine of them from Company A alone. Tryphena Cundall was upset that the regiment had advanced farther south, "How it makes the heart ache to think they have gone further off and we know not where." The men were encamped near the sight of the Battle of Hampton Roads, and could see the mast of the U.S.S. *Cumberland* in the distance; the vessel was sunk by the C.S.S. *Virginia*. The men were issued larger tents and prepared to again perform picket duty; however, this time the Seventh would not suffer from the same privation as they had at Falmouth.[19]

The date February 14, 1863, was one many in the regiment had been awaiting for a long time. The schooners *Elizabeth* and *Helen* finally arrived. The vessels were docked at Acquia Creek as the Seventh left for the Peninsula. As such the next day was spent off loading the vessels. The delay was unfortunate; all of the perishable items had been destroyed. In the box sent from Moosup Valley, both Harrington and Potter were upset to find all of their pies rotten. He cautioned his wife to use more care in the packing, "If there ben two thicknesses of paper between each pie I think they would have kept good." Harrington continued to gain weight. Some of the men in the regiment were still ill with the disease contracted at Falmouth, and death still occurred, though not on the same level as at Falmouth. Isaac Cundall finally received a shirt from his mother, but, much to Tryphena's dismay, the shirt was stolen. The health of the Seventh continued to improve as the men changed their diets. Large amounts of clams and oysters were available and the officers allowed the men to venture into the mud flats to collect them; thus, their food had some resemblance to traditional southern Rhode Island fare.[20]

The Seventh remained encamped near Newport News into March as they again performed picket duty and improved their health; still only 250 men were present for duty. A private wrote that the regimental hospital "is enough to make any one heart sick." March 17 was celebrated as Saint Patrick's Day by the few Irish members of the Seventh. They joined in several horse races and a musical performance under the direction of Brigadier General Michael Corcoran. On March 18, the Third Division of the Ninth Corps was detached to return to Norfolk, the move including the detachment of the Fourth Rhode Island. Martha Young continued to miss her husband Emor, serving in Company C.

Discharged to accept a commission in an African-American regiment, Sergeant Samuel Farnum drowned on his way home from the war.

She wanted to travel to Virginia to serve as a nurse. Emor fired back that she could not as there was no room for her in the tent, "with thousands of men of the roughest kind." He also did not want his wife to come because she might become ill. Young continued to insist that "I want to stay long enough to see this rebellion put down so that my Children will never have to go through what I have been already." In Company A, Charles Slocum wanted desperately to return to Richmond and resume farming. He thought soldiering was reducing his life expectancy. In addition Slocum thought there were too many "shoulder straps" in Newport News. Lieutenant Colonel Church was promoted to command of the Eleventh Rhode Island and left the Seventh.[21]

On March 18, another round of commissions was announced in the Seventh. Second Lieutenant Peckham received his much coveted bar as a first lieutenant and left Company E for B. Company D was reduced to thirty-eight men, although those wounded at Fredericksburg returned to duty, along with the ill. On March 19, the First Division of the Ninth Corps paraded past the Second Division as it marched to the steamers. The orders came down on March 22 for the regiment to prepare to march. Private Benjamin E. Wells was disgruntled in a manner similar to every other member of the Seventh. The Seventh was in the field for seven months and had not yet been paid. Wells wrote that he wanted to return home to farm, hoping at the very least to return by another winter. Upon seeing a comrade discharged for illness, Wells wrote, "I wish I could gone with him." The men needed the money; indeed, some families in the small villages of western Rhode Island were on the verge of starving. As to Private Wells, "I don't kerr I shank go onto another fight until i be paid off." Colonel Bliss apparently heard his men's pleas. He would not take his regiment anywhere until they were paid. On March 25, the Seventh received orders to take the steamer *Swan* to an unknown location. Late in the day, the paymaster finally arrived. The officer called each man forward and paid him five and one half months' pay; for a private this was $76.40. Many sent the amount home, keeping only several dollars for themselves. It was almost midnight before the regiment was completely paid off; $45,000 was paid to the Seventh. After his resignation, President Lincoln placed Ambrose Burnside in command of the Department of the Ohio, with headquarters in Kentucky. Burnside wrote to the president that he needed reinforcements; the general even specified which troops he wanted. As such, his Ninth Corps was detached from the Army of the Potomac and ordered west.[22]

Sergeant James B. Spencer of Warwick died of tuberculosis at Newport News. Courtesy of the City of Warwick.

7

River of Death

Before you get this I may be no more, but I believe in destiny. Prepare for the worst and hope for the best.
— First Sergeant John K. Hull, June 12, 1863

A storm broke over the bow of the *Swan* as the steamer carried the Seventh Rhode Island north from Virginia. In seven months, the troops of the regiment had learned to become soldiers, fought in a horrific battle, and survived the elements. Now they were going west, back under Burnside's command and to what many hoped would be easy duty. The storm brewed all day as the regiment steamed up the Chesapeake toward Baltimore. The Seventh arrived on March 27 to a welcome sight; merchants came to peddle their wares. Steward Peckham bought an expensive pair of the newly adopted hospital steward chevron; they were green in color, bearing a caduceus on each arm. After being recently paid, many were willing to trade the funds for pie and other edibles. Following their departure from the steamer, the men marched through the city to a waiting train and started on their journey.[1]

The Seventh boarded a series of cramped, stifling, uncomfortable box cars; many in the regiment were forced to stand as the train pulled out of Baltimore. The next day, the Ninth Corps stopped at York, Pennsylvania, for coffee. Four months later their brothers changed the course of history in a small town thirty miles to the west. In the afternoon, the trains arrived in Pittsburgh. Near the station, a large banner was posted with the words, "All Honor to the Heroes of Roanoke, New Bern, South Mountain, Antietam, and Fredericksburg," in reference to the battles the Ninth Corps had fought in. As the Seventh debarked from the train, the crowd started cheering the regiment. Isaac Cundall claimed, "It is honor enough for one man to belong to the 7th." The regiment arrived at Cincinnati on March 30, to another bountiful meal.[2]

The Ninth Corps was sent west at the specific request of their former commander. As they arrived in the city the men were quickly ferried across the Ohio River into neutral Kentucky. In the autumn of 1862, a large Confederate force under Braxton Bragg attempted to wrest the state for the Confederacy. His army was repulsed by Federal forces near Perryville in early October. As Ulysses S. Grant, the Federal commander in the West, set his army into motion to capture Vicksburg, he brought all of the Union forces in the area with him. With his headquarters in Cincinnati, Ambrose Burnside, in command of the Department of the Ohio, was responsible for the defense of Kentucky and to protect the loyal citizens against Confederate raiding parties.[3]

The Ninth Corps was assigned to Lexington, Kentucky, a small city of 10,000 inhabitants that was largely pro-Union and full of slaves seeking protection. The Seventh was ordered to camp in a large field outside of the city. Initially the citizenry did not appreciate the presence of a large number of New England troops in the area, claiming that they were all "abolitionists." In time the people of Kentucky grew to appreciate the Ninth Corps, as they were more disciplined and less likely to rampage than their western comrades. Erecting their shelter tents, the Seventh set about to build their first official camp since leaving Camp Bliss. The slaves called the soldiers, "Uncle Sam's men." The slaves again swarmed to the Seventh selling their wares, which were purchased with zeal. The regiment tore down many of the local fences for firewood. The citizens of Lexington were glad to receive the protection because the city had been captured the previous year. In addition Morgan and his guerrillas were almost always operating nearby. One day a young slave boy arrived near the Seventh's camp. Captain Edward Allen adopted the boy as his servant, naming him William. William Allen later traveled with Captain Allen to South Kingstown where he joined the Fourteenth Rhode Island Heavy Artillery, a black regiment then forming. Some of the Seventh's enlisted men were discharged to accept commissions in the regiment. William Allen died as a Rhode Island Volunteer in New Orleans in 1864. The Seventh remained at Lexington until April 8.[4]

The regiment began a march toward Winchester, Kentucky. The trek started at 8:00 on the morning of the ninth and continued till 7:00 that night; the Seventh traveled twenty-three miles, fatiguing all who participated in it. Some of the men thought they could make the trek easier by removing their shoes, causing all of them to have blisters. The straggling was so great that when Sergeant Hull called the roll of Company G that night, there were only five men present. As to Sergeant Hull's condition, "I as you may suppose, was foot-sore, lame and very much fatigued." Only the field and staff officers were mounted, allowing the line officers to share in the misery with their men. Those that arrived that night built small fires, boiling water to wash their feet in. The next day the master of Captain Allen's servant arrived looking for his slave. The man asked Colonel Bliss permission to search for the slave but the colonel denied the request, saying he was the only one that could search for the boy.[5]

The new location near Winchester had yet another positive impact upon the morale of the Seventh. Many thought it was among the most beautiful locations they had ever witnessed. Though Rhode Island with its jagged coastline, forests and open meadows was the home of these men, Kentucky offered something that many had never seen. Rhode Island was a poor place to farm, with its large masses of rock and other debris left behind during the last glacier period. The soil of Kentucky was rich and dark while the grass was tall and green. In Rhode Island, most planting did not occur until the end of April; in Kentucky the slaves claimed that the growing season arrived three weeks before Rhode Island. First Sergeant Hull claimed, "The fields are as green as they are in R.I. in June." There was but one article that the men did hate in Kentucky. This was the macadamized roads which made marching difficult. The people of Winchester were one-half pro-Confederate, a quarter Unionists, and a quarter neutral. The Federal supporters brought Kentucky whiskey to the men in the Seventh nearly every day. One soldier claimed in a letter after writing about the drinking, "You need not show this part." The men were sore after the march from Lexington, but did not "grumble" as Sergeant Hull said. The regiment continued on picket, constantly on watch for Confederate guerrillas.[6]

A finely dressed officer in a double-breasted dark blue tunic appeared in the Seventh's camp on March 14. He was Lieutenant Colonel Job Arnold. Arnold came to the regiment to replace Lieutenant Colonel Church. Rather than promoting Major Tobey to the rank, Governor Sprague, in one of his last acts of office, promoted Lieutenant Colonel Arnold. Arnold was a veteran of the First Rhode Island and had fought at New Berne, Fort Macon, Washington, and Kingston, North Carolina, with the Fifth Rhode Island. Arnold was cheered by the men in the regiment as he assumed his duties. By March 16, Nagle's Brigade left Winchester and marched south pass Boonsboro, the home of the legendary Daniel Boone. Some of the men discovered his fort, used in the Indian conflicts in the late 1700s. The Seventh was marching toward Richmond, another Unionist stronghold in central Kentucky and wherever the Federals went in the state, they were welcomed by the native inhabitants.[7]

Richmond was reached on April 19. The next day the men encamped at a field with gruesome sites. It was here on August 30, 1862, that Federal forces were defeated at the Battle of Richmond. William Hopkins noted bodies and debris still littering the field. The Seventh sent one company out on picket while the men huddled in their shelter tents during a rain storm. The people were pro-Union and continued to keep the regiment well provisioned. Peleg Jones watched as Unionists poured in each day from eastern Tennessee to escape the threat of being drafted into the Confederate army. The Seventh had garnished a good reputation for itself, "We have the name of being the best behaved troops," one soldier commented. Hospital Steward Peckham spent a large amount of money on a dutch oven for the use of the hospital detachment. Assigning one of the assistants to carry it, he told the man not to abandon it under any circumstances. In addition, he purchased a wide-brimmed straw hat and wore it throughout the rest of the campaign. William O. Harrington found himself detached to cook for the officers of Company K, a duty he enjoyed. The weather continued to be warm as the men drilled constantly. Many soldiers returned to duty following their recovery from wounds or illness. By April 20, 397 officers and men were available for duty, the most since December 12, 1862.[8]

Lieutenant Peleg Peckham continued his quest for promotion with the one person he could find to listen to his complaints. Captain David Kenyon was a neighbor of Peckham, living in Richmond, Rhode Island. Kenyon resigned in March and returned to Rhode Island to take command of the Eighth Rhode Island; a militia regiment called into state service to guard Narragansett Bay from a potential Confederate attack. Peckham wanted Kenyon to press for a captaincy in the Fourteenth Rhode Island. Each Saturday the men were excused from duty to prepare for Sunday inspection. On Sunday, the chaplain held service followed by an inspection. Here Colonel Bliss and the field officers walked down the ranks as they looked at the weapons and knapsacks of the men; those who failed were bound to be assigned to extra duty. Chaplain Harris Howard could be located only on Sunday to perform his services; when the men went to find him the rest of the time he was nowhere to be found.[9]

Marching orders were again received on May 1, but the weather proved to be unsatisfactory, and the Seventh remained encamped until the third of May when they marched the fifteen miles to Paint Lick. The site was named after an old Native American tactic to hunt deer by placing scent at a location where the animal would lick it, thus making the deer easier to kill. Colonel Bliss received a leave of absence on May 1, and he left for Providence. This gave Lieutenant Colonel Arnold his first test of leadership in the Seventh. The regiment remained encamped at Paint Lick for one week, allowing many to explore the area. Drummer Hopkins, in his ever-expanding curiosity into slave culture, found George Harris, the man who told Harriet Beecher Stowe about his experiences in bondage; Harris's story became the basis for *Uncle Tom's Cabin*. Following another march on May 11, Nagle's Brigade was assigned to Lancaster, Kentucky. During the march, the air became filled with dust kicked up by the marching columns, turning the blue uniforms of the men to white with dust. The men heard a rumor spreading throughout the army that Hooker had advanced on Fredericksburg and defeated Lee. In reality it was the complete opposite; Lee defeated the Army of the Potomac again at a small clearing in the woods known as Chancellorsville. Lieutenant Peckham continued to pester Colonel Kenyon for the commission; this time he attempted to bribe the colonel. Peckham was no longer just aspiring for a captaincy, he wanted to become a field officer. Tryphena Cundall again worried that Isaac would be unable to survive the rigors of marching, "I do not know how he will stand the heat so far south." Private Isaac Cundall wrote to his brother Edward that his health was well, but he failed to receive his mail from home. Like many in the Seventh he continued to be amazed at the scenery around him and the already advanced growth of the crops. Cundall entertained thoughts of moving to Kentucky after the war to farm.[10]

A major change for the First Brigade, Second Division, occurred on May 21. Brigadier General James Nagle resigned his commission and returned to Pennsylvania; he was suffering from ill health. Nagle again returned to service in late June, organizing the Pennsylvania militia during the Gettysburg Campaign. He was replaced by Colonel Simon G. Griffin, of the Sixth New Hampshire. Griffin was a veteran commander, and one well liked by his men, having fought at both battles of Bull Run, in North Carolina, and at Antietam and Fredericksburg. In addition, Brigadier General Robert B. Potter of New York was assigned to the command of the Second Division. Major General John G. Parke, a close associate of Burnside and a veteran of the North Carolina mission, took command of the Ninth Corps. The Seventh Rhode Island remained encamped at Lancaster until May 22. This day they marched the short distance of sixteen miles to Crab Orchard. Because the majority of the regiments in the brigade were from New England, the new encampment was designated Camp New England.[11]

Crab Orchard served as the center of activity in central Kentucky. It was one of the prime sources from which the salt pork eaten by most Federal soldiers was raised. The men had to constantly be on alert to prevent food from being eaten by the pigs. One night, a hog attempted to break into Drummer Hopkins tent to steal his haversack. As the young musician never was engaged in combat, and carried no weapon, he fought back with the one weapon he did possess: a three-tined fork. Hopkins managed to stab the pig behind the ears, thus forcing it back and saving his food. Private Harrington continued serving as the cook for Company K's officers; only First Lieutenant George Wilbur was on duty making his life easier. The men continued to supplement their rations by fishing in a local stream, while resorting back to "hard bread, salt pork & coffee." Fleas infested the soil near the camp, and the men detested their biting ability; one could not even sit down without being bitten. The officers enjoyed their time at Crab Orchard by racing each other on horses at a nearby track. Colonel Bliss returned on the twenty-seventh while the health of the regiment continued to improve dramatically. However, the pleasant duty at Camp New England was about to end.[12]

On June 1, Colonel Bliss went to brigade headquarters and returned with orders: The Ninth Corps was to prepare to move once more. Quartermaster Stanhope took the time to issue a new garment to the men. The coat was officially named the fatigue blouse, but it was called a sack coat by the men. It was a loose, four-button, dark blue coat that was more comfortable than the dress coats that had been issued in Providence—those coats were long since worn out. As with every move the Seventh made, the men wrote home to inform their families. This move, however, would be unlike any the regiment had ever made. The men were ordered to reduce their baggage to "one change of underclothes, one extra pair of shoes, sixty rounds of cartridges, & eight dayes rations." Rumors began to spread through camp as to where the men were going.

Some speculated Burnside would march into Tennessee while others thought they would travel to Vicksburg. With no other reinforcements available, Ulysses S. Grant called for the Ninth Corps to reinforce his position. He had been besieging the city for a month, but still more men were needed. The men continued to make preparations as they knew a hard campaign lay before them. On June 3, Private Harrington noted the temperature was 105 degrees, hotter than it ever was in Rhode Island. He was upset with his wife for not mailing his children's photos; Harrington had yet to see his nearly year old son, William. The Seventh left Crab Orchard on June 3 with ten days of rations carried in their knapsacks. The next day was particularly brutal and hot as the Ninth Corps marched twenty-one miles, passing by the grave of General William Nelson, shot by General Jefferson C. Davis. The men were up at 3:30 in the morning of the fifth as they marched to Nicholasville.[13]

Brigadier General Robert B. Potter commanded the Second Division, Ninth Corps, from Jackson to the end. Courtesy of the USAMHI.

The Seventh camped for the night. In their second experience with the paymaster, he again visited at night, paying the men for two months service. Isaac Cundall took the time to scribble a note to his brother, informing him he was keeping the funds as he did not know when he was going to receive them again. He also weighed in the rumor that was continuing to make the rounds in the regiment; the men did not know if they were going to Mississippi or Tennessee. "I think that we are going to Vicksburg to reinforse Grant," he wrote. June 6 constituted another tough day for Company A. Private William Bentley was killed in a boiler explosion on board a train. The Twelfth Rhode Island left the brigade and was sent to guard Hickman's Bridge; their nine months of service would end in several weeks. In their seven months in the brigade, the Twelfth had fought and died alongside their brothers in the Seventh, but had developed a poor reputation. In a harsh letter to Colonel Kenyon, Albert Perry wrote, "They was tip top blowers but darn poor feighters." In Company G, Sergeant Hull finally started to complain of the long marches the Seventh was undertaking. After listing what he was carrying in his pack, he claimed, "If that ain't making a mule of a man I don't know what is." That afternoon the Seventh boarded a train to Cincinnati. Here they again met their beloved general. Burnside wanted to lead his corps into Mississippi but the request was denied. He remained in Cincinnati making plans to defend the state from John Hunt Morgan's Confederate raiders.[14]

The Seventh arrived at Cairo, Illinois, on June 8 to another refreshing supply of fine food. Cairo was situated on the southern tip of Illinois and was bristling with defenses. Steward Peckham described the city as "a small, filthy disgusting place." It was from here that all supplies and men left for the western armies. The Mississippi was the lifeline of the West. If Vicksburg could be captured, the Federal forces would effectively cut the Confederacy in two. Officers and men scurried about again reducing their supplies and mailing letters home. Some men turned in their knapsacks, carrying only small belongings in a blanket rolled up and slung over their shoulder. Sergeant Hull, like the other first sergeants, was forced to carry his knapsack to hold the important company books he was responsible for. Captain Nathaniel Low served in the Eleventh New Hampshire, assigned to the Second Division. Low and Major Tobey were good friends and the two often rode together. In a letter to his wife, he complained about the orders issued to the line officers. "Line officer's baggage to be cut down, all that means a devil of a long march. It is going to be very tough on us line officers I tell you." Corporal Samuel G. Brown only carried a blanket, bottle of ink, note book, and a pair of spectacles. While at Cairo, Private Adams Murray of Company E decided he was tired of the Seventh and took "French leave." Indeed Murray was not only disgusted with the Seventh Rhode Island but the United States as well — he deserted to England. About midnight, Colonel Bliss led 310 Rhode Islanders onboard the steamer *Dove* docked in the river. The ship cast off as the Seventh Rhode Island again sailed south into the unknown.[15]

A "gray dawn" appeared over Cairo, Illinois, as a fleet of twelve transports carried two divisions of the Federal Ninth Corps down the Mississippi River on June 9, 1863. The men were bound for Vicksburg, Mississippi, to participate in the battle to finally open the entire river to Federal navigation. The fleet proceeded slowly down the river; some of the men experienced seasickness on the steamer north from the Peninsula, but this journey was relatively calm. During the first night on the river, several members of the Seventh went around to their sleeping comrades and

Commissary Charles Hopkins insured the Seventh's soldiers were well supplied with food.

stole their food. Private Uz Cameron of Company G was known as a sleep walker. During the night he stumbled from the deck into the water and was crushed by the paddlewheel; his remains were never found. Colonel Bliss also had another dilemma facing his officers. With such a large number of new officers and with various dates of commissions, he again had to designate the companies in line. This time he appointed the companies by the date their commanding officer was commissioned. From the left the companies were posted as: D, H, I, K, G, F, A, C, E, B.[16]

The flotilla passed Island Number Ten, the site of an important Federal victory the year before. The ever-dutiful Sergeant Hull noted his first viewing of the United States Colored Troops that were garrisoning the island. These men had yet to prove themselves in combat, and some in the Seventh looked down upon them as no more than slaves with firearms. Colonel Bliss ordered each company to take its normal turn at picket. Rather than placing each man out on duty, the men loaded their weapons and waited for the guerrillas on the hurricane deck of the

Surviving his Fredericksburg wound, Alonzo Jenks rose to the rank of first sergeant. Courtesy of the USAMHI.

Dove. The raiders could fire on the Federals safely from the side of the river. As the Seventh passed Memphis, they could see a monument erected several years earlier to President Andrew Jackson. Inscribed upon the shaft were the words, "The Federal Union, it must and shall be preserved." The Confederates had chiseled most of the words away. By June 12, the armada was half completed with its mission. The men broke out in song, singing "John Brown's Body" while fishing for catfish. Chaplain Howard composed a song about the Ninth Corps as they sailed down the river. On the thirteenth, the Seventh received fire from the long awaited Confederate guerrillas. First Sergeant Hull was washing a shirt when a bullet hit the boiler, six feet from where he was standing. After a five-day journey, Vicksburg was reached on June 14.[17]

Major General Ulysses S. Grant, the Federal commander in the West began his investment of Vicksburg in May. Following the defeat of the Confederates at the Battle of Jackson, Confederate commander John C. Pemberton brought his army into the bristling Vicksburg defenses. The city was the last major obstacle in opening up the Mississippi River. Grant had hoped not to have to lay siege to but capture the city quickly. Launching several assaults in late May and June, the Federals were repulsed with severe Union losses. Grant then began a standard siege operation, chocking off the city from resupply, while moving ever

MISSISSIPPI CAMPAIGN

Philip Laino

closer to the enemy. Day and night his artillery bombarded the stricken citadel against a dejected, demoralized enemy who refused to surrender. By the middle of June, the siege was finally taking its effect upon the Confederate defenders.

After debarking on June 16, the Ninth Corps prepared to go into camp. Many of the Westerners shouted at the Rhode Islanders the names of the battles in which they had been defeated, including "Fredericksburg." The Rhode Islanders yelled back, "Burnside sent us down here to show you how to fight and drive the rebs." Private Joseph Taylor spent two days trying to find the regiment. On June 15 he saw his brother on a naval transport in the river. Without asking permission, Taylor went to visit him. After completing his visit, Taylor returned to the shore to find the Seventh departed. He followed a Regular battery, but upon asking the western troops where the Ninth Corps was camped, they replied that they had never heard of the corps. Taylor eventually found the Seventh, but upon returning to camp he was arrested by Colonel Bliss for straggling. The colonel dismissed the private and then talked with Captain Percy Daniels, insulting him for allowing a private soldier to straggle. As the men settled into their new surroundings, Sergeant Hull had a premonition of his death: "Before you get this I may be no more." The water in Mississippi, like that at Falmouth, was stagnant, and almost totally undrinkable. One soldier com-pared it to a "frog pond."[18]

The weather in Mississippi was a problem for the Seventh from the start; it was the rainy season and mosquitoes and fever again became serious concerns for the regiment. The Seventh moved and encamped near Hayne's Bluff in Milldale, being held in reserve as Grant advanced closer to the city. Many of the men developed a type of illness known as Yazoo fever, named after the Yazoo River. It was a form of yellow fever that devastated the regiment, caused by the mosquitoes that infested the swamps. Captain Lyman Jackman described the Yazoo as "thick with green slime and death malaria." Even more disturbing to some was the fact that the name Yazoo meant "river of death." The men in the Ninth Corps were a poor choice to be brought into Mississippi. The majority of them were from New England or Pennsylvania and the men were highly susceptible to catching the tropical diseases in the extreme South. A further cause of illness was the presence of ripe blackberries. William O. Harrington claimed the men ate large amounts of the fruit, in addition to green

Residing in South Kingstown, Private Horace Healey died of Yazoo fever in Mississippi. Photo courtesy of the Pettaquamscutt Historical Society, Kingston, R.I.

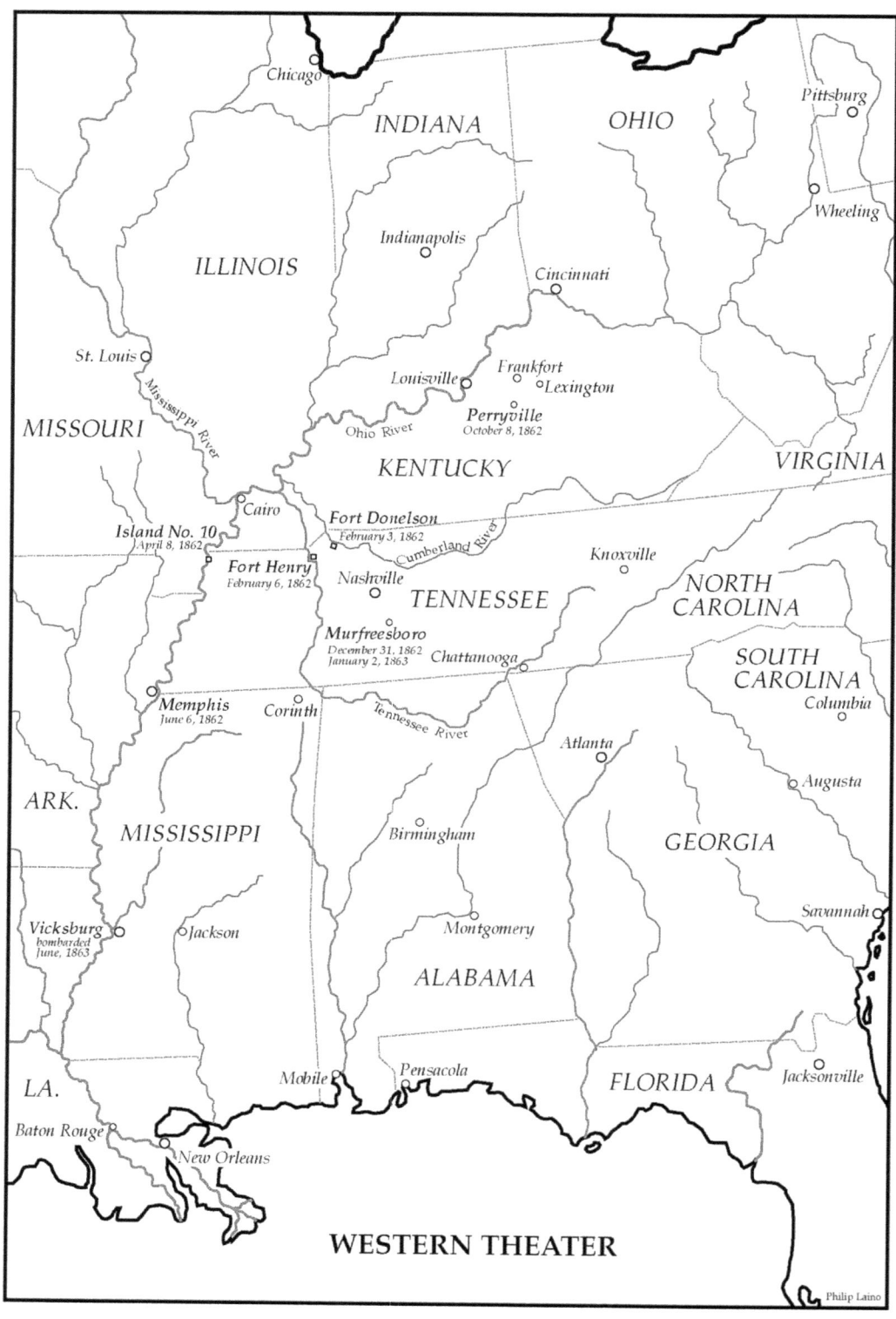

WESTERN THEATER

corn, causing chronic dysentery that wasted many of the men. By the end of June, 119 men were absent sick; the regiment again began the process of losing men from a climate that the Rhode Islanders were unused to. Company A was detached to help dig trenches along with the Sixth New Hampshire. The Seventh was camped ten miles from the city as they took their time to catch catfish, weighing up to eight pounds, in the Big Black River. Sergeant Hull commented, "We caught nice ones." The rain fell as if the men were fighting in a rain forest. The continuous tropical storm drenched the men constantly in their wool uniforms.[19]

On June 25, they were awake at 3:30 A.M. and, by the end of the day, had marched thirty miles to the east when Grant heard that Joseph Johnston was approaching from that direction. Only seventy-five men were capable of making the march in ranks, as the rest of the regiment caught up during the night. On this day the Seventh watched a battle that decided the fate of Vicksburg; the Union forces captured a hill, the key to the Confederate defensive positions. The marching orders were countermanded and the Seventh went into camp. The regiment encamped near an orchard that proved to be infested with rattlesnakes. Several of them were killed, allowing the men to keep the tails as a souvenir. The men marched to yet another encampment and began to construct breastworks. The labor was intensive for many in the extreme heat. As with his few complaints, William O. Harrington enjoyed the duty: "I have never felt better in my life." The mail failed to come to the regiment, allowing many to again wonder why it was so slow. Ever the keen observer, Private Harrington called the area "the most romantik places around here." The Ninth Corps began to feel as though they were not needed at all. Indeed, they were relegated to protecting the rear rather than fighting in the main lines around Vicksburg. One New Hampshire soldier vented his frustration to his wife, 1,500 miles away in Boston. He wrote: "Gen. Grant does not need us at all & it was a perfect Tom fools sending us out here so far."[20]

Captain Ethan Jenks was a veteran officer, promoted for gallantry at Fredericksburg to the captaincy of Company I. He was a native of Foster and an acquaintance of several of the men in Company K. On July 2, 1863, he returned to the encampment after supervising a wood-cutting detail. Colonel Bliss summoned the captain to his quarters to inform Jenks that he was dismissed from the service effective immediately. Colonel Bliss did not give any mention as to why Captain Jenks was being dismissed. He turned over his accounts to his lieutenant, boarded a steamer, and proceeded to Providence to settle the account. The first notice that Captain Jenks had of his dismissal was on June 9, when he noticed he was not in a listing of Seventh officers in the Rhode Island papers. This was in addition to not receiving his pay in Kentucky. This action had an unsettling effect upon all of the other officers in the regiment; if one of them could be dismissed for no just cause, so could the other officers. In a sign of solidarity, every officer in the regiment signed a letter that appeared in the *Providence Journal*. In the account, the officers praised Captain Jenks's bravery in giving all of his "distinguished soldierly qualities." The officers further stated that they hoped the government would settle the matter and "anxiously look forward to his speedy return." After traveling to Providence, the captain went to Washington. Here he was told that a mention of his court hearing was issued in early May; however, Jenks could not read it as he was in Kentucky. The specific charge leveled against him was that the captain had enlisted a man he knew was physically disabled in order to gain the required number of enlisted men to receive his lieutenant's commission. The man was Private James A. Briggs, a small man, but one who was thought to be able to maintain the rigors of army life. Briggs became ill at Pleasant Valley and was sent to Washington, finally receiving a discharge in June. Through a clerical error, Captain Jenks was ordered dismissed from the service. Under a special order by Secretary of War Stanton, Captain Jenks retained his rank, and he was allowed to take his place in the company line. He returned to the Seventh in September.[21]

The eighty-seventh birthday of the United States of America dawned on July 4, 1863. In Vicksburg, Mississippi, the United States forces finally achieved what they had been waiting forty-seven days to see. At 9:45 in the morning, white flags appeared on the Confederate works as the Southerners finally yielded to the Northern forces. General Grant met with Pemberton to discuss the surrender terms; Grant accepted nothing short of a full and complete unconditional surrender. The 30,000 Confederates were paroled on the promise that they would never again take up arms against the Union. Along the Federal line, the men began shouting "Battle Cry of Freedom," a popular song about the Union cause. Captain Low of the Eleventh New Hampshire exclaimed, "It is enough to make a fellow crazy. Hurrah! Hip! Hip! Hurrah!" With the victory at Gettysburg and Vicksburg, the tide of war finally turned in favor of the United States. Grant was not one to rest when victory was achieved; Johnston and the Army of Tennessee were still prowling somewhere to the east. After he learned of the fall of Vicksburg, Johnston set his army in motion back to Jackson. Grant dispatched William Tecumseh Sherman and 50,000 men to pursue and defeat him.[22]

The Union forces marched slowly toward Jackson, only fifty miles distant. The Big Black River was crossed on July 6; however, there was no bridge available for use. A heavily loaded artillery caisson broke the span. The only craft present could bring only six men across at a time. Due to the twenty-four-foot depth of the river, it could not be forded. The march was largely uneventful for the Seventh, except for discovering a hornet's nest that was accidentally burned, allowing the insects to fly around stinging the men, who were forced to abandon their dinner. Jackson was reached on the night of July 10 as the men abandoned their knapsacks to rush forward. Lieutenant Frederic Weigand and a platoon of Company G were left behind to guard the packs. When Stephen Peckham found the lieutenant, he was under a tree reading a book about railroads, taken from Jefferson Davis's library. On July 11, Colonel Bliss took command of the Seventh and Sixth New Hampshire and destroyed nearly a mile of railroad track running into Jackson. The process consisted of burning the wooden railroad ties and then heating the iron rails over them. The heated rails were then bent over a tree, thus preventing them from ever being used again. The Ninth Corps approached Jackson from the north and waited for action.[23]

At 2:30 in the morning of July 12, the Confederates began peppering away at the Seventh Rhode Island. Within a moment the entire battalion was awake and preparing for battle. After several hours, arms were stacked, but Confederate cavalry approached the camp between the pickets and were able to report back with information. The Confederate artillery opened fire, creating a hazardous location in the ranks. At 8:00 the Seventh advanced to the front. The regiment deployed under fire, exactly as they were trained. Company B stood in its position, as the other companies swung from the left and ran into position. Here they rested on their arms all day, under constant Confederate fire. For picket duty that night, Colonel Bliss assigned Company G to the hazardous task. With no other officers present, First Sergeant John Hull led the company forward into the darkness. The following morning he cautiously walked the picket line, recalling his men to the Seventh's main line. As Hull approached Sergeant Henry Tisdale of the Thirty-Fifth Massachusetts, a shot ran out from a Confederate sniper in a tree. Sergeant Hull was hit in the chest and died instantly. The faithful chronicler of the Seventh's travels was no more. Captain Allen eulogized the young man in a letter to his father: "As a soldier he was faithful and ever at his duty, and as first sergeant of his company he was like a father — kind and ever attentive to the wellbeing of his company." As First Sergeant Hull was killed, Private Jonathan R. Clarke was shot in the head; he was also from South Kingstown.[24]

The fighting now became general all along the Seventh's line. Abel B. Kenyon went down, shot in the hand while loading his musket, Nathan Rathbun received a mortal wound to the arm, and Oliver Congdon was hit in the cheek. As the Confederates shelled the Rhode Island line, Captain William Joyce ran to check on Captain Allen. Joyce had developed a reputation for being a "dapper fellow" and always appeared clean and polished, despite the muddy roads and Mississippi swamps. As the enlisted men hugged the ground for protection, Captains Allen and Joyce stood upright and talked for half an hour while the battle raged around them. Private Jared J. Potter of Richmond had never been under fire, having been ill during Fredericksburg. A bullet clipped his scalp, stunning the young man. His only comments on the engagement were "it was a hard fight." First Sergeant William Barstow commanded a platoon in Company A and fired into an advancing Confederate line,

A teacher from South Kingstown, First Sergeant John K. Hull was killed at Jackson. Photo courtesy of the Pettaquamscutt Historical Society, Kingston, R.I.

driving back the enemy. The Confederates retreated in haste back to the city. For the second time in combat the Seventh Rhode Island stood and held its ground; this time it had the satisfaction of repulsing the Confederates. In the middle of the night, Colonel Bliss ordered Adjutant Sullivan to take Company D out to reinforce the picket line. He and Lieutenant Fuller Dingley set the company in the required area, but took a wrong turn in the dark. Both men were captured by the Confederate pickets. They were quickly whisked away to Richmond, Virginia. Sullivan did not rejoin the regiment for nearly two years.[25]

The following day, Colonel Bliss sent a detail out to recover the bodies of Sergeant Hull and Private Clarke. They were wrapped in their military blankets and hastily buried in a shallow grave in an apple orchard. After the burial, the men returned to the picket line. Corporal Manuel Open marked the graves with a rough wooden marker. Benjamin Hull desperately wanted to travel to Mississippi and retrieve his son's body. The state was still in Confederate hands and he could not successfully accomplish the task. Sergeant John Webster mailed home Hull's knapsack adding the note, "He was liked by all." For the Seventh, Jackson was a victory, and one that came at a low cost. Two men were killed outright, two were mortally wounded, eight men were wounded, and two officers captured. The men were somewhat shell shocked, having remained under fire for forty-eight hours.[26]

The Confederates evacuated Jackson on July 16 and retreated into Tennessee. The Ninth Corps remained to help tear up some additional railroad tracks. The Thirty-Fifth Massachusetts was the first into the city as they and other Federal soldiers ransacked the capital. The Seventh remained on picket north of the city. Stephen Peckham traveled close to the city, and among his observations he noted, "The Mississippi State Lunatic Asylum is the finest building I have ever seen in this state." On July 20, the Ninth Corps received orders to turn around and march back to Milldale. The heat was stifling, and the Seventh was suffering from poor provisions. Many of the enlisted men and half of the officers were severely ill from the climate. The shoes of the Rhode Islanders fell apart as they marched the fifty miles. Some stripped off their sky blue trousers and threw them alongside the road, marching in their cotton drawers. The clothing of the regiment was so depleted that some wore civilian suits. The following day, Private Joseph H. Holbrook collapsed at the side of the road and died of exhaustion. All the men had left to eat was a single piece of hardtack besides the fruit, which caused even more medical problems. By July 24, the last survivors of the Seventh straggled into Milldale as the regiment again established a camp. In a report of the Battle of Jackson, Colonel Bliss again praised his regiment:

> The conduct of the regiment during the expedition has been praiseworthy, and credit is due them for their gallantry in repelling the sortie of the enemy and for the soldier like manner in which they have submitted to the many privations and fatigues they were turned out, and remained in readiness to repel the attack of the enemy. They have suffered severely from the intense heat and debilitating effects of the climate. Some of the marches were long, with but little water, and many of the men were barefooted and without proper clothing, and at times all were on half rations.

For the Rhode Islanders, the Mississippi odyssey was only beginning.[27]

After hearing the news of the victory at Jackson, Grant set about to reward the Ninth Corps commanders for their role in ensuring success in the battle. Colonels Zenas R. Bliss, Simon G. Griffin, and John Hartranft were all nominated for promotion. Hartranft was the colonel of the Fifty-First Pennsylvania and led his regiment during the storming of the Rohrbach Bridge at Antietam. Colonel Bliss was told that this time the promotion was coming for sure. Griffin and Hartranft went so far even as to order the coat of a brigadier. Even with Grant's personal endorsement, none of the officers received the promotion. When he returned to Kentucky, Colonel Bliss began to hear a rumor that he would never be promoted to brigadier general due to an earlier incident. This was in reference to the dishonorable surrender of the Eighth United States in 1861. Colonel Bliss was only a first lieutenant in the incident and was not responsible for the actions of a lieutenant colonel. All of the officers involved in the incident were never promoted in the volunteer service to any rank above colonel and so, for the second time, Colonel Bliss did not receive his merited promotion because of the Washington political machine.[28]

While the regiment was engaged in the Jackson Campaign the surgeons were engaged in a battle of their own. Nearly 150 men were left ill at Milldale, and the number was rising everyday. The climate, combined with the mosquitoes and "stagnant pools from which horses refused to drink," continued to reduce the Seventh. Private J. Weeden Burdick, a popular member of Company A, died of Yazoo fever on July 16. His death broke the bond between the three men from Hopkinton who were connected to Burdick through marriage. After the war, Abel B. Kenyon returned to Mississippi and brought Burdick's remains back to Rockville. Corporal Roswell H. Potter followed on July 22. Henry Godfrey and Joel C. Maxon were more fortunate; they were discharged and allowed to die at home in Hopkinton. The men were allowed to rest on July 24, enjoying a feast of salt pork. The water continued to be "very poor." Colonel Bliss deployed guards around the wells while men continued to drink from the Yazoo. He had sent Captain Theodore Winn home in July to enlist men to fill up the decimated ranks of the regiment. In addition to the heat and water, the rain was having a telling effect. Many of the poorly constructed articles of clothing simply rotted off of the men. The illness became a growing concern as men continued to be sent to the hospital each day. During dress parade on the twenty-sixth, the men were nearly naked; no supplies could be located. The food continued to be poor; Drummer Hopkins described the hardtack as "musty and wormy." The rations were made in Cairo and shipped down the Mississippi, often arriving full of weevils and mold. By July 30, the Seventh Rhode Island was unable to muster any men for duty. Private Harrington expressed what many in the regiment were feeling: "I have seene enough of Mississippi."[29]

On July 31 Grant finally relieved the Ninth Corps, permitting them to return to Kentucky. He praised their conduct during the campaign, especially for the action at Jackson. The New Englanders finally won the affections of the Westerners, who learned first hand how well they fought. In the Seventh, the suffering from illness was worse than the regiment

Private Henry Godfrey was discharged due to Yazoo fever and died thirteen days later in Richmond. Photo courtesy of the Town of Richmond, Rhode Island.

had experienced at Falmouth. Isaac Cundall again became ill with Yazoo fever in addition to being covered in boils while some men were too weak to eat the poor food they were receiving. One soldier commented, "The men fear if they tarry much longer all will perish from the climate." Finally the steamer *David Tatum*, a "large but old and shabby craft" arrived to take the First Brigade, Second Division north. The steamer got underway, but could not proceed as it was overcrowded. The Ninth New Hampshire remained behind as the steamer finally began the journey north on August 9; it would be another trying experience for the Seventh.[30]

The illnesses suffered by the Seventh Rhode Island took several weeks in their course to finally kill the soldier it infected. By the time the regiment left Mississippi, the grim reaper again returned. Private Thomas Ray Kenyon of Company A died of typhoid on the ninth; during the night his body was buried on the riverbank. On August 12, Benjamin Peckham died and with two other Seventh soldiers was buried at the mouth of the Arkansas River. Private Peleg Jones had the unfortunate task of burying his friend at night underneath a tree. The medical staff attempted to do everything they could to help the sick. There was no medicine but whiskey, which did not help. Only three commissioned officers remained well enough to command their companies; Lieutenant Peckham finally received his wish and became an acting captain. Private Jones recorded, "The men fall sick each day." With Colonel Griffin ill, Colonel Bliss again took command of the First Brigade. Captain George Wilbur almost died of chronic dysentery, only being kept alive by Stephen Peckham's constant attention. The voyage up the Mississippi took the lives of five members of the regiment. Drummer Hopkins became ill with Yazoo fever in commenting that he suddenly became cold. Suffering from a headache and pale in the face, he lost all control of his muscles. It was from this horrid disease that so many Rhode Islanders were lost.[31]

By August 17, the Seventh had arrived back at Cairo, Illinois, after a two-month sojourn in Mississippi. Many felt that the campaign was unnecessary because the Ninth Corps was not even fully used for the purposes for which it was enlisted. Lieutenant Peckham wrote, "In two months service under Grant the 9th Army Corps lost 66 killed and fifty percent sick with disease." Nearly 3,000 men in the corps were ill. The seemingly invincible Private Harrington continued to be in excellent health.[32]

On August 20, the Seventh arrived in Cincinnati in a pitiable

Private Nathan Rathbun was mortally wounded at Jackson. Courtesy of David Rathbun.

condition. They were embarrassed due to their wretched look; one citizen bought a Rhode Islander shoes out of his own pocket. Almost every enlisted man was barefoot and some were wearing rags; the officers were not much better. Captain Allen and several other officers who had received furloughs during the campaign promptly returned to Rhode Island. Major Thomas Tobey also left on sick leave. Chaplain Harris Howard resigned in July, leaving the men without a spiritual adviser. Even more disturbing, two of the Seventh's surgeons took their furloughs as well, leaving the regiment with one doctor and a pharmacist. Some clothing was issued to the Seventh while the men enjoyed a bountiful breakfast. After several days of rest, the regiment proceeded to Camp Nelson, where they encamped in a field still suffering from loss. Again, Company G suffered heavily. In a letter to Harrison Steadman, who served in the Twelfth Rhode Island, Sergeant Winfield S. Chappell wrote:

> The Mississippi Campaign was one of hardship and suffering. The heat was awful and the water at best was no better. We left many of our Company in Miss., poor boys. They have gone and I trust they are in a happier world. That we were sorrowful at there loss wil not in no means begin with our feelings. It was hard for us, very hard indeed, and thousands of times have I thought of them and mourned their loss. Oh, think only a little more than a year ago they left their homes full of life and hope with the expectation of returning. Their hopes are blasted and their bodies now rest in Southern soil.[33]

8

Kentucky

We have truly learned that the soldier's life may be arduous to the extreme.
— *Hospital Steward Stephen F. Peckham, August 14, 1863*

Two months in Mississippi destroyed the Seventh Rhode Island Volunteers. From an initial strength of 310 entering the campaign, only 100 remained fit for duty. Yazoo fever, dysentery, malaria, and typhoid had cut through the regiment like a knife through butter. The campaign had a greater impact on the regiment than both Fredericksburg and Falmouth. The surgeons were overwhelmed with illness; nothing could be done but give the men whiskey. After only one year in the field, Rhode Islanders were again needed to answer the call.[1] Many in the regiment hoped that the men of Rhode Island would rise up and join the service. Albert Perry and Elisha Palmer wrote to their former captain, David R. Kenyon, about the problems facing the Seventh. They, like all of the men in the regiment wanted the people of Rhode Island to "com with their musket on their shoulder to join the 7th Rhode Island to make one strike for the 'Star Spangled Banner.'" The men already in the regiment were unanimous in one regard — they did not want any of their relatives enlisting in the service. William O. Harrington was pleased that his brother Sanford did not enlist. His other brother, Josiah, continued to serve with the Eighteenth Connecticut in the Shenandoah. One of his comments rang true for the regiment. "We have left some of our boys in every state we have been it makes me feele sad to think of the past & how many brave boys have left there bones in rebbeland." The Seventh was in such a reduced state that they were not even considered a combat effective regiment. Only 100 Rhode Islanders remained, but the officers and men of the Seventh who remained now considered themselves veterans.[2]

Like the other states in the North, Rhode Island was compelled to issue a draft in July 1863. The majority of those pressed into service were non-native Rhode Islanders, mainly from New York, who joined to receive the large bounties being offered, but never joined the regiments. All of the men were assigned to the Second and Fifth Rhode Island Infantry. Many of those drafted paid the three hundred dollar commutation fee, or sought a substitute from New York. Isaac Cundall's brother Edward was drafted, despite having already served in the Ninth Rhode Island; he paid the three hundred dollars for a substitute. In addition, Governor James Y. Smith issued orders to raise the Third Rhode Island Cavalry, consisting of 1,500 men. His motives were purely political as he could gain support by issuing commissions to prominent men supporting the Republican cause. Few commissions were issued to the veterans who had proven themselves in combat. The raising of the new regiments meant that the ranks of such decimated regiments as the Seventh Infantry and the First Rhode Island Cavalry, which was captured almost in its entirety during the Gettysburg Campaign, were never brought up to full strength, allowing the veterans to continue to perish. Nearly half of the Third Cavalry came from states other than Rhode Island, while a quarter of the enlisted men were the despised bounty jumpers who practiced their craft again. The Third Rhode Island Cavalry was sent to the swamps of Louisiana where, like their brothers in the Seventh, they died by the score due to disease.[3]

By September 1863 the Seventh Rhode Island was a veteran combat regiment that had proven itself at both Fredericksburg and Jackson. The only solace to their two months in Mississippi was the personal

Private William Tourgee died of Yazoo fever in Kentucky. Photo courtesy of the Pettaquamscutt Historical Society, Kingston, R.I.

thanks of General Grant and the two battle honors on the regimental colors: "Vicksburg" and "Jackson." As a veteran regiment, many of the men did not want to see their ranks filled with bounty jumpers and draftees that would bring disgrace to the Seventh. Palmer and Perry wrote, "We do not expect to have our ranks fill up with such poor men as cant raise 300 dollars." Captain Theodore Winn was unsuccessful in attempting to enlist men at home, while the other officers failed to induce any Rhode Islanders into the service.[4]

Following their arrival in Kentucky, the regiment waited for several days trying to regain its health. On August 23, they took a train to the pleasant camp near Nicholasville. The camp was clean and fully provisioned, and a running stream supplied fresh water. The location was named Camp Parke in honor of the Ninth Corps commander. Dr. Corey and Steward Peckham attempted to treat the 150 sick men in the camp. By August 31, nine men died of dysentery and Yazoo fever, including First Lieutenant Albert L. Smith. On September 1, only ninety men were present for duty. Lieutenant Peleg Peckham served as the commander of Company B, Adjutant, and Officer of the Day as there were few company officers left. He claimed many of the men were "sick and drunk." In addition the Seventh became known as the "Sunburned heroes" for their actions in Mississippi. Drummer Hopkins reported, "Men are dying off rapidly." Dr. Corey became ill and was unable to complete his duties. Only Stephen Peckham remained to care for the sick; each day his supplies of whiskey and quinine dwindled until none were left. He called upon the surgeon of another regiment but little aid could be given. Peckham claimed, "We have truly learned that the soldier's life may be arduous to the extreme." The men were paid off on September 4. Rather than sending the pay home, many spent the small amount on eggs, butter, and chickens in a vain attempt to gain their health. Sergeant William T. Wood died on September 10 and, as with most of the deaths, the loss was reported by Captain George N. Stone to the family. His brother Henry was dispatched to Lexington to retrieve his body and return it to Apponaug. For Henry Wood, the task was especially difficult, only eight months earlier he had traveled to Falmouth to bring the remains of George W. Wood home to Warwick. George was a member of the Twelfth Rhode Island; both brothers died of dysentery and were buried together in Apponaug.[5]

The gravely ill men were transferred to Camp Denison in Cincinnati. Here the surgeons attempted to treat the men to the best of their ability. Quinine worked somewhat to break the fever of those suffering from malaria and yellow fever, while the others waited in agony for the end. By October 1, 150 men of the Seventh Rhode Island had been transferred to Camp Denison. The campaign was disastrous for the Seventh; forty-five Rhode Islanders lost their lives due to the Mississippi Campaign. Private Darius Hopkins received a discharge to return to Scituate, but he died at the camp on September 26. Corporal Charles P. Nye was one of the fortunate members of the regiment during the campaign. He gained more weight and considered himself "fat as a hog." His companions in Company K were different, the company brought thirty-five men into Mississippi; nine men died due to disease, almost all of them from Foster and Scituate. In Company K seven men were discharged on account of illness: such losses were typical.[6]

While the Ninth Corps was in the South, Burnside again added to his reputation by driving Morgan's raiders out of Ohio into Kentucky. Morgan and a large proportion of his men were captured in Ohio. Burnside's next plan was to take the Ninth Corps into eastern Tennessee, in a move reminiscent of the spring campaign in Kentucky to protect the Unionists there from Confederate raiding parties. He quickly attempted to reorganize the Ninth Corps for the campaign, but it proved to be in vain because there were hardly any men available for duty. Upon learning of the reduced size of the Seventh Rhode Island and Ninth New Hampshire, the two regiments were allowed to return to Kentucky for a much needed rest and reorganization. Burnside marched the Ninth Corps to the Cumberland Plateau, over the mountains into eastern Tennessee, finally coming to the relief of loyal Unionists in the area. The only men from the Seventh involved were those detached to Battery D, First Rhode Island Light Artillery. Instead of marching to Tennessee, the severely depleted regiment was ordered to Lexington, Kentucky and, instead of marching the distance, a train was again procured to transport the men.[7]

The Seventh arrived in Lexington on September 10 to return to the duty they began in the spring. Rather than pitching their tents, the regiment was assigned to a large warehouse that served as the headquarters of the Forty-Eighth Pennsylvania. The citizens continued to supply the regiment with whiskey, which caused some insubordination among all of the men in the regiment, both officers and enlisted men. Captain Percy Daniels and Lieutenant Peleg Peckham were arrested by General Willcox for "using indecent language to some ladies." Some of the men on picket found stills in the forests, which led to more problems from abuse of whiskey. The on and off illness of Isaac Cundall finally subsided and he was able to return to duty. Each day troops passed through Lexington on their way to join Burnside in Tennessee and the Army of the Cumberland as they met the Army of Tennessee in combat along the Chickamauga in Georgia. William O. Harrington enjoyed the "lite duty" the men performed, but was upset at the course of the war; the Union forces were again defeated at Chickamauga while the Army of the Potomac failed to follow up on the victory at Gettysburg.[8]

The black citizens in Lexington continued to seek the protection of the Federal forces. Captain Allen led a detail that captured 500 of them and employed the former slaves in government operations. Unable to find the required number by searching local farms, Captain Allen and Company A surrounded a black church on a Sunday and found 100 strong, young men. Under the Emancipation Proclamation, slavery and the slave trade was still legal in Kentucky. One Seventh officer remarked that the bidder of a particular slave girl should feel embarrassed for purchasing the girl. The auctioneer claimed the presence of the Federal troops reduced his profits nearly 95 percent. As the men performed the menial tasks in Lexington, they could view the fruits of Burnside's victory in Tennessee. Corporal Charles P. Nye served with the provost guard at Nicholasville; on September 21, he watched as Confederate prisoners were escorted to the camp on their way to prison in the North. His description of the prisoners gives the stereotypical appearance of a Confederate soldier in the West. He wrote: "They was the hard lot of looking men that I ever saw they looked so that they ought to have a good scrubbing with soop and watter."[9]

Colonel Bliss received a leave of absence and returned to Rhode Island. This time, his intentions were personal. He was married in October and tarried for several weeks before returning to the Seventh. Despite being gravely ill, Lieutenant Colonel Arnold again took command of the regiment with zeal and attempted to reorganize the men into soldiers. New clothing was issued while the men bathed and washed constantly. Dress parade and drills continued to restore the soldierly characteristics for which the Seventh was known. Arnold set up competitions among the companies for "neatness of dress and equipment and soldierly bearing." The ever-complaining Lieutenant Peckham continued to vent his frustrations to his confidant, David R. Kenyon. In his latest ranting, Peckham again lost all faith in President Lincoln. He claimed, "honest is a misnomer to his name," upon learning the president had suspended the writ of habeas corpus. The regiment continued on their tour of picket duty, but found the task difficult, especially with such a small number of men; the privates were required to "turn out" every other day for the duty. It became evident that they would remain at Lexington into the winter; especially welcome was the barracks, instead of the leaky, cramped huts the men had barely managed to live through at Falmouth. No reinforcements arrived, although the sick trickled back to the Seventh, restoring the regiment to almost 125 men. The health of the men improved somewhat, as they changed their diet from hardtack and salt pork to fresh meat and soft bread.[10]

Private William O. Harrington became one of the fortunate men to be dismissed from the monotony of guard duty. He was assigned as the cook of Company K, a duty he enjoyed. By the beginning of November, the company gained enough men to finally become a respectable command for recently appointed Captain George Wilbur; his company mustered thirty-two rifles. Harrington finally received several small photographs of his children while requesting warmer clothing for the winter months ahead. Despite his volunteering for the Seventh, Harrington continued to wish he was at home picking his apples, "I allmost immagin myself at home farming." A fire broke out on November 11, which the regiment responded to in a "timely and invaluable" manner. Despite being in service for a year, the Enfields continued to be polished for every parade, although the rifling and cones were starting to show the effects of two battles.[11]

Thanksgiving in 1863 was finally celebrated in a manner befitting the Rhode Islanders native heritage. Only one year earlier the men had subsisted on hardtack and turnips as they waited to cross the Rappahannock. Now the men had turkey and beans, while several young ladies brought in pails of milk. The sick were treated at Transylvania College to a feast of turkey, pie, and soup while the bands played the sad tune, "Home Sweet Home." The men had much to be thankful for, especially the survivors of Fredericksburg, Jackson, and the diseases that seemed to follow the Seventh everywhere. For a brief moment it resembled in a small way home as it was in Rhode Island.[12]

December 1863 was a cold dreary time in Lexington as the regiment continued with the monotony of performing picket and guard mount constantly. The Seventh had finally received an issue of warm clothing. The sick continued to return and the health of the Seventh improved greatly. The forests around Lexington were severely depleted, while firewood commanded a high price. The men continued to purchase food from the local farmers to supplement their meals. Chicken was very popular with the men, as they could be purchased for fifteen cents. Lieutenant Colonel Arnold issued orders against drinking whiskey; none could be found in camp. Some of the farmers brought the liquor to the Seventh by inserting the bottle in the chicken, which was seldom discovered by the officers conducting the search.

The situation in the West finally seemed to be turning after Chickamauga. Grant defeated the Army of Tennessee at Chattanooga, while Burnside thrashed Longstreet at Fort Sanders in late November. Battery D, First Rhode Island Light Artillery, and Roemer's New York Battery were responsible for the successful defense. In a letter to his wife, Emor Young claimed the New Yorkers were "our deliverour," after saving the regiment at Sulphur Springs and performing invaluable services with the Ninth Corps at Fredericksburg and in the West. Ever the tactician, Young theorized about the moves of the 1864 campaign. He believed the Army of Northern Virginia would never be "whipped" along the Rappahannock; instead, Meade had to flank Lee. Burnside's victory in Tennessee gave him additional public support in Rhode Island; however, some of the men in the Seventh never forgave their commander for the slaughter he brought upon them a year earlier. Private Young recalled it as a complicated political game. He wrote: "I do not think any General can satisfy the Government for they sit at Washington and give them orders and if he

A musician from West Greenwich, William P. Hopkins devoted his life to retelling the story of the Seventh Rhode Island.

obeys he is defeated." The Seventh continued to enjoy their duty at Lexington, being pleased with the availability of fresh supplies and the monthly appearance of the paymaster. However, as the snow and rain began to build up, the mud returned, leaving some in the Seventh to rename the encampment Camp Mud, Number Two; still, Lexington was a far better place than where the regiment had spent the last winter. Lieutenant Peleg Peckham continued to complain about his lack of advancement; he was next in line for a promotion to captain and had been commanding Company B since the Mississippi Campaign ended. He claimed in another letter to David R. Kenyon, "My patriotism is love of money." Although some complained about their duty at Lexington, the Seventh was about to receive a Christmas surprise.[13]

Marching orders were received on December 24 to travel the twelve miles to Nicholasville, where two companies of the Seventh had already been deployed guarding prisoners under Captain Allen. Nearly twenty men became sick from the change in climate, after moving out of the barracks, and had to be returned to Lexington. The Seventh's destination was again to reinforce the main Ninth Corps lines around Knoxville, but, still understrength, the orders were countermanded. On Christmas, the men ate their standard army meal while listening to the fireworks and celebrations of the citizens. For some in the Seventh, the loud explosions brought flashbacks to Fredericksburg. The Rhode Islanders marched on steadily in the worsening weather through rain and snow. The regiment was going to garrison a line of communications in eastern Kentucky. The only protection against the elements was the pathetically small shelter tents. Private William O. Harrington reported, "The regt is very much dissadisfied with the moove." Straggling again became an issue as the men marched in the cold of winter, "I dont think that half the boys will be found when they are wanted." By New Year's Eve, the temperature dropped to what William Hopkins reported as "twenty degrees below zero."

Lemuel Briggs was one of the fortunate survivors from South Kingstown's Company G. Photo courtesy of the Pettaquamscutt Historical Society, Kingston, R.I.

A large fence was found and the Seventh built a raging bonfire, much to the dismay of the farmer whose fence was just destroyed. The New Year broke cold and hard as the Seventh attempted to evacuate their tents, which were frozen solid. William H. Jordan, a private in Company K, was among the cold Rhode Islanders making the journey "in the very worst of weather in the winter through the roughest of the country." He witnessed the men freeze as they attempted to complete the march. During the night, two men in Company D had frostbite on their feet. The food was expended; Company D collected five dollars for a "good sized pig." Ever the observant anthropologist, Drummer Hopkins recorded his observations of Kentuckians in the mountains. They lived in "rude, windowless, log cabins, with such a low doorway a tall man is obliged to stoop on entering." By January 5, 1864, the Seventh Rhode Island had arrived at its destination, the Cumberland River. They marched fifty miles in the middle of winter through the worst of weather. Private Jordan claimed, "we have had a tough time in getting here." Some were surprised that no member of the regiment died during the march. The Seventh was assigned to Point Isabel, a fortified position guarding a key ford and bridge over the Cumberland River. Colonel Bliss returned from his leave and took command of the post. Each company set up its own camp without regard to army regulations; the only point was to keep the regiment alive and together. The position was renamed Point Burnside as this is where the Ninth Corps commander crossed into Tennessee. Here the Seventh remained for several months.[14]

Owing to their isolated position on the Cumberland, the supply trains often could not travel over the rough roads to Point Burnside. Hardtack became a valuable commodity and was eaten "to the last crumb." The freezing weather continued bringing snow and ice almost every day. Jared J. Potter built a roaring bonfire each night for Company G. The men slept around the fire as if they were the spokes to a wheel. The sleeping arrangement had both an advantage and a disadvantage; "we baked one side & froze the other." In order to survive the harsh elements at the exposed position, the men finally were allowed to build the huts they were so used to occupying during the winter. The food problems continued for some time but the local black population again supplied the Seventh. On one occasion, upon ordering a chicken pie, the men were disturbed to find the food was indeed a chicken pie, but contained the whole bird; including the feathers and the feet sticking up through the crust. Foraging parties were organized under Captain Jenks to ride into the countryside in search of fresh provisions. In one of the few letters to leave Point Burnside, First Lieutenant Peckham continued to pursue a captaincy. This time he offered Colonel Kenyon 500 dollars for the commission. It was a prestigious position; the double bars of a captain paid one hundred dollars per month. The officers of the Seventh camped together, leaving the first sergeants to care for the men each night. By February, 200 men were on duty, creating some sense of a regimental formation.[15]

With little to do at the Point, the men took the opportunity to explore the area and to wait for the spring campaign to begin. Several of the men were allowed to go home for thirty days on a furlough. Those selected had been with the Seventh through all of the campaigns, diseases, and weather conditions; they deserved to receive the gift. This reduced the amount of officers present for duty. Lieutenant Peckham was forced to take command of both Companies B and C as they began to corduroy the roads around the post by chopping logs so the wagons did not sink into the mud. Some of the regiments around the Seventh were among those that had first been formed in 1861. During the summer of 1864, their three years of enlistment would be over. As such, they were given the option of enlisting for an additional three years. For this, these "veterans" would be given a bounty of $700 and a thirty-day furlough. William O. Harrington believed that the men who reenlisted could receive the funds "quite easy." Harrington was among the growing number who believed that the war would be over by Christmas 1864. Despite the high bounties being offered in Rhode Island, no recruits enlisted in the Seventh, but men returned from the hospital each week. Private Emor Young was pleased with the scenery at Point Isabel, noting the rocks that rose several hundred feet above the river. The cold continued to have an effect upon the regiment, causing colds and pneumonia. Ever curious to know about the life of a Federal soldier, Martha Young asked her husband about the picket duty and other daily routines of army life. He replied, "Just think of it, march al day then lay down for the night upon the cold ground; many have frostbitten toes ears and fingers."[16]

In Hopkinton, Tryphena Cundall continued to pray for her son, Isaac. He was constantly in and out of the hospitals for various ailments. With the surgeons back from their furlough, Stephen Peckham had little to accomplish. He became good friends with Captain Jenks of Company I. After returning from his court-martial, Jenks became the best liked of the Seventh's company commanders. He was very similar to Colonel Bliss in disposition being "quiet, pure, and simple." Promoted for bravery at Fredericksburg, Jenks was thirty-six years old. In 1861, he had served with the First Rhode Island fighting at Bull Run alongside Lieutenant Colonel Arnold. In 1862 he raised thirty men for the Seventh and was awarded with a commission. Major Thomas F. Tobey returned to Rhode Island and was discharged on February 9. Despite his being a junior captain, many of the enlisted men hoped Jenks would become the next major.[17]

By the middle of February, the supplies had finally arrived at the Point, allowing the men to "get enough to eat." Some men set traps along the river to catch fish. Private Young's wife feared he would reenlist for another three years. Young did not want to upset his wife, but he was sick

Sergeant Jesse Carr of Exeter served in Company F. Courtesy of Katie and Luane McDonald.

with the disease that eventually killed him. He did not reenlist, affirming, "You want me to hold out firm and not enlist again have no fear on that account." The dirty water which had so plagued the regiment at Falmouth and in Mississippi subsided as the men found a spring near camp. The Seventh continued to build their quarters while Colonel Bliss brought his wife Martha to visit the camp; she was warmly received by the regiment. Washington's Birthday was celebrated with a flag raising as the men fired their muskets and the artillery roared from the heights above the Cumberland. On February 27, Colonel Bliss reported to the men on developments taking place in the regiments around them; it was time to decide if they were going to reenlist or not. The Rhode Island government gave a bounty of 300 dollars, while the United States contributed 400 dollars. In addition, two dollars were added by each town, for a total of $702 for the reenlisted veteran. Furthermore, the new enlistment started from the time the man reenlisted. As a bonus, a forty-day furlough was offered that could be spent at home. The men gathered together in their huts to debate the option. It was becoming clearer that the war would end soon. However, if the regiments were maintained after the war to become part of the force garrisoning the South, it meant another three years away from home. The Rhode Islanders felt as though they had already done their duty; it was time for other men to rally around the colors. In one and a half years of service, the Seventh had marched hundreds of miles and fought in two battles, in addition to losing hundreds by disease. They left their comrades buried in nine states. Private Young's wife Martha continued to pester her husband not to enlist. Her pleas were given added urgency when 175 members of the Fourth Rhode Island reenlisted and returned home. Emor Young replied, "let them list, for my part I shall not." In addition, Young wanted to move to Kentucky after the war.[18]

In March 1864, the Seventh continued with what seemed to be endless tedium in picket and guard duty along the Cumberland River. Officers and men continued to come and go daily, returning and traveling between Rhode Island and Kentucky on furloughs. By the middle of the month, rumors began to spread through the camp that the Ninth Corps was being recalled to Virginia. Emor Young hoped the rumors were not true, "I am well contented to stay here the rest of my three years," he wrote. On March 25, the Seventh received orders to move to Annapolis, Maryland, where the Ninth Corps was reequipping and outfitting itself for the spring campaign in the East. The march began on March 27, as the men left Point Burnside, singing "My Old Kentucky Home." Before leaving, they raided the tent of a sutler, who had been charging the men exorbitant amounts of money for the items he was selling. Captain James N. Potter attempted to stop the attack but was hit in the head. By March 30, the Seventh arrived at Camp Dick Robinson for the third time. The roads were again full of mud, sucking the boots off some men. On April 3, the entire First Brigade, Second Division was reunited for the first time in several months at Covington.[19]

Lieutenant Colonel Job Arnold would eventually die of the illness he contracted in Mississippi.

A train took the Seventh from Covington along much of the same route they had traversed exactly one year earlier. In their time in the West, over fifty additional names were added to the Seventh's growing list of deceased members. Lieutenant Colonel Arnold, still suffering from a lingering illness, followed his regiment, but was forced to yield the command. Arnold traveled home to Providence, where he resigned his commission in May. The beloved colonel finally succumbed to the illness in 1869, becoming the last Rhode Islander to die from the effects of the western campaign. Lieutenant General Ulysses S. Grant arrived from the West; he was a new ray of hope to end the war in the East. The Ninth Corps rendezvoused at Annapolis, Maryland, where Major General Ambrose Everett Burnside reorganized his forces to begin the campaign to finally defeat the Confederacy.[20]

9

Return to Virginia

We charged their works, we lost heavy but gained nothing.
— *Private Jared J. Potter, May 18, 1864*

    The fourth spring of war came to a divided America in April 1864. For three years the killing had gone on, with no end in sight. In the Army of the Potomac, encamped at Brandy Station, Virginia, 80,000 men waited for the slaughter again. After losing battle after battle for three years, President Lincoln finally found a general who led his army to victory in the East. Grant took command of an Army of the Potomac radically changed from the one that the Seventh Rhode Island had last seen struggling to survive at Falmouth. After being defeated at Chancellorsville, they fought Lee to the death at Gettysburg and won more victories in the fall of 1863. After refitting over the winter of 1864, the Army of the Potomac waited for the spring to arrive.

    Burnside brought his Ninth Corps from Kentucky and Tennessee in a poor state of preparedness and strength. Only 6,000 men returned with him, while reinforcements streamed into the vast Annapolis encampment daily. Annapolis was well known to the original members of the corps; it was from here Burnside had successfully launched his North Carolina expedition two years earlier. The veteran regiments, such as the Seventh Rhode Island; Sixth, Ninth, and Eleventh New Hampshire; and Forty-Eighth Pennsylvania provided a model for the new recruits learning how to become soldiers.[1]

    The Third Division of the Ninth Corps, which had been left at Newport News, was broken up and its regiments transferred to other corps. The Fourth Rhode Island was stationed at Point Lookout, Maryland, guarding Confederate prisoners. The Second Division was completely reorganized. The two New Hampshire regiments were transferred to the Second Brigade, along with Colonel Simon Griffin. Two Massachusetts regiments, the Fifty-First New York, and Forty-Fifth Pennsylvania were added to the First Brigade along with the Seventh Rhode Island and Forty-Eighth Pennsylvania. The First Brigade of the First Division consisted of new regiments, composed of veterans from Massachusetts. Six Michigan regiments joined the Third Division, robbing the Ninth Corps of its "Yankee" heritage. The Fourth Division also added a new element to the corps. The soldiers in the Fourth Division were not only fighting to preserve the Union but for their own freedom as well. These men were U.S. Colored Troops organized into two brigades under Brigadier General Edward Ferrero. The officers were white, many of whom had previously served as enlisted men in other regiments and had to pass a test of leadership proctored by Major General Silas Casey. In total the Ninth Corps mustered 25,000 officers and men. Burnside added a new symbol to his corps as well. When Hooker took command of the Army of the Potomac, he had established a system of badges for recognition among his corps. Each infantry corps and its supporting artillery were given a specific shape; the Second Corps wore a trefoil, while the Sixth Corps carried a Greek cross. Each division was assigned a color, red for the first, white for the second, and blue for the third division. Burnside's symbol for his corps was a shield with a fowled anchor and crossed cannon, along with a "9" made of a piece of rope. The symbols represented the naval origins of the corps during the North Carolina Campaign. Initially Burnside wanted the badges to be made out of gold bullion, but it soon became evident that the enlisted men would not be able to receive them. Instead, they cut the shape of a shield out of scrap wool and sewed it to their forage caps. The black soldiers in the Fourth Division wore green as their division color.[2]

The Seventh took time at Annapolis to again bolster its ranks. Those who had been at the hospital and on detached duty continued to stream in, bringing the command up to 250 officers and rifles. Colonel Bliss was sent to Alexandria, Virginia, on detached duty, in addition to the second captain, Percy Daniels. In nine months at home, Captain Winn had forwarded no recruits to the regiment. The only hope for reinforcement lay with those veterans willing and able to return from the hospital to the front. Many had already been transferred to the Veterans Reserve Corps or discharged, reducing the aggregate strength of the regiment. Hospital Steward Peckham had taken a furlough while the Seventh was at Covington. He took his time to collect additional medicine and supplies for the regiment. While the Seventh was encamped, a circus was in town, allowing the men time to view the show.[3]

Ambrose Burnside designed this badge to be worn by members of the Ninth Corps. *History of the Sixth New Hampshire.*

The officers thoroughly drilled the Seventh again to a high degree of proficiency. As with all organizations that did not frequently participate in close order drill, the Seventh only needed several hours to again prove that they were among the best. On April 13, former Major Tobey arrived in camp to look after his old regiment. He was cheered by the men. After regaining his health in Providence for several months, Tobey enlisted in the Fourteenth U.S. Infantry, but was commissioned a second lieutenant. He used his political connections through John Hay to help Colonel Bliss in his pursuit of a star. In Company C, Private Young was among the few who did not welcome the appearance of the major. "I will not cheer for any man but when peace is proclaimed," he said. On the same day Burnside rode through the camp, like Major Tobey, the general was again warmly received by his men. As for Private Young, "I held my tongue and kept mum." While the Seventh was encamped at Falmouth, Martha Young had sent her husband a pair of boots and, to her surprise, Emor still wore them. While the Seventh remained at Annapolis, Grant came from Brandy Station to confer with Burnside and to review the Ninth Corps. Upon seeing their new commander for the first time, one Rhode Islander commented, "I must say that it looks as though the Government had chosen a curious looking man for a military leader."[4]

Discharged due to the disease he contracted in Mississippi, Major Thomas F. Tobey later joined the Regular Army and served until 1900. Courtesy of the USAMHI.

April 20 was a busy day in the camp of the Seventh Rhode Island. Marching orders were again received. All baggage was turned in while the men were issued new uniforms. Many chose to abandon their cumbersome knapsacks to again carry rolled blankets filled with a few personal belongings. The men were worried about the strength of the regiment. Only 250 men were present, with more than 200 in hospitals. These men continued to be discharged and transferred to the Veterans Reserve Corps. If the Seventh did not maintain a paper strength of 400 men, they faced being consolidated with another regiment, losing their identity as the Seventh Rhode Island. The body of Sergeant Henry Morse was sent to Glocester. Morse was one of the few members of the regiment to accompany Burnside to Knoxville where he had contracted typhoid. Private Young wrote, "he was beloved by all in the company although he had not been with it for a long time." Lice were a pest that had followed the Seventh since they arrived in the field in 1862. Some soldiers pinched them with their fingers while the majority boiled their clothing to get rid of the "devels." Captain Theodore Winn finally returned to the Seventh on April 22 to take command of the regiment. The line officers were issued with shelter tents while the quartermaster removed the large wall tents. At 9:30 in the morning of April 23, the Ninth Corps marched out of Annapolis on its way to Washington. The new regiments, unused to marching at all, pitched their supplies along the road, allowing the veterans to resupply themselves with what was needed.[5]

President Lincoln and General Burnside held a review of the corps on April 25, as the men crossed the Potomac and again entered Virginia, encamping at Alexandria for two days. On April 27, the Ninth Corps turned south and began their march to reinforce the Army of the Potomac. The Seventh was detached as flankers, probing the sides of the road for enemy activity. The twice contested field of Bull Run, where Rhode Islanders had started the battle and brought glory to their state, was reached on April 28. The men were told that this was the last opportunity to mail letters home. William O. Harrington wrote, "we are looking for hot worke before many days."[6]

The Ninth Corps continued to march, occasionally hearing the sounds of firing in the distance. Colonel Bliss remained at Alexandria, transferring new regiments to the Army of the Potomac. Captain Percy Daniels hurried from the city and was appointed to command the right wing of the Seventh. On the morning of May 4, the Army of the Potomac left Brandy Station and crossed the Rapidan to attack Lee. Like the Ninth Corps, the Army of the Potomac had received a facelift. When the Ninth Corps left, there were seven infantry corps present; now only three corps comprised the Army of the Potomac, containing 25,000 men each. Burnside's Ninth Corps posed a problem. Under the rank system, both he and Major General George G. Meade held the same rank. Burnside outranked Meade, having been commissioned in April 1862 after capturing New Berne. Under an odd set of orders, set forth by Grant, Burnside reported directly to the lieutenant general, not having to take orders from Meade. The men in the Army of the Potomac looked with disdain at the soldiers in the Ninth Corps. While they had fought and died by the thousands at Chancellorsville, Gettysburg, and Mine Run, the Ninth Corps had performed relatively easy duty in the West. Just as they had done in Mississippi, the Ninth Corps had to prove themselves again in combat.[7]

Grant's plan of attack was almost identical to Burnside's plan of two years earlier. Using his massive 100,000 man army to defeat the enemy, he would slide continually around Lee's flank. In this manner, Grant avoided direct contact with the Army of Northern Virginia while moving into position to finally capture Richmond. Standing in his way was Robert E. Lee and the 70,000 veterans of the Army of Northern Virginia. Although the force suffered massive casualties, including many veteran commanders, the Confederate army again fought with the same zeal that had carried it through three years of war. Grant's plan of attack began as his men crossed the Rapidan River and converged near the Wilderness Tavern. Moving west along the old Chancellorsville battlefield, the Army of the Potomac found the Confederate forces in the thick undergrowth of a forest simply called the Wilderness. In two days of hellish fighting, Federals and Confederates fought each other in a seesaw action. The woods caught on fire, as the two forces exchanged point-blank musket fire in a swirling mass of confusion. It was a seesaw engagement until Confederate reinforcements arrived on May 6, repulsing the Union forces. Another bloody day for Rhode Island came on May 5 with the Second Regiment losing a quarter of its strength. After two days of indescribable combat, no ground was gained by either side. It was a draw in which the Army of the Potomac lost 18,000 to Lee's 7,000.[8]

While the Army of the Potomac was fighting at the Wilderness, the Seventh Rhode Island had the task of guarding the wagons of the Second Division, Ninth Corps. Ever the wandering soldier, Private Hartford Alexander of Company E followed a regiment he thought was the Seventh. Alexander fought in the May 5 battle along with the Forty-Eighth Pennsylvania. This was the second time Alexander had fought away from the ranks of the Seventh; previously, he had charged up Marye's Heights twice at Fredericksburg. During the night of May 5, Colonel Bliss rode from Alexandria to take command of the First Brigade. Despite being seriously ill, the colonel took command and led the men into action on May 6, earning his third nomination to become a general and a brevet in the Regular Army to lieutenant colonel. A brevet was an honorary promotion, allowing the recipient to wear the uniform and title of the new rank but not to receive the pay that accompanied it.

The fighting raged two miles from the Rhode Islanders, leading one Seventh soldier to write, "We listened to the sound of battle and frequently could see the smoke." When the black-pow-

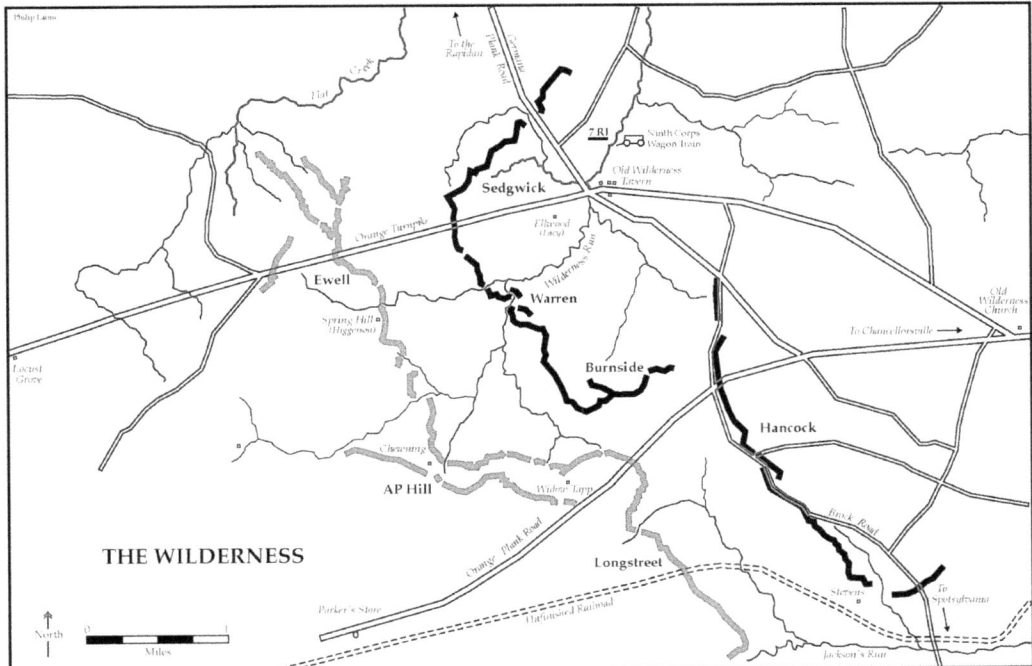

der muskets were fired, they produced huge clouds of white sulphuric smoke. In the hellish combat in the undergrowth and fallen timber of the Wilderness the two sides often could not see each other, making the fighting even more mentally challenging for the participants. Early on the morning of May 6, the Seventh was relieved from guarding the trains and crossed the Rapidan at Germanna Ford. The river was 125 feet wide and three feet deep. Each man stripped himself and then dried off in the hot May sun. Sergeant Decatur M. Boyden was severely wounded by a piece of stray Confederate artillery, becoming the only casualty suffered by the Seventh at the Wilderness. The Seventh proceeded to the Wilderness Tavern still being held in reserve.[9]

The wagon train crossed the Rapidan on May 7 and the Seventh was recalled to guard them. Here they also guarded several hundred Confederate prisoners. Drummer William P. Hopkins noted, "The men themselves were lank,

Assistant surgeon Albert Sprague practiced medicine for fifty years.

yellow, long limbed, rough-haired fellows possessing the hardihood of wild animals." During the night, the regiment encamped near the Wilderness Tavern, noticing body parts and skulls that appeared to be looking directly at the men protruding from the ground from the

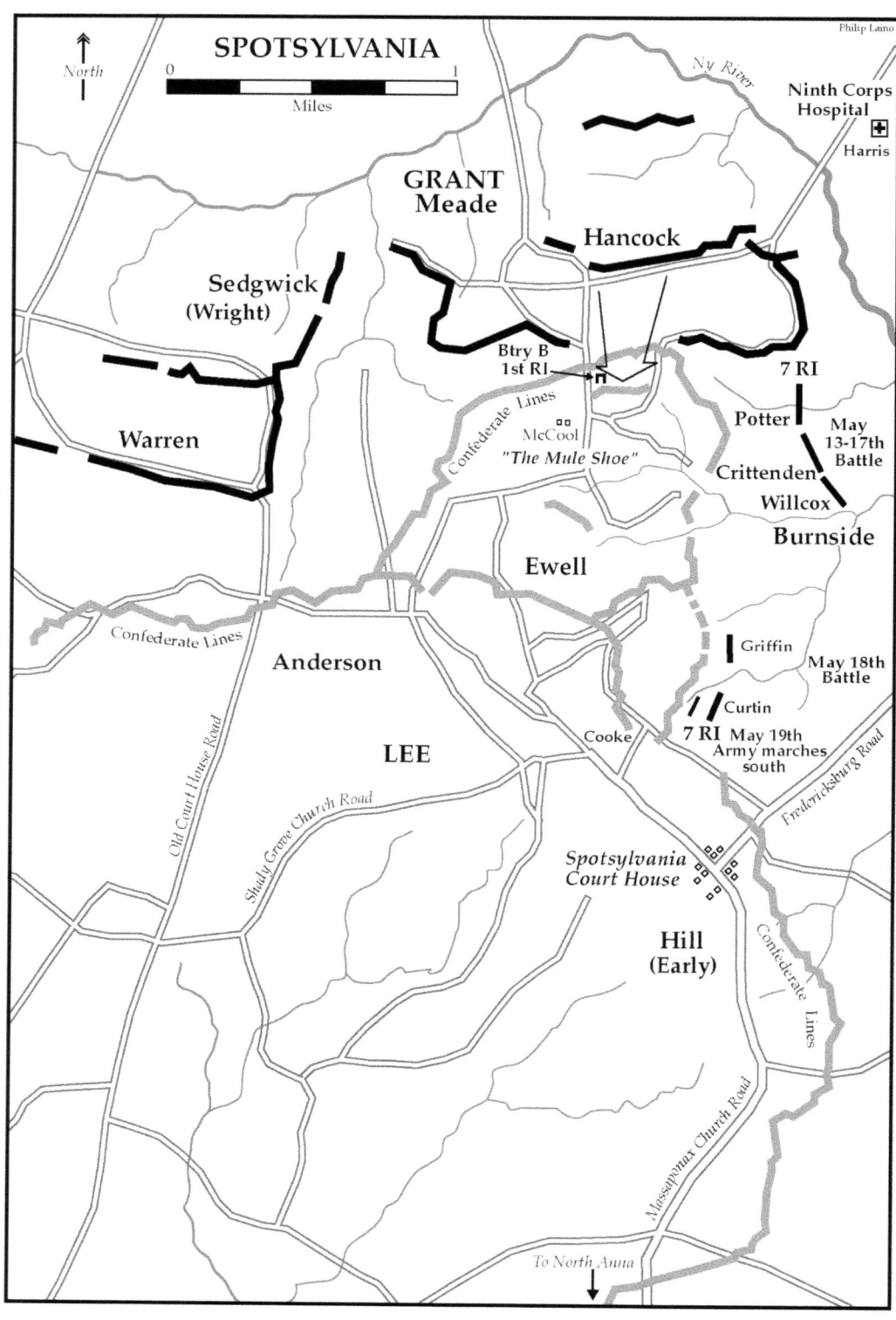

Battle of Chancellorsville. Burnside took the opportunity to organize a central hospital to treat the wounded. Under the command of Major Harris of the Seventh, the plan was designed so that the injured could be treated quickly at the front before moving to the larger hospitals in Washington. In addition, those suffering from noncritical injuries could quickly be bandaged up and returned to the regiments. Harris was well suited for the task, having more real-life combat medicine training than any other surgeon in the Ninth Corps. Steward Peckham claimed, "In both military medicine and surgery he had wide experience." Assistant Surgeon Sprague and Steward Peckham were also assigned to the hospital, leaving Dr. Corey to treat the wounded Rhode Islanders on the front line. During the day, Grant decided on a fateful course. After being defeated at every battle before, each commander of the Army of the Potomac had returned to Washington. This time, however, after suffering 20,000 casualties Grant decided to turn south to a small crossroads village called Spotsylvania.[10]

Ever quick to move, Lee moved his army into the area first, as it was on the road leading directly to Richmond. Here the Army of Northern Virginia built a series of impenetrable defenses. Deep trenches were constructed to completely shield the defenders. They reinforced with earth, branches, logs, and sharpened sticks. Into the entrenchments Lee placed his infantry and artillery creating a position that was even more defensible than the line that was at Marye's Heights two years earlier. The main lines were placed around the high ground near the McCool House. The best troops in the Army of Northern Virginia — the Stonewall Division — were stationed here. They continued to build the defensive position, which took the shape of an inverted letter "u." The attacking Federals named the position the Mule Shoe salient. On May 8, the Seventh awoke to see their brothers in the Second Rhode Island marching past them as they attempted to cut off Lee's line of retreat. By May 9, the Seventh was detached from the wagon duty as the Fourth Division of the Ninth Corps took over the task for the entire army. The Ny River was crossed as Grant threw a brigade against the Spotsylvania entrenchments; it was beaten back with heavy losses. Again, only one man was wounded in the Seventh, by a piece of shell. The wounded staggered back to the rear as the dead were collected and laid out in long rows, a small piece of paper pinned to each jacket to tell who the man was. On May 10, the Ninth Corps suffered a significant loss. Brigadier General Thomas G. Stevenson, commanding the First Division was killed by a sharpshooter. Dr. Harris commandeered the Harris House as the surgeons waited for the gruesome work ahead. It had been a year and a half since the Rhode Islanders viewed such slaughter; their relatively safe duty was about to come to a tragic end.[11]

"The rain poured in torants," one Seventh soldier wrote on May 11. The regiment moved into position and built a line of breastworks of fallen timber and limbs; no injuries occurred. During the night, Colonel Bliss was attempting to jump his horse over the swollen Ny River when the horse fell on the bank, nearly crushing the colonel. Bliss received a severe sprain to his ankle, which led to his removal to Washington for a month. The injury troubled Colonel Bliss for the rest of his life. Command of the First Brigade fell to Colonel John I. Curtin of the Forty-Fifth Pennsylvania.[12]

Thursday, May 12, 1864, was a day long remembered by all those who lived through it. Early in the morning, Major General Winfield S. Hancock and the 15,000 soldiers of the Second Corps broke through the Confederate defenses around the Mule Shoe, capturing an entire division. Battery B, First Rhode Island Light Artillery, charged along with the infantry, firing point-blank blasts of double canister right into the works to drive the Confederates from their positions. The shattered Southern forces retreated to another line of entrenchments a half mile to the rear of the Mule Shoe and began to fortify them again. Hancock attempted to pursue, but the Ninth Corps, which was supposed to be on his right flank, received conflicting orders

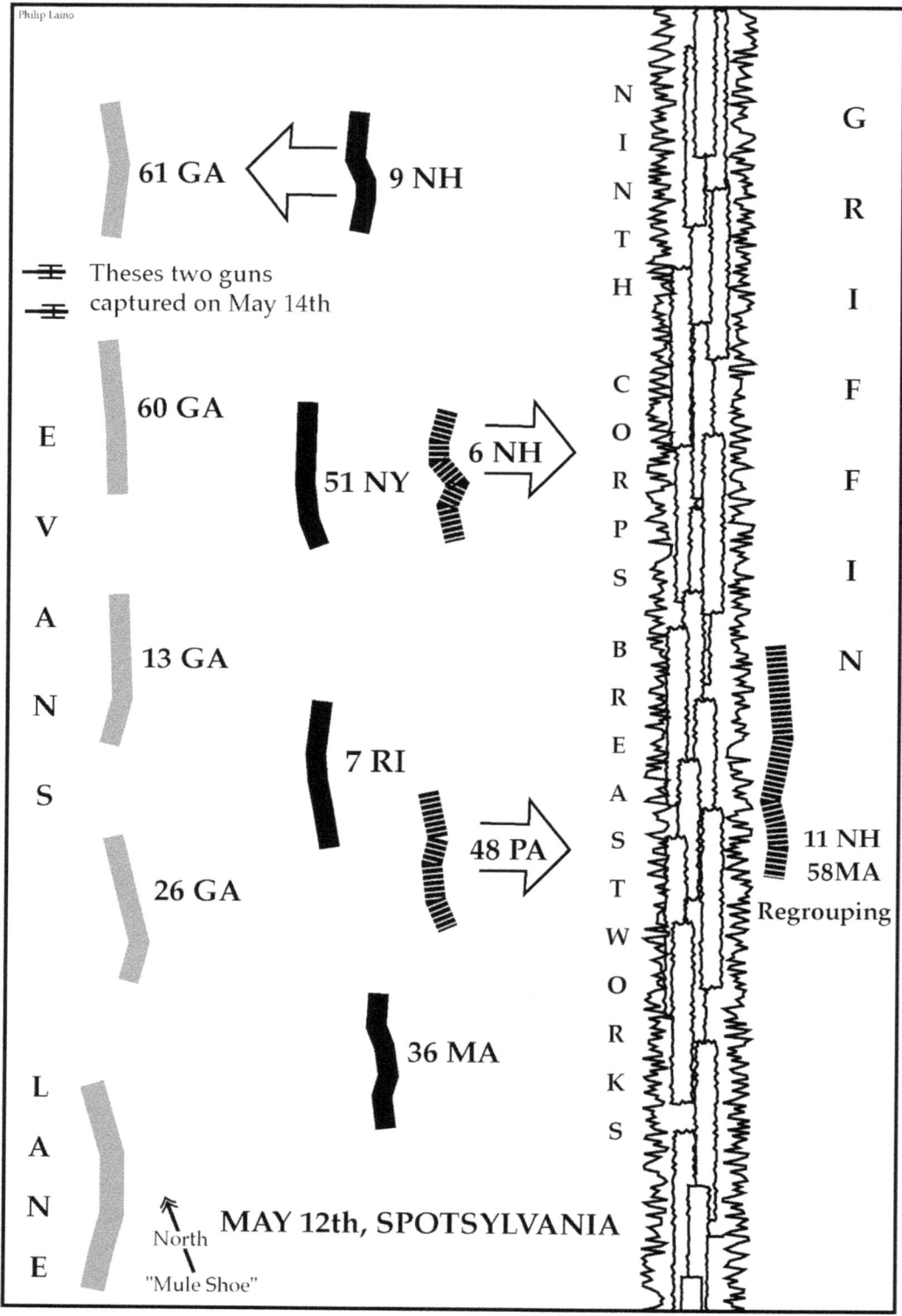

and marched out to the right. Receiving orders to advance at 3:30 in the morning, the Second Division moved into position on the right of the Second Corps, but a huge gap developed between the two formations.

Due to the fatiguing marches, only 225 officers and men were present in the ranks. The rain continued to fall as the men attempted to keep their powder dry. For twenty hours in the pouring rain at the Mule Shoe, American killed American with bayonets, clubs, and swords in a slaughter unparalleled during the war. With a loud cheer, the Second Division of the Ninth Corps charged the Confederate lines, capturing 100 prisoners and two cannon. During the attack, the Ninth Corps line became separated from the Second Corps. A fierce Confederate attack, led by Richard Ewell then began to fight back against the Ninth Corps. The Seventh and Fifty-First New York they moved forward amid a heavy fire at 6:30 A.M. Around this time, the Sixth New Hampshire and Forty-Eighth Pennsylvania were forced to retreat. Into the gap Colonel Griffin placed the New Yorkers and the Seventh. Private Peleg Jones watched as the Ninth New Hampshire charged, unsupported, and was "cut to pieces."[13]

The firing grew more intense as Captain Theodore Winn ordered the Seventh to open fire against the Georgians in front of them. Private Augustus Joyeaux was shot through the hand while loading his Enfield. He yelled out in broken English that he would rather die in the French army than lose his hand as an American. Private George Simmons, a farmer from Foster, was killed with a shot through the head while his neighbor Esais Pray had his jaw fractured. The bullets were again flying around the Seventh. Private John W. Luther received three separate wounds to the back, arm, and hip, leaving him an invalid for the rest of his life. In the pouring rain, powder became wet, as the men cursed and scrambled to find additional cartridges to keep up their fire. Tongues and hands became blackened as the enlisted men bit open the bitter tasting cartridges and rammed the bullets down the barrels of the muskets.

Lieutenant Frederic Weigand received a painful wound to the hand. Patrick Burke was shot through both legs. The officers maintained the line, plugging up the holes and yelling commands to their men. Private Benjamin T. Sisson was shot in the thigh; upon binding the wound, he went back into line with Company E, where he was shot through the heart and killed instantly. The day was perhaps hardest on the village of Rockville in northern Hopkinton. Benjamin R. Austin and Isaac N. Saunders were killed, while Abel B. Kenyon was shot in the hand. Of the three brothers-in-law who joined the regiment, only Kenyon was left. The majority of the wounds suffered by the Rhode Islanders were in the arms and upper body, indicating the Confederates were aiming high.[14]

Only eight officers were present with the regiment, allowing some companies to go into action commanded by their first sergeants. Captain Winn commanded the battalion, while Captain Daniels took command of the right, and Captain Jenks the left companies. The fight lasted for an hour before more Confederate reinforcements arrived and the Seventh remained in their position as a stalemate ensued; they could neither advance nor retreat. The Ninth Corps received additional ammunition while continuing to build a line of breastworks out of any material available. Cups, hands, and bayonets were all utilized in the effort. The men paused momentarily to eat several pieces of wet, moldy hardtack, "seated on the grass, perhaps in the blood of a comrade." During the night of the twelfth, the bodies of the dead were collected and the wounded were sent to the Ninth Corps hospital. In his first performance as a regimental commander, Captain Winn performed with the same ready decisiveness as Colonel Bliss. In his report of the battle, Daniels praised the regiment for their behavior during the action. "Great credit is due to the officers and men for their gallantry in undauntedly facing that storm of shot and shell." Compared to other regiments in the corps, the casualties

Shown after the Battle of Spotsylvania, these simple barricades were similar to those erected by the Seventh throughout the Overland Campaign. Courtesy of the Library of Congress.

were relatively light: six killed and twenty-four wounded. For the Seventh Rhode Island the Battle of Spotsylvania had only started.[15]

During the night of May 12, the regiment was under arms as picket firing erupted all night long. On May 13, the Seventh continued to build a series of breastworks. Positioned on the extreme right of the Federal line, the Ninth Corps was in a vulnerable position from being flanked; it was exactly this maneuver that the Confederates attempted. The men felt as though they had fortified their position enough, and they became "careless." Adjutant Darius I. Cole was shot in the shoulder, dying a half hour later. He was only the fourth Seventh officer to be killed in action to date. Corporal Francis W. Potter of Company C was killed while six other enlisted men were wounded. Sleep was finally gained on May 14, but the men awoke at 3:30 in the morning to a loud firing in their front as the rain finally stopped. The Confederates retreated to a new series of lines but left two artillery pieces in between the lines.

The Rhode Islanders wanted to rush forward to capture them but they could not due to sniper fire. Finally, Federal artillery opened fire, allowing two companies of the Seventh to run forward and drag in the coveted trophies. The casualties for May 14 were two killed and two wounded. The Seventh remained in position on the fifteenth as Captain Jenks took command of the picket line and recovered the remains of several members of the regiment; the bodies were shipped back to Rhode Island. Unable to find any shovels to entrench, several entrepreneurial privates began digging with pieces of hardtack crates. Sharpshooters, posted in the trees in front of the Seventh's position, continued to be a problem, firing at anything that moved. They managed to severely wound Private Michael Crowley.[16]

Reinforcements, taken from the heavy artillery regiments garrisoning the forts around Washington, began to arrive on May 16. These soldiers had been in the service nearly as long as the Seventh, but were used to performing in parades

A farmer from Foster, Ethan A. Jenks was considered by many to be the Seventh's bravest officer and saved the regiment from destruction at Spotsylvania.

and other garrison duties around Washington. Now in their bright blue uniforms with polished brass fittings, these soldiers came to reinforce the mud-caked and soaked men in the Army of the Potomac. There was a full moon on the night of May 17, as Captain Jenks led a company out on a diversionary raid, resulting in the death of Corporal Lyman Whitcomb. Orders to leave the trenches were given on the morning of May 18, as the Seventh moved forward into what would again be another storm.[17]

Before leaving Spotsylvania, Grant decided to launch one more attack to crush Lee. The Second Division of the Ninth Corps also moved south to help cover the movement. At 3:00 in the morning the Second Division left its entrenchments and started forward to attack the Confederate works. Many in the corps were upset about leaving the defenses that they had perfected for a week. If a large-scale engagement occurred, the men would be in the open and without protection. As the Sixth New Hampshire advanced, Captain Lyman Jackman recalled, "we felt that is was almost sure death." As he advanced Captain Winn announced he was deathly ill and left the field. The command of the Seventh passed to twenty-three-year-old Captain Percy Daniels; this would be his first test as a battalion commander. Although Daniels was the second captain, many were afraid of going into battle under an untried officer. During the training of the Seventh, Daniels was faulted many times for being "immature." Stephen F. Peckham wrote, "Too young to command himself, much more to command others." The Seventh was on the extreme right of the Federal line. They marched through a swamp, followed by a thick woodlot, and then into a dense set of underbrush. At daybreak the Rhode Islanders witnessed the sight they feared most.[18]

The Confederates had not retreated, but simply reorganized and reinforced their already impenetrable line. The Seventh had to charge up a hill, lined with infantry, while contending with a battery posted on their flank. The hill was fortified much like Marye's Heights; ironically it was being held by Cooke's Brigade of North Carolinians, the same Confederates the Seventh faced at Fredericksburg. Worse still, there were only six line officers and 169 men in the Seventh's line. As the sun appeared the Confederate artillery opened up upon the Rhode Islanders. The first few shots flew overhead as Captain Daniels attempted to comprehend the situation around him. The next shot struck the knapsack of Private James Robinson, throwing him to the ground. The third shell, fired from a twelve-pound Napoleon cannon, landed in the middle of Company H and exploded. Arms and legs flew through the air as six men were hit. Sergeant Samuel E. Rice lost a leg and an arm. The musicians had been detailed to act as stretcher bearers to bring the wounded to the rear and then to the Ninth Corps hospital. They rushed forward in an attempt to save Sergeant Rice. As the young man was being carried away he turned to Company H and said, "Boys I can't be with you any more, go in." This inspired the soldiers in the regiment as they attempted to advance. One officer, looking on, recalled the grisly scene in a letter to the *Providence Journal*, "You would have realized some of the horrors war can bring." Sergeant Rice died three hours later at a field hospital; his last words were: "Tell them all at home, I die like a man." Rice was buried on the field while his family spent the little money they had to erect a stone to his memory in East Greenwich. The shell killed two other members of Company H while severely wounding the other three men.[19]

Using their instinct, the men dropped to the ground to try to escape the fire. Another shell struck the Color Guard, killing Corporal Manuel Open and mortally wounding Corporal Isaac Nye. Open was a German immigrant from South Kingstown who was detached to the guard because he was tall. Corporal Daniel B. Smith, another member of the Color Guard, had his "bowels torn out" by a shell. Only Sergeant Samuel Simpson carrying the U.S. flag and Sergeant John B. Stoothoff, holding onto the Rhode Island colors, remained. The men again pulled out bayonets and cups and began scratching into the earth to attempt to build a breastwork. The Seventh was in an exposed position, receiving fire from their front and left flank. This was the worst fire the Seventh had faced since Fredericksburg. The artillery shells continued to rain down upon the Seventh's position, knocking tree branches and hot pieces of iron into the thin line. The minié balls whizzed by the entrenching regiment as they frantically dug in. Occasionally they heard the unmistakable thud that no one wanted to hear—a Rhode Islander had been hit. Sergeant Amos Lillibridge reached for a large rail to throw in front of Company A's position but was shot through the head. The Confederate defenders now charged the Seventh's line in an attempt to drive back the Rhode Islanders.

Captain Edward Allen, a faithful correspondent of both the *Narragansett Times* and the *Providence Journal* wrote, "Their masses rushed on to our lines only to be driven back with terrible slaughter."[20]

The Confederates were not repulsed, but rather regrouped. Captain Daniels ordered the men to fix bayonets and prepare to assault the Confederate works. One New Hampshire soldier, who was watching, commented, "It was hopeless to carry the works in the face of a murderous fire." First Lieutenant Albert A. Bolles was shot through the foot, yielding his company to Sergeant Jonathan Linton. Captain James N. Potter was shot through the leg and left the field. The captain left the Seventh as well, heading for a draft camp in New Hampshire. Preparing to give the order to advance, Daniels did not notice a critical threat on his right flank. General Potter had

Percy Daniels nearly destroyed the Seventh at Spotsylvania. USAMHI.

pulled back the rest of his division without notifying Captain Daniels. The firing continued to knock the Rhode Islanders out of their ranks. Private Charles O. Browning suffered a massive wound to the chest. A ball passed through Lieutenant Edward Morse's face. All along the Seventh's thin line, Rhode Islanders continued to face a withering fire as they closed ranks and continued with the deadly work. After a year of badgering David R. Kenyon, Peleg Peckham finally earned his captaincy, leading Company B. In July, he was rewarded by President Lincoln, becoming a major by brevet for his actions this day. The three remaining line officers in the Seventh continued to yell out "Steady men, Hold your ground." The Seventh then prepared to charge.[21]

Bringing the musket from the shoulder to "port arms" and placing the rifle directly across the chest the Seventh went in yelling "Hurrah." The firing intensified as the Rhode Islanders pushed on. Sergeant Nathan G. Follansbee recalled, "I saw a number of comrades cut up in an instant." The Seventh was surrounded. Captain Daniels in the heat of the battle became disoriented, unable to issue any command. If the Seventh remained where it was any longer, it would be destroyed. Although he was only commanding the left wing, Captain Jenks knew what needed to be done. Against Daniels's orders, he gave the command for the Seventh to fall back, thus saving the regiment from annihilation. Completely cut off and surrounded, the Rhode Islanders ran for a series of rifle pits vacated by a Pennsylvania regiment in their rear. The charge was costly for the Seventh; there were only three officers and 126 men left.

Sergeant Amos A. Lillibridge was killed at Spotsylvania. Courtesy of Kris VanDenBossche.

Colonel Curtin left the Seventh in its position as he constructed rifle pits in the rear. At nightfall, the men finally were pulled off the line, and they filed to the rear. As the wounded Rhode Islanders were carried to the Harris House, they told Stephen Peckham plainly why the Seventh was routed from the position; it was because of Captain Percy Daniel's "reckless incompetence." Instead of pursuing the charge, Daniels simply froze, allowing the Seventh to take the amount of casualties it did. One Rhode Islander recorded, "Daniels never forgave Jenks for the affair at Spotsylvania." The Seventh Rhode Island lost ten killed and thirty wounded.[22]

Unable to write home for three weeks, the men took the lull in the battle to tell their families of the unbelievable sights that they had just survived. The Seventh had survived the slaughter at Fredericks-

Federal soldiers dig in along the North Anna River on May 25, 1864. Courtesy of the Library of Congress.

9. Return to Virginia

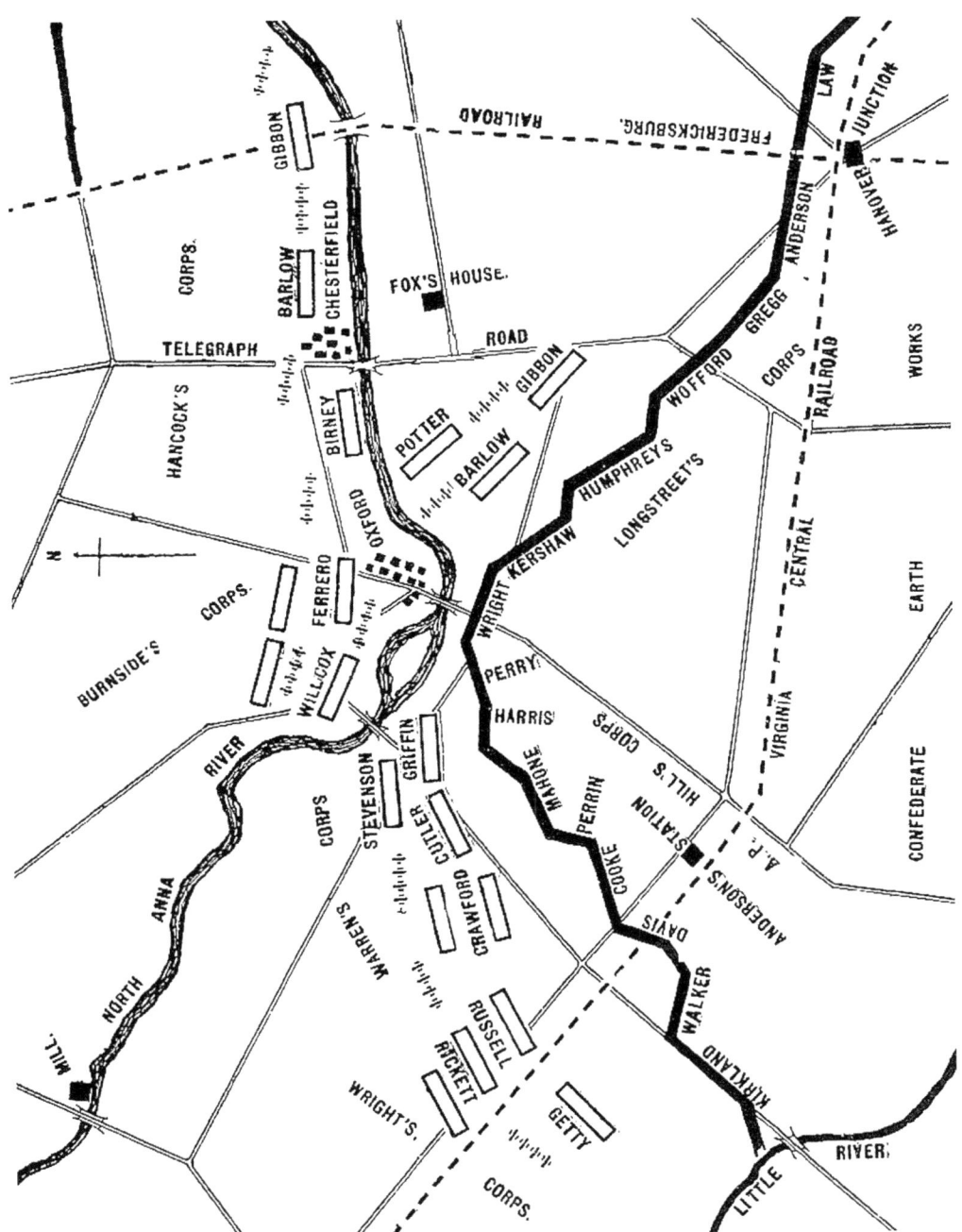

Battle of the North Anna River

burg and seen the results of the Battle of the Wilderness. However, this latest bloodletting was like nothing that these Rhode Islanders had ever witnessed before. In one week, fighting in the trenches around Spotsylvania, 30,000 Americans were killed, wounded, and missing. In the Seventh Rhode Island, twenty-one men were dead while sixty-three were wounded. The small hospital that Major Harris and Steward Peckham established was overflowing, as the patients waited outside in the elements to be treated. The city of Fredericksburg was filled to capacity with both wounded Federals and captured Confederates. Those fortunate enough to be transferred to a larger facility might be sent to Portsmouth Grove, in Rhode Island. Private William O. Harrington finally managed to pen a short letter to his wife Eunice. The small town of Foster had already lost heavily in the Seventh's previous campaigns. Now George Simmons was dead while three men were wounded. Harrington's friend, Edward S. Lewis, a resident of Glocester, was also wounded. "We fight them some wheare along our lines every day." In Hopkinton, Tryphena Cundall continued to pray that God would spare Isaac in the bloodbath that the Seventh was engaged in. Private Peleg Jones's only comment in his diary about the charge was that "it failed." The body of Corporal Isaac Nye arrived in Coventry in June. After a service at the Knotty Oak Baptist Church, his remains were solemnly laid underneath a pine tree in the Manchester Cemetery. Carved into the top of his marble monument was the flag he swore to defend as a member of the Color Guard and the words "mortally wounded May 18, 1864 at Spotsylvania Va."[23]

After the battle the men went out of the entrenchments to view the debris of the battle. Stephen Peckham saw trees ten inches in diameter cut down by the Rhode Islanders fire. Orders were again issued to move out on the nineteenth, but the Ninth Corps was ordered to rest for two days as the battered regiments struggled to regain their strength. The wounded and sick continued to stream in from Washington and Annapolis. Sergeant Winfield S. Chappell, long expecting a promotion to second lieutenant, was surprised to become a first, replacing Lieutenant Cole. Grant moved out of his lines around Spotsylvania, again trying to slip around Lee's flank, skirmishing again at the Po River. Lee moved his army to the south, away from Grant's eyes, as he set about to cover the approaches to the North Anna River.[24]

The Seventh crossed the river on the twenty-fourth and promptly began building a series of breastworks. The men were becoming adapted to the task as it was the only way to safely protect their bodies from the large volume of lead the Confederates shot into the regiment. Lee attempted to trap Grant at the North Anna on May 23, but, due to the large number of casualties his own forces had taken, he was unable to launch a successful attack. The Army of the Potomac lost 40,000 men in three weeks. Ambrose Burnside finally agreed to waive his seniority over George Meade, as the Ninth Corps was formally integrated into Meade's force "for the good of the service."

The Confederates counterattacked along the line on May 25. Captain Peckham ran to each squad

A veteran of the Mexican War, Color Sergeant Samuel F. Simpson was killed at the North Anna River. Courtesy of Katie and Luane McDonald.

of men urging them to reinforce their breastworks, some of which were six feet tall. Private Chester L. Franklin, a tall farmer from Exeter, was mortally wounded as a minié ball hit his spine. During the fighting Private Hugh McNulty retired to build a small fire to boil the first coffee Company D had in a week. A minié ball hit the pail he was using to cook the beverage in, spilling the contents on the ground. McNulty secured a musket, announcing he was going to kill the Confederate who ruined the company's relief. The private joined the firing line, using the Enfield "vigorously." Color Sergeant Samuel F. Simpson was shot through the head as he reached for a branch. A former friend of Stonewall Jackson, the sergeant collapsed onto the American flag. Only Sergeant Stoothoff, carrying the Rhode Island flag, remained of the Seventh's Color Guard. Before the day was over, two more men were wounded.[25]

For three weeks the Seventh Rhode Island had been under fire constantly losing men at an alarming rate. Although tired and sore from the digging and marching they cheerfully followed their commander to an obscure Virginia tavern called Cold Harbor.

10

"If it takes all summer"

I dont know how many we have lost in all.
— *Private William O. Harrington, June 2, 1862*

    A small, mud-caked force of 150 men trudged slowly south from the North Anna River in late May 1864. This was all that was left of the Seventh Rhode Island. Speaking in their usual, distinct accent by dropping "er" from most every word, the men wondered where their travels would take them. After crossing the Rapidan with 250 men, death had taken twenty-three members of the regiment while the rest were wounded, fatigued, or detached. Despite taking massive casualties, Grant decided to pursue the battle and continued to follow Lee.

    Robert E. Lee and the men that comprised his Army of Northern Virginia were fighting for the very survival of the Confederacy. Barricading every river crossing and inflicting thousands of casualties on the Army of the Potomac, the Rebels were only prolonging the inevitable; there was in effect no stopping the Federal onslaught. Reinforcements continued to stream in to the Army of the Potomac, but none came to the Rhode Islanders. Every day rivers were crossed and battles fought as Grant followed his plan to continuously turn Lee's flank. The Federal commander did not back down, proclaiming, "I intend to fight along this line, if it takes all summer."

    In Rhode Island the effects of the May campaign were already beginning to be seen. Each passing day brought news that a loved one or neighbor had been shot in Virginia. Tryphena Cundall continued to count her blessings that Isaac was not hit. In Foster, George Simmons was buried on a small hill overlooking the Ponagansett River. He was fortunate; the majority of those killed were buried where they fell, a simple marker made from a hardtack box to mark their gravesite. After the war, they were interred in the National Cemetery on Marye's Heights. In a rare case, the body of Lieutenant Darius Cole was not returned to Rhode Island, but was interred alongside several other officers in the cemetery. As the majority of the men were mortally wounded and died later, the Adjutant General's office in Providence was swamped daily trying to complete the necessary paperwork required of the office. So far Rhode Island had sent 20,000 men into the field — a tenth of the state population. South Kingstown continued with its almost constant process of mourning the boys in Company G. South

10. "If it takes all summer"

Marching south from Spotsylvania. *Battles and Leaders of the Civil War*

Kingstown was the unfortunate home to two companies. Company E of the Second Rhode Island lost half of its strength between the Wilderness and Spotsylvania. As the war progressed, the tired citizens of Rhode Island kept waiting for it to end.[1]

The Seventh and the Ninth Corps moved out from the North Anna and crossed the Pamunkey River. There was no food at hand, allowing the men to grumble as they tried to find scraps in the recesses of their well-worn haversacks. Private Jared J. Potter was pleased to locate some tobacco at an abandoned house one night and enjoyed the aromatic taste. On the twenty-ninth, the regiment encamped in a quiet location for the night, the first real sleep in over a week. Captain Jenks spent every night commanding the thin picket line that was the first line of defense in the thickets and swamps of central Virginia. Every night, the weary soldiers built a series of breastworks while keeping the Enfields loaded and nearby. On May 30, the Seventh supported the Fifty-Eighth Massachusetts and helped to drive the Confederate picket line nearly a mile. By the end of May, the Army of the Potomac was within twelve miles of Richmond. They now knew that Lee would fight for every inch of ground to preserve his capital.[2]

As the Seventh marched closer to Richmond, their story was the same each day: March a short distance, entrench, listen to the battle, and wait. William Hopkins, who had recorded the people the Seventh encountered with remarkable accuracy, was surprised to see that the young women of the area "are most ardent advocates of the Southern cause." He also noted the effect of the war on the region; it was here in the early summer of 1862 that McClellan had been repulsed in the series of battles that had required the Seventh to enter the field. By June 1, the church steeples of Richmond were in sight. During the night Captain Allen took command of what was left of Company A and led them out on picket duty. Sergeant John H. Rowley found himself caught in the open and was struck in the finger by a rebel ball "two

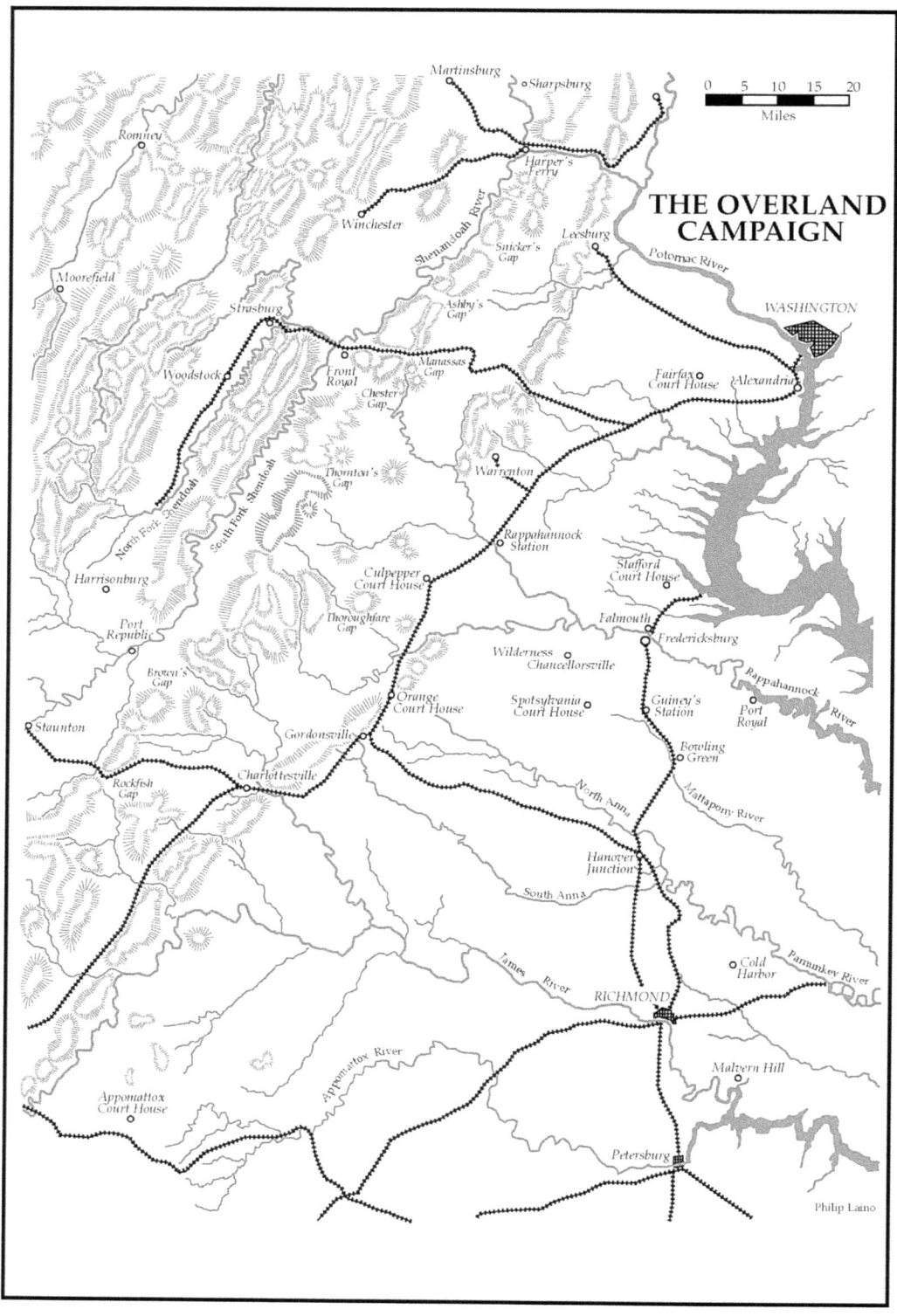

10. "If it takes all summer"   109

The Seventh remained in hastily dug trenches like this throughout the Overland Campaign. *Battles and Leaders of the Civil War.*

rods distant." The recently promoted Captain Peckham was relieved of the command of Company B and was attached to the staff of Colonel Curtin. His official title was assistant adjutant general, a glorified secretary's position that required him to collect all reports and to make sure the orders were passed down along the line.³

As Grant pushed on, Lee countered with every maneuver he could think of to try to block the massive Union force. Although his Army of Northern Virginia had taken thousands of irreplaceable casualties, hundreds continued to reinforce his main line, being taken from rear echelon positions. The Confederate commander knew that if Grant managed to cross the James River, the only option for him would be to lay siege to Richmond, a move that would ultimately end in a Confederate defeat. With enough forces now at his disposal, Lee set out to make a final effort to try to defeat the Federals. He chose Cold Harbor, named after a small tavern nearby. His men took whatever entrenching tools were available and began to build another set of impenetrable defenses. Digging down into the red-yellow claylike soil, the trenches were constructed to provide immense protective covering for the rebel defenders. They were reinforced on top by notched logs to protect their heads. In addition, the trenches were built back at right angles so that all of the line could be covered. Grant had no choice but to launch a head-on assault.

On June 2, the Seventh built another series of entrenchments near Mechanicsville, where in 1862 the Seven Days Battles began. The Seventh remained in the entrenchments while sending out small detachments to find and occasionally meet the Confederate line. On the morning of June 2, Company K was dispatched to search the area to their front. William O. Harrington had finished with his tasks as the cook for Company K, which took him out of the firing line and picket duty, when he sat down to write a letter to his family. The firing had been going on all day, as the two sides probed each other's lines. As he wrote the letter,

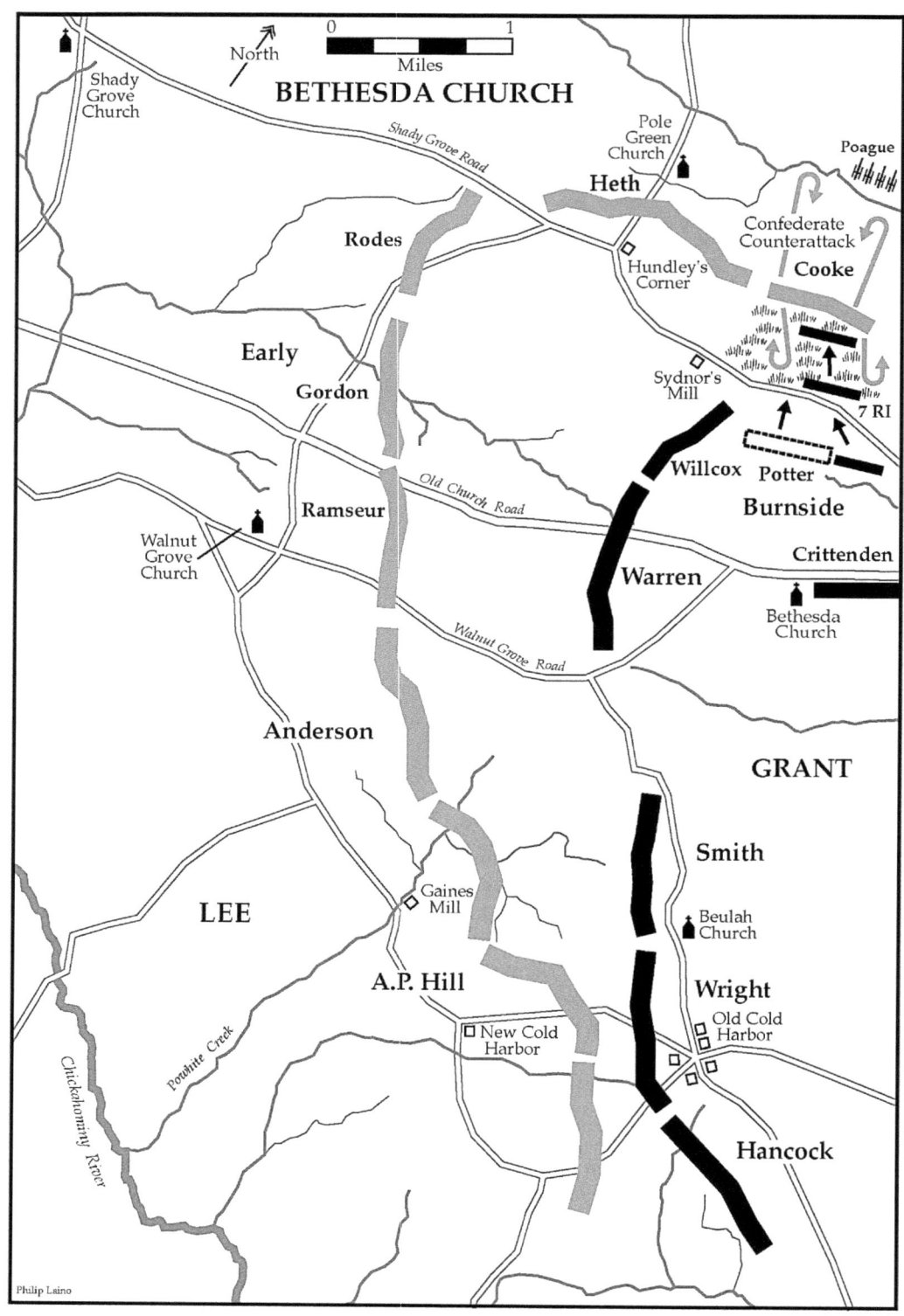

Harrington noticed the patrol of Company K returning from its mission. As Private Harrington was in the middle of his letter he looked up to see a blanket being carried by four men. In it were the remains of Corporal Edward S. Reynolds, shot through the head. The effect had a powerful impact on the unlucky private, "Now both of my boys are gone killed the other wounded I dont know how many we have lost in all." Sergeant George Potter, his other friend, received his second wound at Spotsylvania and was in Washington recovering from the wound. Reynolds was buried in a shallow grave near the Seventh's position. William Weldon received a painful wound to the face. Captain Peckham was riding in front of the lines when he found three Confederates. Drawing his .36-caliber Colt revolver, Peckham ordered the men to drop their weapons and took them prisoner. Private James W. Gavitt was on picket duty when he saw two men near his position. Thinking they were Federals, he went up to them and found they were Tennesseans; the men took Gavitt prisoner. Pretending to bend down to tie his shoe, the bewildered Rhode Islander grabbed one of the Confederates' weapons and hit him over the head. Gavitt then threatened to bayonet the other man from the Seventh Tennessee; instead, he took both men prisoner and brought them back to brigade headquarters. As the day progressed, Grant tested the Cold Harbor defenses. The Ninth Corps remained in their positions around a small clearing named Bethesda Church. The remainder of the Army of the Potomac moved to the left and prepared for the assault. The Confederates attempted to charge the Ninth Corps line, but were repulsed by Federal artillery. They drove in the pickets of the Ninth New Hampshire, who ran back shouting, "Hurry up and get out of here." The Rhode Islanders ignored the calls and stayed in position. During the remainder of the day, the Seventh remained under constant fire from Confederate artillery as they attempted to boil their coffee. A favorite pastime while waiting in these unnerving moments was to pass around copies of the *Providence Journal*, the largest Rhode Island newspaper. The paper always appeared at interesting times, including during the Battle of Jackson. During the night, First Sergeant William H. Barstow led a twenty-man picket detail into "a wooded, wet swamp."[4]

On the morning of June 3, 1864, Lieutenant General Ulysses S. Grant gave the order that would produce 7,000 Federal casualties. The Seventh was again positioned near the extreme end of the Federal line. The month of active campaigning had significantly reduced the Seventh to only 150 officers and rifles. During the six weeks of fighting, the Seventh Rhode Island became lost in the swirl of combat that was occurring around them; few of the Providence papers carried stories from the regiment although Stephen Peckham was a regular correspondent to the *Providence Journal*. During one letter he wrote, "The history of the little band known as the 7th Rhode Island has been very little of individuals in the campaign." The regiment was up at 4:30 in the morning and rejoined the First Brigade line, having been detached for several days guarding their own front. For eight miles along the line, the Federals gallantly attempted to break the Confederate lines. The veterans did not pursue with vigor, knowing the fruitlessness of such a charge. The new regiments from the Washington defenses almost made it to the Confederate lines in moves reminiscent of earlier battles but they were shot down by the hundreds. The Seventh Rhode Island remained in their position until early morning when Colonel John Curtin passed the orders to his brigade commanders. This was Captain Percy Daniels second attempt as a regimental commander. Because of the small force, Daniels commanded the right companies and Captain Jenks the left. Most of the companies were so reduced that now sergeants and second lieutenants commanded them. Company F only mustered fourteen men. At 8:00 A.M. Colonel Curtin gave the orders for the regiment to advance forward.[5]

A steady rain fell as the men advanced in line of battle across the plain to the Confederate positions. As soon as the Rhode Islanders were in view of the Confederates they came under fire. Little did the men in the Seventh realize, but for the third time in the war they were engaging Cooke's North Carolinians. Advancing at a quick pace, the regiment passed into a swamp that was up to the knees, followed by a march into a patch of thick woods and underbrush. The rush brought the Seventh two miles to their front. The regiment then saw the first line of Confederate works, which they charged and captured. The Carolinians broke and ran to their second line of defense as the Rhode Islanders dug in to their position with cups and bayonets. Here they came under fire from a Confederate sniper positioned in a tree. The men instantly took cover behind their own trees as they scanned the canopy looking for the sharpshooter. First Sergeant Barstow received a wound to the stomach. The Seventh named the Confederate "Pinkie" to pass the time. His next victim was Sergeant George W. Congdon, who was killed by a shot to the head. Corporal Michael Flaherty was also killed by a head shot. The men fired wildly at the tree line as they attempted to shoot the sniper. The wayward Private Hartford Alexander lost his taste for battle as he stepped out from behind his tree to reload his musket. Pinkie fired another shot that killed the young man who had been with the Seventh every step of the way. Eventually the men in the Seventh saw Pinkie's position and Company B fired their weapons simultaneously: "There was no more sharpshooting from that angle."[6]

After dodging the sniper fire, the Seventh charged into the second line of defenses built by Cooke's men. Here they encountered stiff resistance from the grey defenders. One officer commented, "it was a terrible fire." The Seventh Rhode Island fired their Enfields with deadly effect, engaging the Confederates at distances of sixty yards in the open field. The fire hit Company F like a scythe through rye; five men were killed and two were wounded. Fully half the company became casualties. Corporal Nathan B. Lewis took command of the shattered force of Exeter and North Kingstown men. Privates Potter Straight and Palmer G. Perkins, both neighbors and farmers from Exeter, were killed in that small town's bloodiest day of the war. The Rhode Islanders continued their deadly work for which they now received $16 per month. When the sixty rounds were expanded, more were brought up from the rear and the men continued firing. The fighting was so intense, one Seventh officer recorded 111 holes in a one-foot diameter pine tree. Second Lieutenant Samuel McIlroy, in command of Company I, received a painful wound to the thigh that never healed. Private William O. Harrington saw another neighbor killed as Private Oliver Wood was shot. He was buried near the Connecticut border in western Foster. Like many in his regiment, his stone was marked for eternity, "killed at Cold Harbor." In the Seventh's shrinking battle line, the clinking, methodical sound of the ramrods could be heard as the muskets were capped and fired as fast as the tired men could load the black powder-fouled weapons. Officers and sergeants walked up and down their company lines screaming at the top of their lungs while the musicians dragged the wounded to the rear.[7]

The North Carolinians pulled back as the Seventh entrenched near the second line. Private Ira W. Grant was shot in the chest and died a half hour later. Captain Daniels vividly recalled the battle in a letter to Brigadier General Edward Mauran: "All day, like the swelling and ebbing of the voice of the winds, the noise of battle now rose to a hurricane and sank in a whisper, but at dark we were as well protected as our foe, and our bullets had made them shy." The men dug frantically to secure the position; the Confederates could counterattack at any time. Because the rifle-musket only fired one shot before being reloaded, some men collected all that could be found. One member of Company D secured eight of the weapons and exclaimed: "Let them come on, now, I'm as good as a gunboat." At five o'clock, the Confederates counterattacked for an hour, but could not drive the Rhode Islanders from their secure position. Private Robert Hanning was saved when he was shot in the chest. The bullet was stopped by his photograph album and pocket watch. The muskets were again fired with effect, resulting in the death of a Confederate colonel. In total, the Seventh claimed twenty dead Confederates from the effects of their fire. Private Harrington wrote, "The fight has been very heavy."[8]

For the Federal forces all along the Cold Harbor front, June 3, 1864, brought failure. No significant breakthroughs occurred and thousands of casualties were taken. Ever the clear and concise diarist, Jared J. Potter recorded: "We charged the swamp + drove them from one line of works + put up works in front of their second line we lost heavy." The Seventh slept on their arms again through the night of the third. Again Lee could not press his victory due to the defensive lines the Federals were building. On the morning of the fourth, the battle-weary men awoke to find the Confederates in their front to have silently evacuated the lines in the middle of the night. Advancing into the abandoned works, the men discovered bloating bodies and dead horses littering the ground. Near the Confederate lines they found a small log cabin where an old woman had been hiding during the engagement. The men of the Seventh located several bushels of sweet potatoes, which were taken. During the day, the customary after-battle roll calls were given. For its small size, the Seventh had suffered terribly in the battle: Fully a third of the regiment lay dead or wounded on the fields of Bethesda Church, including fifteen killed. In September of 1862, one company of the Seventh was larger than the size of the regiment now. Drummer William Hopkins commented, "It was about this time when the ranks were so reduced there seemed to be no Seventh Regiment." If the regiment continued to take casualties at this rate, the regiment would disappear or they would be consolidated.[9]

The lines remained in place throughout the fifth and sixth of June. On the fifth, four officers returned to the regiment from their wounds. Captain George Wilbur was still sick and could hardly walk; nevertheless, he returned to command Company K. Captain Daniels remained in command of the regiment. In his second engagement, Daniels had demonstrated his ability to handle a regiment in combat. This still did not erase the memory of Spotsylvania, but it marked an improvement over the earlier engagement. With their lieutenant colonel and major gone, and the colonel ill, the Seventh knew that promotions would soon be coming to the regiment. Many hoped Captain Jenks would be raised to a higher rank; "he is always at the front," one soldier wrote. William O. Harrington was pleased to receive a letter from his brother Josiah, fighting in the Shenandoah with the Eighteenth Connecticut. The Nutmeg Boys had also lost heavily in their engagements while Dr. Harrington treated the many patients from the battles of New Market and Piedmont, where yet another Foster soldier was killed. Private Harrington was worried about the amount of officers the Seventh now had: "many of our officers are killed or wounded." Two captains commanded each wing of the regiment while four captains and three lieutenants contended with the companies. Captain Peckham was removed because of his staff work while Captain Edwin L. Hunt was ill with sunstroke. Among the officers who rejoined the regiment was Captain George Stone, who had been left behind completing staff duties at Point Burnside. He took command of a picket line on the morning of the sixth, but it appeared as if the Army of Northern Virginia had disappeared once more. Private James Hodson asked the captain if he could go forward a greater distance and search. Captain Stone told him it was dangerous, but did not say no. The private went out a short distance before he was shot in the stomach and bled to death. The Seventh remained in the Cold Harbor entrenchments, coming under stray Confederate artillery fire. They continued to strengthen the existing entrenchments while losing more wounded men. It became impossible for the Confederates to attack them successfully. As the

Corporal Nathan B. Lewis commanded Company F for a brief time after Bethesda Church and went on to become one of the most successful veterans of the Seventh.

men waited for the next battle to come, they began to look back at what forty days of continuous fighting had brought to the Union. Over 50,000 men were dead or wounded in the campaign, while Richmond was so close the church bells could be heard. The campaign had severely fatigued the Seventh Rhode Island, which lost 60 percent of its strength. Captain Edward Allen wrote, "We have been marching and skirmishing incessantly, and our losses have been severe." Another soldier in the regiment proclaimed, "it has been hard work." Despite the severe losses, the Seventh had added to its reputation as a regiment that ranked among the best. As the conscripts and new regiments broke and faltered around them, the Rhode Islanders stood firm. Although he was no longer directly involved with his regiment, Colonel Bliss's doctrine of discipline and courage had showed in the small band in the entire campaign. Under the command of experienced officers such as Captain Ethan Jenks, the Rhode Islanders again proved themselves as veterans.[10]

The Seventh remained near Cold Harbor until June 12 when they marched thirteen miles to White House Landing. Grant had again succeeded in driving Lee south, but at a loss of 10,000 men. Now he was going to attempt to capture Richmond from the south through the important railroad junction at Petersburg. The men marched into low-lying valleys and through forests filled with the fragrant smells of early summer. Stephen Peckham took notice of the "beautiful birds" that flew around. The Chickahominy River was crossed on the fourteenth. During the day, an unfortunate accident occurred. As the Seventh was constantly engaged, the muskets were always loaded, even when forming the tepee-like stacks made when breaks were taken. One stack fell over, accidentally wounding Private John McDonough in the back. Five days of rations were received on the fifteenth, and after a march of thirty miles, the Seventh Rhode Island became the first regiment in the Ninth Corps and the first in the Union army to cross the James River. The river was spanned by a 1,800-foot pontoon bridge, which was crossed at 8:15 in the morning. On the far side of the river, the men could see the city of Petersburg. Confederate general Pierre Beauregard had built thirty miles of defenses to protect Richmond and Petersburg. Like the other series of trenches, they were impenetrable and were heavily defended by the entire Army of Northern Virginia. Just as in his previous assaults, Grant sent his entire army forward to be repulsed again. After two more days of bloody assaults Grant decided that he would have to lay siege to the city. For the Confederacy, the end had begun.[11]

The Ninth Corps made its initial charge on the sixteenth, but Captain Daniels did not receive the orders to support the charge, so the Seventh remained behind. On the afternoon of

Captain Edward T. Allen accidentally shot himself in the leg at Petersburg.

June 17, the Second Division of the Ninth Corps charged an outer earthwork, capturing six hundred prisoners, six cannon and part of one of the main railroads running into the city. Nine enlisted men were wounded in the Seventh. Chaplain Augustus Woodbury wrote, "They burst upon him with the fury of a tornado." Day and night the Confederate artillery kept up a heavy bombardment against the entrenching Federals. It became clear to the men in the ranks that a siege was going to begin. During the eighteenth, the Seventh charged again and made it to within 100 yards of the Confederate works before it was repulsed. Private Peleg Jones commented, "It was a strong position that we could not carry." The remainder of the day was built digging entrenchments. Captain Edward T. Allen returned from the picket line at dusk and was inspecting his pistol when the weapon went off. The captain was struck in the leg and carried to the hospital where Dr. Corey dressed the wound. For Captain Allen, the Civil War was over. Plagued by the effects of the wound, he resigned his commission in September. Now his brother, Edwin, serving as the sergeant major would be alone. Private James G. Kenyon helped his captain to the rear. Upon returning to the picket line, he was killed.[12] Captain Jenks commanded the Seventh's picket line again on the night of June 19. Near midnight he was conversing with a sergeant when he was hit in the shoulder. The wound was not serious, but it was painful. The captain was transported to a field hospital eight miles

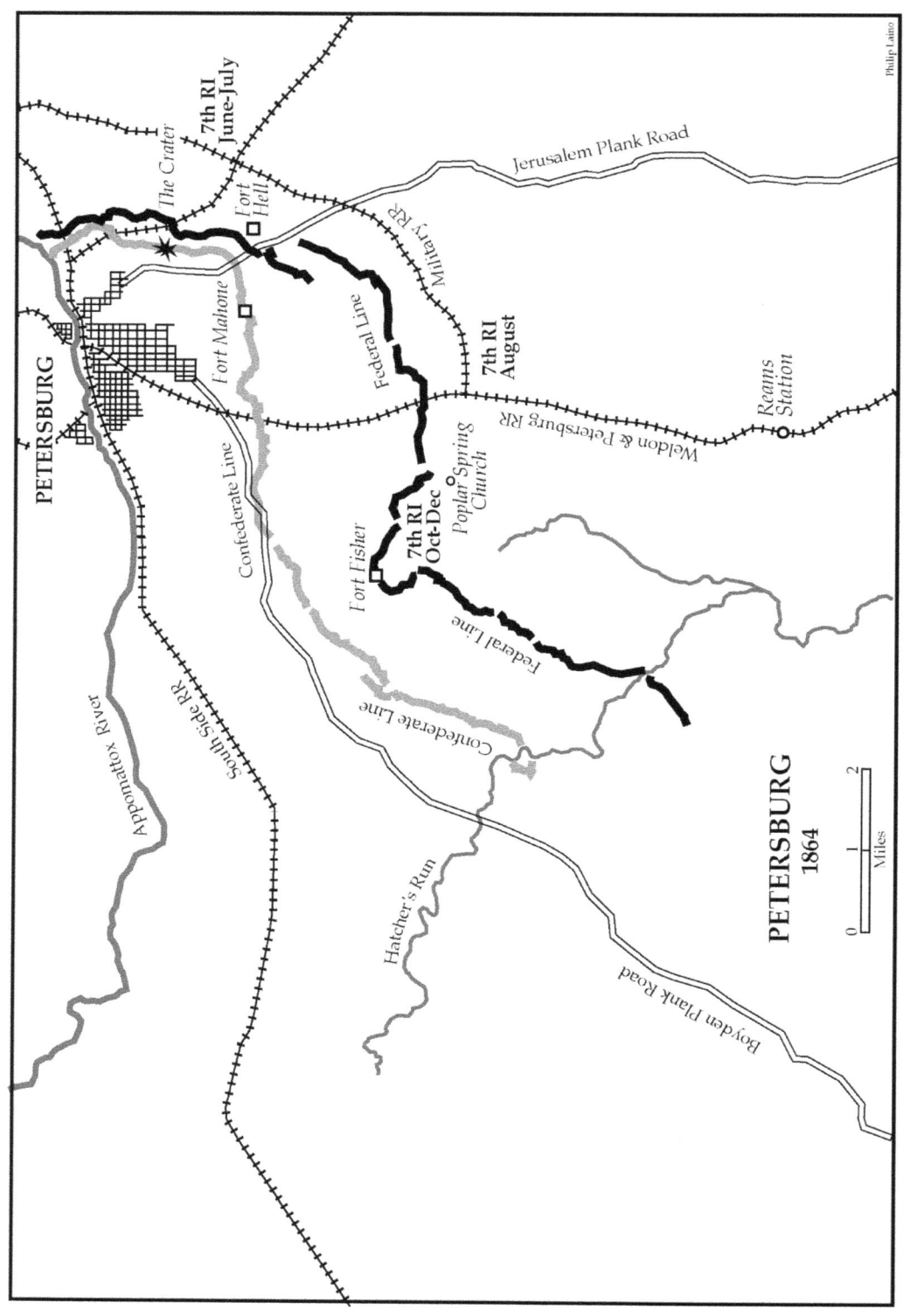

to the rear, near the James River. The sights were sickening to Jenks. "O such misery as I see there." Captain Jenks returned to his command a week later, but he remained ill. The sole remaining original captain of the Seventh resigned his commission on June 25; Theodore Winn was severely ill and retired to his home. With Captain Jenks temporarily disabled, Captain Daniels had no other senior officers present. Indeed June 20, 1864, represented the darkest day for the Seventh Rhode Island. Only eighty enlisted men and two officers were present for duty.[13]

In six weeks, the Seventh had lost two-thirds of its strength in the nonstop campaign that was bringing the Confederacy to its knees. In a letter to the Rhode Island adjutant general, Captain Daniels tried to explain where the Seventh Rhode Island was.

> Look on the bloodstained hills, in the desolate valleys, and among the battle-scarred forests from the Rapidan to the Appomattox, and you can see where many of them sleep, and though their places are vacant their names are sacred and encircled with a halo of glory. Many others have returned to their friends maimed with deformities they must carry to the grave, but they, while here, will be cared for and loved, and when they pass away their names shall be remembered. Better, had better, the fate of either than to be worthy the curses of sire or son, or merit the scorn of mother or sister. Hard indeed has been the work and terrible the carnage of the past two months, and not soon shall we forget the 10th, 11th, 12th, 13th, and 18th of May, when we shared in the hard struggle around Spotsylvania, nor the fighting of the 24th, 25th, and 26th across the North Anna. The skirmishers of the 30th and 31st of may and 1st and 2nd of June at Totopotomoy Creek will, too, be remembered, and the bloody charge of the 3rd of June, when one-third of the regiment went down, will never be forgotten. Our hard marches also, which have not been few, have left their impression, as well as the many nights we have used the shovel and pick in the trenches and pits. But through all the Seventh has shown a gallantry, coolness, fidelity, and perseverance worthy her native State, and we hope no Rhode Islander can look on our record with any but the feelings of pride, though his joy must be tinged with sadness for the fallen brave. They have added much to the bright laurels won in previous campaigns, and nobly earned a soldier's brightest reward — the approbation of his superiors. Our decimated ranks tell of the hard work we have done. You would hardly recognize our short line of to-day as all that is left of the 900 that left Rhode Island with us less than two years ago; but though the chances of war have called us to weep over the graves of so many noble comrades, those that remain are true as steel, as has been proven on many a hard-fought field. May the future be as free from dishonor as the past.[14]

No company in the regiment suffered more than Company H. Of the eighty-five men that Captain James Remington had recruited from Warwick and East Greenwich, few were left. The captain himself had recovered from his Fredericksburg wound to join the Veterans Reserve Corps. On the morning of June 20, Private George W. Covill went to collect the rations for his company and said, "Here is Company H." Only Covill remained. No Rhode Island regiment had lost as many men as the Seventh to date. With the draft again underway in Rhode Island, the draftees were again assigned to the senior regiments, while the Seventh received none. In the midst of all of the losses, Company K did receive one welcome addition. Sergeant Charles Colvin had been ill nearly nine months from Yazoo fever at Portsmouth Grove when he returned on June 17.[15]

The Seventh continued doing the one thing that they were used to doing: digging. The First Brigade dug in around the railroad that was captured on June 16. One officer commented, "The line in the rear of the railroad was strongly entrenched and strengthened with traverses, abatis, and covered ways." Abatis were sharpened sticks that pointed toward the Confederate lines as a last line of defense before the attackers got to the main entrenchments. The Ninth Corps was positioned in the center of the line with the Second Corps on the right and the Fifth Corps deployed to the left. In three days of combat, the Ninth Corps lost 1,000 men. So far during the campaign, 10,000 men had been lost. Under an agreement, the regiments remained in the trenches for two days and spent two days recovering in the rear. Private Harrington remained behind the lines boiling coffee for Company K. He had to travel to the front trenches daily with a pail of the hot liquid to serve his comrades. After a month in the hospital, Harrington was pleased to see his friend George Potter return from his Spotsylvania wound. Occasionally small truces occurred along the line as the men exchanged small pleasantries and met as Americans between the lines. One day William Harrington invited the Virginians in front of him over for coffee. The Confederates declined because they thought he had a weapon. Like most in the regiment, Harrington thought continuously of his family, writing, "it does seame funny to think that I have a boy all most two years old that I have not seene I oftine see the rest of you in my dreams night before last I was having a good time when the cannons made so much noise that they waked me up and I found that I was on the field in Va instead of being at home in RI." With such a small amount of men, picket duty became increasingly dangerous, with the Seventh being called every night. The weather became unbearably hot as the small band of Rhode Islanders struggled to perform their duty.[16]

In one week in the trenches, eighteen more men were wounded. They included Private Henry Harkness, a thirty-two-year-old carpenter from Coventry, serving in Company K. On June 26, he was shot through the stomach. Harkness was evacuated to Washington where he was discharged from the service. During his stay in the hospital, the "U.S." cartridge box plate from his box was stolen. The hapless private was charged ten cents for its loss. Returning to Coventry, Harkness used his skills as a carpenter to build a small house for his family and decorated it with his wartime trophies, including a small U.S. flag he carried in his knapsack. Constantly thirsty from his stomach wound, Harkness dug an eight-foot well in his yard and

Constantly thirsty due to a severe wound received at Petersburg, Henry Harkness dug an eight-foot well in his yard.

Promoted from the ranks, Lieutenant John McKay commanded the five remaining men in Company H. Courtesy of the USAMHI.

drank from it for the rest of his life. In the Petersburg trenches the heat continued to bore down upon the men. If they so much as raised a head or limb above the entrenchments, instant death or injury could occur. The Confederates introduced a powerful new weapon: short-range mortars. The weapons had an unnerving effect upon the Seventh, as the men could see the slow moving shells fly through the air and explode. Drummer William P. Hopkins noted, "When their shells explode midair, the noise is as of thunder, and we seem compelled to watch them, whether we wish to or not." On June 30, Sergeant John McKay was promoted to lieutenant and took command of Company H. The company consisted of one corporal and four privates. Such were the fortunes of war.[17]

Even with the reduced strength of the Seventh Rhode Island, the small force that remained was allowed either a lieutenant colonel or a major, but not both. Captain Daniels had been in command of the regiment since May 18, beginning at Spotsylvania where he badly bungled the Seventh's bayonet charge. Only the quick-thinking reaction by Captain Jenks had saved the Rhode Islanders from destruction. Now Governor James Y. Smith set about to reward the two senior officers of the Seventh with promotion to higher rank. The task presented a problem. Both captains were commissioned on the same day: March 1, 1863. In Colonel Bliss's reorganization of the regiment, Daniels had commanded the second company, with Jenks's Company I as the eighth company. As was the case at Fredericksburg and by tradition, Daniels had seniority over Jenks. Nearly every officer and enlisted man in the Seventh hoped that Jenks would be commissioned as the next commander. Governor Smith wrote a commission as major and mailed it to the Seventh in the middle of June: it was given to Captain Jenks. The commission arrived when the captain was recovering from his wound. As with all mail issued to the regiments, it was first stopped at division headquarters where it was inspected for contraband. The inspecting officer this day was none other than Captain Peleg Peckham. Despite his earlier misgivings about Daniels, the captain had helped Peckham in his quest for promotion. Now he rewarded that patronage by holding the commission at division headquarters for two weeks. Jenks received word that the commission was coming and waited every day for it. Governor Smith discovered that Jenks had not been mustered in at his new rank. Therefore he issued a commission as lieutenant colonel to Percy Daniels. Daniels was orphaned at age six and attended school in Vermont to become a civil engineer. Despite his upbringing, he still had considerable political support in the Republican Party. Captain Jenks was a "simple farmer" from Foster and was not involved in the political machine. In addition, Jenks was thirty-six to Daniels's twenty-three. Many considered him more mature and capable of leadership. As soon as the lieutenant colonel's commission had arrived at division headquarters, Captain Peckham rode to the Seventh and delivered the commissions. Daniels immediately went to Captain Henry R. Rathbone at Ninth Corps headquarters. Rathbone was the commissary of musters and swore Daniels in as the lieutenant colonel of the Seventh. This had an unsettling effect on the officers and men. Jenks was denied the command because of Peckham's subversive activities. Hospital Steward Stephen Peckham had been detached from the Seventh since the Wilderness. He heard the rumors and was distressed that his friend was denied the much warranted rank. Many years after the war, Peckham traveled to Jenks's farm. He said, "I asked Jenks if it was true, and he said it was." Ethan Amos Jenks was entitled to wear the gold leaves of a major, but not the pay that accompanied it. He eventually earned a brevet of major for his actions at Spotsylvania while the Seventh's reduced numbers never allowed him to be mustered into the new rank. Major Jenks remained in command of the right wing of the Seventh till the end of the war.[18]

As the men came to terms with their new lieutenant colonel, they also became used to the surroundings around them. Each day the breastworks were strengthened as the men struggled to adjust to their new home. The slightest movement of a head or arm above the works could bring instant death or injury; the result was that at least one Rhode Islander was killed or wounded each day. Due to their extremely reduced strength, it became evident to division commander Robert B. Potter that the Seventh Rhode Island was no longer an effective combat regiment; they could barely muster 100 rifles. As such, the regiment was pulled out of the trenches and sent to Second Division Headquarters. Here the men were assigned as engineers. Their duty was to complete the mundane tasks they had been accomplishing for two months. "We worked on the fortifications, made gabions, dug trenches, and repaired roads," noted Private Peleg Jones in stating, "We are put in the engineer corps." In the prewar Regular Army, the engineers were considered the most elite of U.S. soldiers; the top West Point graduates were assigned to it, while those who graduated at the bottom of the class were assigned to the infantry, such as Colonel Bliss. The dangers posed by being in the front trenches did not last long, however, as the regiment was in them every day constructing the works. On July 4, a general truce was declared along the line. The men cheered wildly while singing the "Star Spangled Banner," and the Confederates countered by singing their songs. The trenches were only 600 yards apart, so American met American, trading coffee for tobacco, while discussing the war. At dusk the firing resumed. Rain had not fallen since Cold Harbor, placing water at a premium. The Seventh discovered a spring that they relished. Each day the Confederates bombarded the lines, sending tree branches and leaves flying into the Rhode Island position. The Union forces responded by firing a thirty-two-pound shell into the city every fifteen minutes; the men called the cannon the "Petersburg Express." Each day the battered remnant of the Seventh looked on the horizon for their relief. Finally one day it arrived.[19]

On July 5, the Rhode Islanders looked to see a familiar site marching toward them — a dark blue flag with a silver fouled anchor and the words "What Cheer" upon it. It could mean only one thing: The Fourth Rhode Island Volunteers were here. The Seventh had not seen their brothers in over a year. After the Third Division left the remainder of the Ninth Corps at Newport News, they remained on the Peninsula during the Gettysburg Campaign and for the remainder of 1863. Late that year, the Fourth was transferred to the prisoner-of-war camp near Point Lookout, Maryland. Here they spent the winter of 1864 guarding Confederates. When reinforcements were called for to join the Army of the Potomac the regiments of the Veterans Reserve Corps were transferred to the Point, as the veteran regiments left for the front. The Fourth was assigned to the First Brigade, Second Division, Ninth Corps. They brought a very welcome reinforcement to Colonel Curtin: 350 officers and rifles. To the Seventh, the most important thing was that these men were Rhode Islanders. The Fourth filed into the trenches vacated by the Seventh and prepared to learn the same lesson. Private Ned Carey claimed, "A man was as well entitled to get killed here, as in the middle of a battlefield." The Fourth named their series of trenches, the "Nine Holes," after a game played at home that was hard to get out of. One day, while playing poker, the "pot," which was full of money, was carried away by a shell. Corporal George Allen had never witnessed such a fight, having been on detached duty when the Fourth was cut in two at Antietam. He was shocked to see a comrade shot down every day, while watching as his Company B shrank daily. Every day the Ninth Corps lost ninety men.[20]

As the Army of Northern Virginia faced their fellow countrymen only 300 yards distant, Lee hoped to relieve pressure on his Petersburg lines by sending a corps of his army north in a vain attempt to capture the depleted Washington defenses. By the middle of July, his men had made it, skirmishing within sight of the city and while President Lincoln watched. The Second Rhode Island helped to fight back the Rebel onslaught with the Sixth Corps. As the men settled into the lines, the Rhode Islanders in both regiments completed their duties —

the Fourth fighting and the Seventh digging. Some men passed the time by playing poker and talking to their comrades, while others came up with more creative means. Using his skills as a carpenter, Private Peleg Jones completed complicated math problems in his diary. As the days passed, Ulysses S. Grant knew that he could not launch direct assaults against the Confederate works without it being beaten back with heavy loss. He also wanted to break the siege quickly. The answer came in late June, from an unlikely source.[21]

The Forty-Eighth Pennsylvania had fought with the Ninth Corps since North Carolina. The regiment was comprised largely of coal miners from Schuylkill County, Pennsylvania. Their commander, Lieutenant Colonel Henry Pleasants, devised a brilliant plan. His regiment would dig a tunnel under the Confederate works, pack it with black powder, and blow it up. After the explosion, the Ninth Corps would charge through the breech in the Petersburg line. The plan had promise and Grant gave his formal permission "as a means to keep the men occupied." The task proceeded quickly as the Pennsylvanians worked around the clock, digging forty feet per day. Rumors spread throughout both sides of the operations, but few knew outside of the First Brigade line. The Confederates knew a mine was being built as well, but they could not pinpoint its location. The tunnel took on a life of its own, as Pleasants's men built the over 500-foot span, hauling the dirt out in hardtack boxes, while a complicated ventilation system helped the men breath. When completed, the miners built two parallel thirty-eight foot galleries, which were to be packed with 12,000 pounds of powder.[22]

First Lieutenant Benjamin Perkins resigned the command of Company A on July 20, 1864.

Burnside's plan, as it had been at Fredericksburg, was fairly basic in its design, but required proper preparation by the division and brigade commanders on the ground. The majority of the brigade commanders were veteran colonels, commanding brigades barely the size of their regiment when mustered in. Of his four division commanders, only Robert Potter and Orlando Willcox were true veteran commanders. James Ledlie was a political appointee, while Edward Ferrero and his Fourth Division had yet to distinguish themselves in the campaign. As such, and because his three white divisions had been slaughtered in the fighting, the Fourth Division would lead the assault into Petersburg. Ferrero would send the men around the exploded crater to keep the Confederates occupied, while the white divisions charged into Petersburg. In the Seventh Rhode Island, each man was assigned an ax, spade, and pick ax as they unfortunately turned in their Enfields to draw the entrenching tools. Colonel Bliss arrived on the twenty-fifth and regained command of his First Brigade. Also on this day, Grant told Burnside that he wanted an assault soon. The following day Burnside presented his plan to Meade and Grant. He would explode the mine in the early morning hours; his black division would lead the assault, followed by the three white divisions. The Second and Fifth Corps supported the assault. The reason the Fourth Division was going to lead the assault was due to their training for the mission and their nearly full strength. The plan also had another motive—black troops had yet to prove themselves in combat in the Army of the Potomac. Augustus Woodbury wrote, "They would wipe off whatever reproach an ill-judged prejudice might cast upon them, and would prove themselves brave men, demanding the respect which brave men deserve."[23]

The mine was charged on twenty-seventh of July, the Fourth Rhode Island helping in its completion. Corporal Allen remembered carrying twenty-five pound bags packed with the explosive through a dangerous space to bring the powder to the mine shaft, where it was packed into the two galleries under the Confederate fort. Colonel Pleasants had asked for 12,000 pounds of powder; instead, he only received 8,000 pounds and small pieces of fuse that had to be spliced together to make the fuse work. At Ninth Corps headquarters, Burnside was carefully laying down his plans for the assault, until a bombshell struck. Meade told Burnside that Grant would not allow the Fourth Division to charge first; instead, he would have to rely on one of the white divisions, which were severely understrength and not trained for the dangerous task. Grant's answer was that if the blacks were defeated, it would appear as if they were being purposively slaughtered. Never a man to be put under pressure, Burnside decided that the three white division commanders should draw lots to see who would lead the assault. The winner was also the least experienced — political appointee James Ledlie would lead his First Division in the charge, slated for the early morning hours of July 30.[24]

The men received the orders to prepare to charge at 2:00 in the morning of July 30. Colonel Pleasants crawled into the tunnel to personally light the fuse, but it went out half way. An unlucky sergeant was compelled to climb into the shaft and relight it, but he made it out in time. Colonel Bliss prepared his brigade, while the Seventh received orders to support the charge; they would carry three entrenching tools each and pass them along if needed to the Second Division. The Fourth would be among the first units to charge; the men were issued sixty rounds of ammunition, and only carried their weaponry and blankets. Every cannon along the Federal line prepared to fire when the charge went off, while the Confederates continued with their picket firing, unaware of the events that were about to occur. The fuse finally burned out into 8,000 pounds of black powder at 4:44 in the morning of July 30, 1864; the result was a sight many never forgot. Corporal Allen, waiting in the ranks of the Fourth Rhode Island recalled. "The sight, most awful to behold, the shrieks of the doomed garrison, the roar and rush of the huge guns and time unfolding over our heads, and the mingled noise and shock of the explosion struck terror into the hearts of our bravest troops." The result of the massive blast was a crater two hundred feet long, fifty feet wide, and thirty feet deep. In the pit lay the remains of 256 dead Confederates, in addition to a battery and tons of debris.[25]

As soon as the explosion occurred, Ledlie sent his First Division in, while he retired to a bunker to await the developments, all the while sipping on whisky with Ferrero. The Second Brigade, Second Division, then charged. Colonel Bliss was sitting on a barrel talking to Captain Lyman Jackman of the Sixth New Hampshire waiting for the Second Brigade to clear out of the line of march before committing his brigade. A Confederate shell hit near Bliss's position, causing the colonel to move his position to the left. The first Union troops into the

10. "If it takes all summer"   123

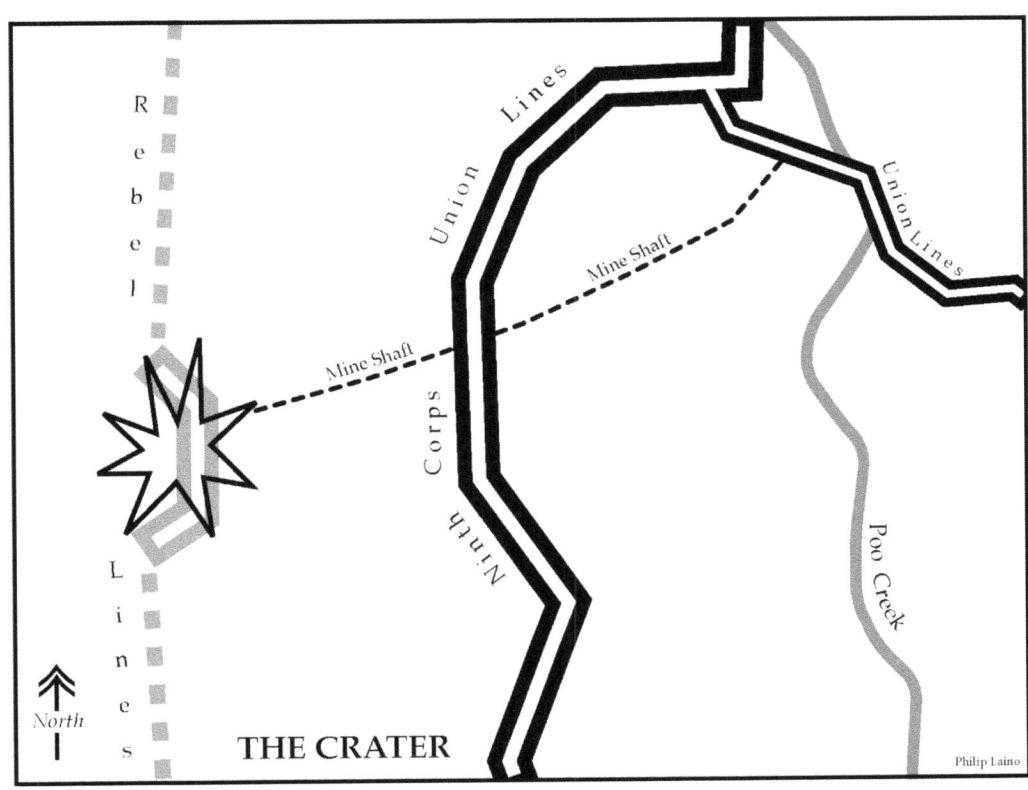

THE CRATER

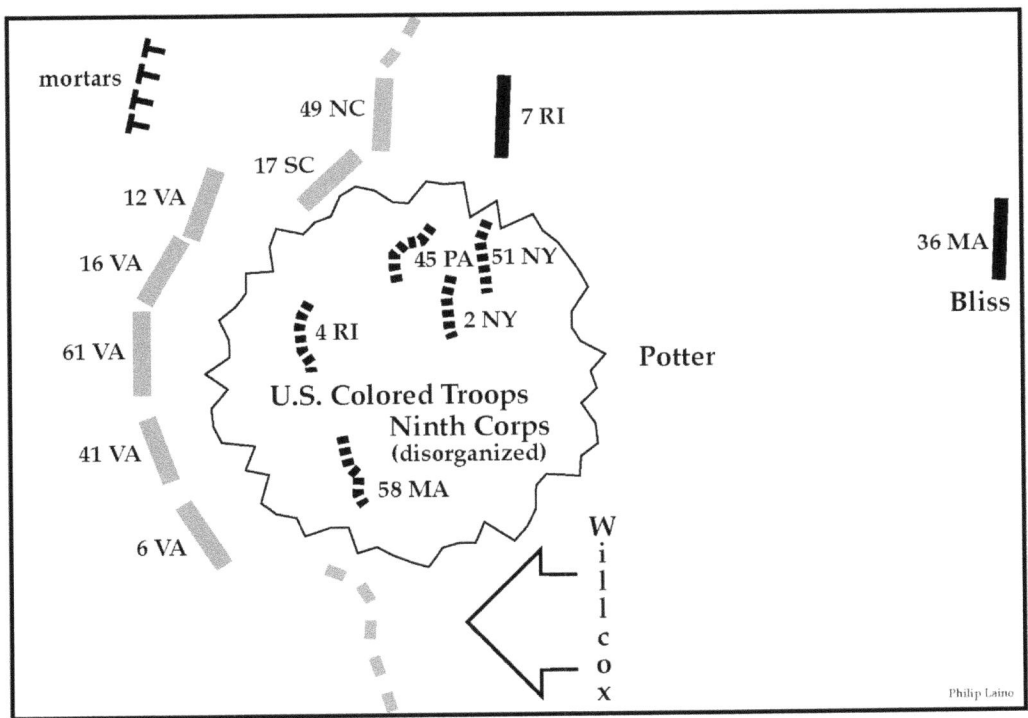

works were sickened by the sight of pieces of bodies blown all over the crater. They stopped to collect souvenirs and to help the wounded Confederates. As Griffin's Brigade charged, Bliss issued orders to his brigade. The Fifty-Eighth Massachusetts, Fourth Rhode Island, and Forty-Fifth Pennsylvania charged the lines first. Lieutenant Colonel Martin P. Buffum yelled out, "Forward Fourth Rhode Island." With the command, the Fourth charged into the crater; instead of going around the position as was planned, nearly all of the Union forces charged directly into the pit. The result was that the Confederates could stand at the crest of the hole and fire down into the Federal position. The Union artillery opened fire all along the line, adding to the confusion in the early morning hours. Among the men rushing forward with the Fourth Rhode Island was Private Elisha R. Watson of Coventry. He recalled the initial charge:

> As we crossed the short space between the lines we got mixed up with some other troops that crossed before us and we had to stop for a minute. As I dropped to the ground a friend of mine saw me when I fell. He said to one of his comrades, "Elisha is hit, he is down!" But no, at that I was up and going forward.[26]

Through the black powder smoke, the Fourth Rhode Island could hear a call that they were shooting into the ranks of their own soldiers. The officers ignored the calls, yelling out, "Give 'em hell. They played that on us at Antietam" in reference to a trick the South Carolinians had played in Otto's Cornfield claiming they were Connecticut men instead of the enemy.[27]

The way to Petersburg was open, as Union forces only needed to push forward to gain the advantage. In the Ninth Corps, one brigade charged at a time, into the crater rather than into the city they were trying to capture, which wasted time and allowed the Confederates to start to bring up reinforcements, including short-range mortars. The Fourth Rhode Island

The Ninth Corps charged into the Crater. *Battles and Leaders of the Civil War.*

laid down in their position in a move reminiscent of the Seventh at Fredericksburg; even more eerily similar, the Fourth was among the units to advance farthest into the pit. Colonel Bliss next sent in the Fifty-First New York and Second New York Rifles. He ordered the Thirty-Sixth Massachusetts to stay behind in reserve. Colonel Bliss himself did not go forward with the charging regiments. Rather, he remained behind to direct the battalions to their proper place; this was the job of a brigade leader as it was up to the regimental commanders to lead from the front. The last division to charge in the Ninth Corps was the Fourth Division. The men were prepared for the action, and they sought to prove themselves as soldiers. Proudly wearing the green shield of the Ninth Corps on their forage caps, the black soldiers and white officers charged in to support their white brothers. The Confederates were enraged at the sight; it was the first time in Virginia they had fought such a large number of blacks. This led them to fight even more ferociously. Even worse for the Union forces, the Confederates leading the counterattack were comprised of William Mahone's brigade; these men lived in Petersburg and the surrounding areas and they now savagely fought hand to hand to protect their homes. In the crater proper, the Fourth Rhode Island was receiving fire from the Forty-First and Sixty-First Virginia. The small dog that Company B had adopted broke from its leash and ran into the works to find the Rhode Islanders, barking at the Confederates; the animal had its fur singed by a bullet. Lieutenant George W. Field rose to his feet and, waving his sword, he yelled out, "Who will follow me?" A dozen men responded. The lieutenant walked one step ahead when he was killed.[28]

The Seventh Rhode Island had been waiting for two hours to receive the call to go into the fight. Lieutenant Colonel Daniels searched everywhere for General Robert B. Potter to order the Seventh forward. Unable to find the general, who had led the Second Division into the fight, Daniels took matters into his own hands. The officers in the front were pleading for reinforcements; it was now or never for the Seventh. Throwing away their tools, the Rhode Islanders took their Enfields, took sixty rounds of ammunition and rushed into the breach. Setting up a firing line on the right of the crater, the Seventh remained in its position until the ammunition was expended. Drummer Hopkins recalled, "We at once opened a deliberate fire which was taken up by those on our right and left, a circumstance not without influence undoubtedly in determining the foe to remain where best acquainted." The loss was light, only five men wounded. In the Crater itself, the Fourth Rhode Island was receiving the brunt of the Confederate attack; they advanced farther than any other Federal soldiers. As a wounded officer was being carried to the rear, he yelled out, "Every man of the Fourth Rhode Island deserves a promotion." As other Union forces were being pushed back, Lieutenant Colonel Buffum gave the command to retreat at 9:45. The Fourth had to retrace its steps back to the Ninth Corps lines, all the while being racked by mortar, artillery, and small-arms fire. It was almost a mirror image of what the Seventh had gone through at Fredericksburg. Some of the officers and men decided to remain behind and be taken prisoner instead of taking the risk of being shot during the retreat. After a half dozen color bearers had been shot down, Private James Welsh took the U.S. flag and raced for the rear. He was closely followed by what was left of the Fourth. Welsh's actions earned him the Medal of Honor. Some men did not hear the order to abandon the works; Private Watson continued the fight, as General William F. Bartlett, whose cork leg was shattered, took command in the Crater itself and tried to organize a last-ditch defense.[29]

The regiment had taken two hundred men into the fighting, and it left ninety-six behind, including two dead officers and a dozen enlisted men. At 10:00, Burnside gave the order for the Ninth Corps to abandon the works and fall back to the rear. For yet another time, a charge had failed.[30]

During the rest of the day, the two sides took stock of their losses and treated the wounded. The weather became unbearably hot, rising to 105 degrees. The Confederates were infuriated at fighting people whom they did not even consider men; that is, the soldiers of the Fourth Division. Some of the prisoners were murdered while the others were carried away into bondage. The loss had been heavy for the Ninth Corps: 428 were dead, while in total the Corps lost 3,828 officers and men. Many senior officers were among the captured. As the wounded were being treated on the night of the thirtieth, Captain Lyman Jackman recalled, "Our hearts were all very sad that night at the loss of so many brave fellows with so little to show for the heavy loss." Even more saddening to the enlisted men, they knew that the charge had failed and that lives had been wasted. For all of Burnside's courage and brilliance in planning the North Carolina expedition and the deliverance of Tennessee, the Battle of the Crater would stand second to Fredericksburg in his career in the Federal army as a failure. If only the proper officers had given the correct orders, many lives could have been saved and Petersburg captured.[31]

For the enlisted men in the Fourth and Seventh Rhode Island, few put blame on their commanders. Private William O. Harrington blamed the failure of the assault on the tardiness of the Fourth Division, even though they were the last to charge. He wrote, "We fought the Rebels yesterday and got whipt the fight began about sunrise by our folks blowing up one of the rebel foarts then they opened on them with artillery and musketry the fight was very severe we drove them out of two lines of there works when they broke and run and that broke the white troops and we ware drove back to our lines with a heavy loss they could not start us out of our own lines but if we had not trusted to the negroes we might have held our ground it is a sad sight to look over the field this morning it is fairly speckled with the killed and wounded." In his diary, Jared Potter simply wrote, "We blew up their works & got wasted." The Seventh was fortunate in this engagement; for their small size, the casualties were relatively light. It was perhaps Lieutenant Colonel Daniels's greatest moment in the war, rushing in to support the crumbling Union line. He was awarded with a brevet of colonel and wasted no time in sewing the eagles upon his shoulders. The sights that they saw in the crater were sickening while the battle had again gone against them. Richmond was so close, but until a new maneuver could be designed, the men were forced to remain in the trenches, waiting. Hospital Steward Stephen F. Peckham helped the Ninth Corps surgeons treat the hundreds of wounded men who were brought out of the crater under a flag of truce. In a letter to his brother, he wrote, "The firing impassed anything I had heard, another disastrous defeat was at hand." Peckham also referred to his regiment as "prime gold." Although only a few remained, they continued to fight with their usual ardor.[32]

Despite being at the front for only a month, the Fourth Rhode Island was reduced from 350 to 125 men. The Fourth had developed a reputation for being a hard regiment to command; every commander became a casualty during the war. The first colonel resigned three weeks after being commissioned. Isaac P. Rodman was killed and William H. P. Steere was wounded at Antietam. Joseph B. Curtis was killed at Fredericksburg and Martin P. Buffum now found himself a prisoner of war. They again filed into the trenches to fight alongside the Seventh. The Rhode Islanders were fortunate to save their colors and many of their men; some regiments were nearly taken in their entirety.[33]

Major General George G. Meade immediately began to look for someone to blame for the fiasco. He found it in General Ambrose E. Burnside and his Ninth Army Corps. The Ninth Corps had been a thorn in Meade's side since the beginning of the campaign, never fully integrated into the Army of the Potomac; the men in the Ninth were more loyal to Burnside than any other commander. While other soldiers despised him, he was the man who made and led the Ninth Corps and he inspired feelings there similar to those felt by the first troops in the Army of the Potomac for McClellan. Meade believed that Burnside had not followed orders and set about to court-martial the officers involved in the defeat. In addition, the U.S. Congress began to organize a committee to investigate why the Battle of the Crater failed. Major General Winfield Scott Hancock and two other general officers created a court of inquiry to investigate. After seventeen days of testimony, questioning all of the senior officers in the Ninth Corps, the court returned with its findings. The officers claimed that the charge had failed because the men did not properly complete their mission; they went into the Crater instead of going around the pit into Petersburg as they were supposed to. In a reference to the actions of the Seventh Rhode Island, the court claimed that there was "no proper employment of engineer officers and working parties and of materials for their use." Instead of carrying their tools into the battle, the Rhode Islanders performed the task of providing covering fire with their Enfields. Five Ninth Corps officers were found guilty for the failure of the battle. Burnside failed to listen to Meade's orders, had not properly employed the engineers, and failed to see that Ledlie's First Division went to its proper place. The career of General Ambrose E. Burnside, which began so gloriously leading the Rhode Islanders up Matthews Hill three years earlier, was over; he never again to receive a field command. Burnside returned to Providence, awaiting orders for the rest of the war.[34]

Other officers cited included Ferrero and Ledlie for remaining behind in a bunker, while Orlando B. Willcox was cited for failing to "exercise sufficient energy in causing his troops to go forward." The court also noted that one officer should have been in command of the attacking force, rather than the individual division commanders. The charge against the fifth officer found at fault came as a shock to all who knew him. For two years of combat his record had been spotless, and he had earned the Medal of Honor, two brevets, and three recommendations for promotion. He was with his regiment in every campaign and had led them into the hell that was Fredericksburg and the Mississippi Campaign. The fifth officer was Colonel Zenas Randall Bliss. According to the court of inquiry, Bliss "remained behind with the only regiment of his brigade which did not go forward according to orders and occupied a position where he could not see what was going on." Colonel Bliss stayed behind with the Thirty-Sixth Massachusetts; he had carried out the orders given to him by General Potter, that is, to support the Second Brigade with his brigade. His actions mirrored exactly those of James Nagle at Fredericksburg. Nagle remained behind with the Forty-Eighth Pennsylvania, allowing his regimental commanders to take the assault forward. Bliss's actions were no different from any other brigade commander during the war. However, the people of the North had grown weary of such slaughter; over 60,000 men had fallen in the campaign. With yet another loss, a scapegoat was needed, and it happened to be on Colonel Bliss. The case against the colonel was based on one witness who said, "Colonel Bliss remained with the last regiment of his brigade, and did not go forward at all to my knowledge." This solitary witness was enough to build a case against Bliss; all of the old officers in the Ninth Corps knew of the colonel's gallantry at Fredericksburg, Jackson, and the Wilderness. Bliss had seen the slaughter at those engagements and he knew that perhaps such an attack was fruitless, but the orders were to attack, and, as a professional officer, he carried them out. Now as a brigade commander, he was carrying out his tasks. Unfortunately for the colonel, like his corps commander, Bliss's days in the Army of the Potomac were numbered. He visited the Seventh Rhode Island for the last time in late August, after receiving orders to report for a desk position in Wheeling, West Virginia. Although Bliss would remain officially the colonel of the Seventh, he never led them in the field again. Now under the command of an incompetent, reckless officer, the Seventh Rhode Island remained at the front, ready to perform their duty.[35]

11

Closing the Gap

We were once and always, the Fourth Rhode Island Regiment.
  — *Corporal George H. Allen, October 3, 1864*

After the Crater fiasco and the subsequent death, capture, or court-martial of so many high-ranking Ninth Corps officers, the Ninth lost the esprit de corps that had carried them through the war to date. Now their ranks were filled with draftees and one-year bounty men rather than veteran soldiers. The casualties were so heavy that the Ninth Corps historian, Rhode Islander Augustus Woodbury, recorded, "Scarcely a moiety of the officers and men remained in those regiments which had left Annapolis with full ranks." With the severe losses, the First and Third Divisions were consolidated into one division, while the Fourth Division became the Third Division. The white troops did not always welcome their comrades; whenever the Third Division appeared, the Confederates shelled them with vigor, causing much distress in the other divisions.[1]

Private Joseph Taylor was awarded the Medal of Honor.

With Colonel Bliss gone, the survivors of the Fourth and Seventh Rhode Island remained in their trenches, trying to protect themselves, while the Confederates bombarded the Federal position constantly. Martha Young wanted to join her husband in the field, and often pressed Emor to describe what a battle looked like. He replied, "Now just think how it would seem to you to hear hundreds of cannon belching fourth their thunders and thousands of small arms then add to this the grones of the dying and you will have a faint idea of a battle. But the reality you cannot know." In mid–August, the Ninth Corps moved from the right of the line to the extreme left, taking up positions near the Fifth Corps camp at the Weldon Railroad.[2]

11. Closing the Gap

Arriving at their new home, the Rhode Islanders remained under fire. Fortunately they found relief in the strong earthworks the Fifth Corps left behind. The men lived underground in structures called "bombproofs" to escape the fire outside. Corporal Allen described them as, "a large hole dug in the ground and covered with heavy logs and earth, looking very much like a tomb. Built strongly, as it should be, it is proof against the shot or shell of the enemy, hence its name." As the men settled into their new surroundings, Grant again made plans. Unable to take Petersburg by assault, he would starve the Confederates into submission. As the city was a railroad center, the Union forces would have to capture the track lines running into Petersburg, including, among the largest, the Weldon Railroad, traveling north from the port of Wilmington, North Carolina. The Weldon supplied Lee with many of his supplies and consequently Grant directed that it be taken.[3]

Private George W. Rathbun served with his brothers in Company H. Courtesy of David Rathbun.

The Rhode Islanders followed the Fifth and Second Corps as they attempted to destroy the Weldon Railroad. Fortunately for their depleted ranks, they were not engaged in the action, but they earned the battle honor: "Weldon Railroad." It took a month to finally shut down one of Lee's major supply lines. On August 18, Private Joseph Taylor of Company E was detailed to act as an orderly at First Brigade headquarters, after Major Peckham's aide was killed. Riding out to deliver messages to the regimental commanders, Taylor became lost in the high brush surrounding his route. He saw three Confederates from the Sixteenth Georgia out on picket duty. Drawing his revolver, he quickly took the three men back to Colonel Curtin, the brigade commander. At the age of seventeen, Taylor became one of the youngest men ever to be awarded the Medal of Honor, although he did not receive the award until Colonel Bliss presented it to him in 1897. Grant continued to push the affair, as the Union forces tried to dig up the railroad. In the Seventh, the fatigue of the campaign was having a severe effect upon the health of the officers; half of them were incapacitated. Major Jenks became severely ill and returned home to Foster for two months of rest. As he was a neighbor of William Harrington, the private gave Jenks some money to bring home to Eunice in Moosup Valley. Harrington was also somewhat distressed because his brother Josiah was discharged from the Eighteenth Connecticut and returned home, deathly ill with a disease he contracted in the service. The biggest battle for the Weldon Railroad took place on August 24–25, at Ream's Station when A. P. Hill destroyed the Second Corps and captured Battery B, First Rhode Island Light Artillery.[4]

While the Seventh was undergoing a constant bloodletting in Virginia, Tryphena Cundall maintained an active life in Ashaway. She traveled to Connecticut and visited relatives in Boston. Each day, Tryphena passed the Oak Grove Cemetery, only established in 1860, where her husband was one of the first to be interred. Although relatively new, the cemetery was already becoming the final resting place for the men from Ashaway who perished in the war. Joel C. Maxon died at home after returning from Mississippi while Charles B. Greene became the first man in the Seventh to perish. In 1861, a dozen men left southwestern Rhode Island to join the Fourth Regiment. Now they returned to Hopkinton. Edwin Gavitt and Davis Crandall were killed at New Berne, while William D. Clarke died of typhoid as the Fourth marched north to Antietam. Benjamin Franklin Burdick and Henry F. Saunders were killed in Otto's Cornfield as they tried to save each other. In the northern reaches of Hopkinton, Henry Godfrey was fortunate to spend thirteen days with his family before he died of Yazoo fever; he was buried near Joseph J. Kenyon and Charles W. Gardiner, who died as the Seventh entered the field. The Burdick family mourned the loss of four relatives who died in the war to date. In effect, Hopkinton was devastated. The results in neighboring Richmond were the same. Throughout Rhode Island, families feared that each day's mail would bring the news that none wanted to hear.[5]

On picket duty, the men again performed the task of being the "eyes and ears" of the Federal army. Because the lines were barely one-half mile apart, each night detachments of six men under the command of a corporal were stationed as an advanced guard. The men patrolled far from the main lines as they attempted to carry out the vital duty. The closeness of the picket lines resulted in many opportunities to trade small items. One day, Corporal George Allen tossed a pocket knife to the Confederates, asking for some tobacco as part of a trade. He was surprised at the honesty of the Southerners as they threw the knife back, along with some tobacco. The rest of September was spent performing picket duty and building roads to bring supplies from the recently established supply depot near City Point. The ranks of the Seventh continued to be bolstered; by September 20, 218 men were present for duty, the most since Spotsylvania. The Seventh had yet to receive any of the recruits and had not seen a deserter since April, even with all of the death

Corporal George H. Allen served in the Fourth Rhode Island and later joined the Seventh.

11. Closing the Gap

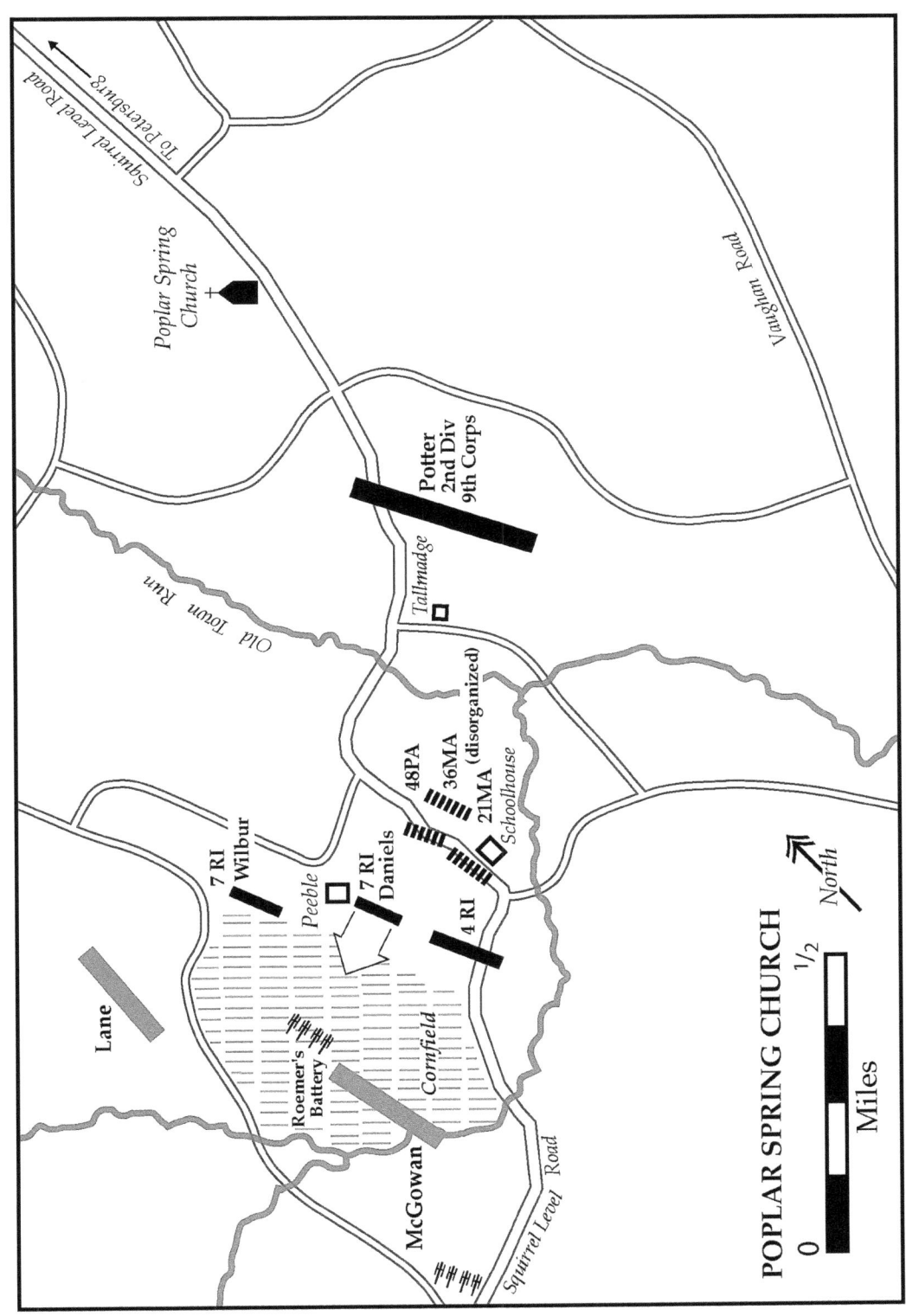

that surrounded them. A high devotion to duty led the men to remain in their positions, even as hundreds fled around them. In a letter to his wife, Emor Young wrote of his continued service to the regiment. "I have stood the firmest, fired the faster, that is what I call duty but some have skuled behing trees both officers as well as privets but that is hat." In late September, Grant decided to launch another broad attack on Petersburg as he attempted to end the war before Christmas. Unfortunately, the First Brigade, Second Division, Ninth Corps was about to lose a valuable regiment.[6]

Mustered into the service on September 30, 1861, the Fourth Rhode Island had fought in some of the war's bloodiest battles, including losing half its strength at Antietam and the Crater. Now their time was up, having served three years. In early 1864, 172 men reenlisted, but the numbers were not enough to maintain a regimental structure. As such, the men in the Fourth would be left in a few days without a regiment. While the veterans of the Fourth tried to find a place in the army, Grant decided to launch another round of attacks in late September. The three years' men of the Fourth were excused from the fighting, but some, including the color guard, volunteered to fight in one more battle. The Army of the Potomac would again attack all along the line, while the Ninth Corps marched toward a small whitewashed church near Poplar Grove, west of Petersburg.[7]

The Seventh advanced at 10:00 on the morning of September 30 toward Poplar Spring Church. The regiment was to carry tools into the battle and act as engineers, but was ordered to form a skirmish line to their front. After an hour, Colonel Curtin directed the men to return to the wagon and collect the tools. The attack lasted all day on the Fifth Corps front, west of the church. On the far left of the Ninth Corps line, the Rhode Islanders were not deployed until after supper. As they waited, Private Stephen A. Clarke of Company K said to his friends, "Now lets have a game of Old Farmer's Lein," in reference to an activity played upon the farm. Daniels divided the regiment into two battalions; he commanded six companies for the engagement, while Captain George Wilbur was given four companies. For the Rhode Islanders, it was a rematch of the Battle of Antietam as they faced the same South Carolinians who had repulsed them in the swirling hell of Otto's Cornfield.

Roemer's New York Battery deployed in front of Daniels, near a cornfield, but was soon receiving fire from a Confederate battery. The Southerners began to fire into the Ninth Corps line, "the crash of musketry being heavy and continuous." In a rolling battle, the Ninth Corps soldiers started to be pushed back by the artillery and Carolinian battle line. The Rhode Islanders fixed bayonets as Wilbur's battalion wheeled to the right in an attempt to stem the flow of retreat. Rushing into action to the left of the Peeble House, Colonel Daniels's horse was shot out from under him. He ordered the six companies to advance and rescue Roemer's Battery, which was losing men at an alarming rate as the South Carolinians closed in upon it. With a loud cheer, the six small companies rushed forward and held the Confederates at bay while Captain Roemer limbered up his command and retired. General Potter, commanding the Second Division, rode up and yelled at the retreating men, "For God's sake move up and help that little Seventh Rhode Island." As usual the Seventh did not run, thus allowing the other units to escape, while Potter desperately tried to rally the wavering line.

Captain Wilbur's four companies advanced up a hill to the right, within musket range of the Confederates, who began firing at them. His command became separated from the entire Federal line. The fire became increasingly heavy as Wilbur ordered the men to lie down. After receiving a few "terrible" volleys, Wilbur's men fell back as best they could. The Confederates wanted them to stop and be taken prisoner, but the Rhode Islanders ran as fast as they could. Captain Wilbur rallied the small battalion as they formed a line and exchanged volleys with the North Carolinians who could not advance because of the stubborn resistance. Private Stephen Clarke, who passed the time before the battle joking with his friends, was shot through the heart; yet another Hopkinton soldier was dead. At dusk, the Ninth Corps counterattacked and repulsed the thin gray line, sending it in retreat toward Petersburg and capturing the field. At nightfall, the four companies rejoined the Seventh.[8]

The remnants of the Fourth formed on the extreme left of the Second Division line. Although their term of service had expired, the Fourth proudly went into the fight, with its Rhode Island flag. Written across its top were the words "What Cheer." These were the first words spoken to Roger Williams by Miantonomi when he arrived in Rhode Island. The Fourth advanced on the left of the Seventh and laid down near a rail fence. A Confederate battery fired into the Fourth, shattering the staff of the U.S. flag and killing two members of the color guard who were due to return home in a few days. After losing three killed and two wounded, the Fourth fell back and posted a skirmish line to cover the Ninth Corps' left flank.[9]

Severely wounded at Fredericksburg, Captain George Wilbur ended the war as the Seventh's senior captain.

The losses at the Battle of Poplar Spring Church were light for the Seventh; four dead and eight wounded. The Seventh was given credit in repulsing the Confederate assault and helping to stop the Federal rout. In his report on the battle, Colonel Daniels wrote. "We again checked the enemy, while, by great exertion, showing the most undaunted bravery and coolness and winning the increased admiration of the entire division." In Foster, Sergeant George Potter's mother became alarmed when he appeared on the wounded list; it would have been Potter's third wound of the war. Fortunately William O. Harrington wrote to his wife that the sergeant was fine. The most significant blow for the Seventh was the loss of Lieutenant Samuel McIlroy. The lieutenant was shot in the left leg, which was amputated. After languishing in agony at a field hospital for three weeks, the lieutenant died. A veteran of the British army, McIlroy was interred with Masonic and military honors in Pawtucket. Commanding Company I since Major Jenks assumed command of a battalion at Spotsylvania, he had received two commissions, but the lieutenant was not yet mustered into the rank. As such, his wife and five children would have to make do with a first sergeant's pension. Hospital Steward Stephen F. Peckham wrote a letter to the *Providence Journal* pressing for McIlroy to be posthumously promoted, as was the case of Sergeant Charles H. Kellen at Fredericksburg.

This woodcut shows Colonel Daniels and his six companies of the Seventh rushing into action at Poplar Spring Church.

Peckham wrote, "His place can scarcely be filled." No promotion ever came. In the same letter, the hospital steward again told the citizens of the Seventh's bravery in battle in stating, "Almost alone we checked the assault of the enemy." The early fall operations around Petersburg were successful. Grant advanced closer to the city while capturing several supply lines running into the stricken citadel. Private Harrington was pleased with what the Seventh had helped accomplish. "The past week we come out here to look after the south side railroad and took one line of the rebels works 2 foarts 7 pieces of artiller and some prisreners the 7th gained the honor of saveing the field the rest run but the 7th stood there ground."[10]

On October 3, the three years' men left the Fourth Rhode Island and returned home. Without a complete organization, it was unclear what to do with the men. With the Seventh down to only 200 men, having gained back 100 from the hospitals, the only logical conclusion was to consolidate the two regiments. Because the Fourth was already mustered out of the service, the new regiment would still be called the Seventh Rhode Island Volunteers. The three most depleted companies of the Seventh — B, D, and South Kingstown's G — were disbanded and their men transferred to the other companies. The remnants of the Fourth were reduced to three companies and designated as Companies B, D, and G. The men in the Fourth considered this an insult, leading one soldier to write. "Though this was our military title, yet we never called ourselves other than as we were *once* and *always*, the Fourth Rhode Island Regiment."[11]

After saying good-bye to their comrades, the three companies moved to the Seventh's camp and began the process of integrating themselves into the new regiment. Unfortunately, they learned the hard way to become accustomed to Brevet Colonel Percy Daniels's command. When the men arrived, the Seventh was busy working on the fortifications by cutting wood from a nearby forest. The Fourth began yelling out, "Build a guard house." Colonel Daniels did everything he could to make the men's existence miserable. Because the Fourth had developed a reputation for being a mischievous regiment, nearly mutinying twice and suffering from desertion, Daniels ordered the veterans to undergo six roll calls per day, rather than the three assigned to the Seventh. Each morning the men had to undergo inspection and dress parade at reveille. Furthermore, he gave the men the most mundane tasks to accomplish, and assigned them to almost constant fatigue details, all while the men slept near the picket line. Eventually, the colonel exclaimed. "If I ever get that Fourth Regiment under my command, *I'll* build a guard house for them that they won't like." After two weeks of this nonsense, Daniels rescinded the orders in an attempt to finally get the Fourth under his control. On October 27, Grant launched another assault on the left, which resulted in the Battle of Hatcher's Run. Like the Weldon Railroad, the Seventh participated, but did not become engaged under fire.[12]

Private James Hoard lost an arm at Petersburg and later became Bristol's first police chief.

As the Federal forces advanced closer to Petersburg. General Phillip Sheridan was dealing a death blow to Confederate forces in the Shenandoah Valley. After the Confederates were repulsed in front of Washington in July, they retreated into the valley, closely pursued by Sheridan. He defeated Jubal Early at every engagement. Early counterattacked in the early morning of October 19 at Cedar Creek. In a seesaw battle, the Confederates attempted to gain the upper hand, but, after Sheridan arrived on the field, the Rebels were repulsed. The news spread quickly through the Petersburg camps. President Lincoln was facing a tough reelection bid in only three weeks. His opponent was former Army of the Potomac commander George B. McClellan, running under the Democratic ticket. For the first time, soldiers in the field would be allowed to vote in the field. They had a tough choice. Lincoln promised to see the war through to the close while McClellan strongly hinted he would negotiate a settlement. To the hundreds of thousands who had already died, this would be an insult to their sacrifice. Lincoln needed military victories, and they came just in time: Cedar Creek and the capture of Atlanta. The Rhode Islanders were thrilled with the victory in the Shenandoah,

Hospital Steward Stephen F. Peckham (far right) praised the Seventh's officers who proved themselves on the field, but ran afoul of Percy Daniels after writing a simple line in the *Providence Journal*. Courtesy of the Library of Congress.

coming on the heels of Poplar Spring; it was a clear sign the war was going to be won by the Union. Upon hearing the news, the men began shouting like Narragansett warriors, which startled some staff officers riding nearby.[13]

Hospital steward Stephen Peckham had been detached from the Seventh since the start of the Overland Campaign, serving at the Ninth Corps hospital with Surgeon James Harris. Although he no longer saw what was happening daily at the regimental level, he was kept abreast of Seventh Rhode Island affairs by the steady stream of wounded Rhode Islanders he treated and through his friendship with Major Jenks. After spending two months at home, recovering from his sickness, the major returned to the Seventh in early November. The only engagement he ever missed was Poplar Spring Church because of the illness. In a letter to the *Providence Journal*, Peckham wrote a simple line that would have deep consequences. "Our old hero, Major Jenks has returned, looking better, but not well. He is one of the few always at the front." The letter was published in the *Journal*, which was always circulated among the Seventh. One day, Colonel Daniels was sitting in his tent talking with Captain George Stone when he read the letter, which was not signed. Daniels took the letter as a personal insult to himself as the regimental commander, in suggesting that he was not performing his duty. He also suspected that Stephen Peckham wrote it. Peckham was ordered to report to Daniels, where he found the paper sitting on the table in his tent. The steward acknowledged that he wrote the letter, but he said he meant nothing against the colonel. Secretly, he "hated" Daniels. The colonel demanded that Peckham retract the statement. Following the exchange, Peckham returned to headquarters to confer with Surgeon Harris. The doctor told Peckham he had nothing to retract. Bolstered by this opinion, he wrote to Daniels stating: "I can find in it nothing to retract and do justice to myself and others." This infuriated Daniels who demanded Ninth Corps commander John G. Parke return Peckham to the regiment immediately. The colonel planned to put Peckham in the ranks, where

Major General John G. Parke commanded the Ninth Corps after the Crater. Courtesy of the USAMHI.

he could be controlled. Surgeon Harris intervened, and he sent Peckham to Philadelphia for the rest of the war. Here his chemistry training from Brown University proved of invaluable service as he supervised the U.S. Chemical Laboratory, making medicine for the Union war effort.[14]

Although the battles around Petersburg in the early fall of 1864 did much to boost the morale of the Rhode Islanders fighting in the trenches around Petersburg, it appeared to the men that they would not be home by Christmas. The Seventh was fortunate though to finally receive an adjutant. He came in the form of First Lieutenant Henry Joshua Spooner of the Fourth. Like most of the Rhode Island officers with a college education, Spooner was a graduate of Brown. In 1862, he graduated and applied for a commission when the Seventh was forming. Instead, he and two other officers were sent to the Fourth as they marched to Antietam. Only two weeks after joining the army, the lieutenant was commanding a company in Otto's Cornfield. Now Spooner served as the Seventh's adjutant, which pleased the men from the Fourth. In Company C, Emor Young sent his old greatcoat home for his son Edgar to wear to school in Chepachet. Like most of the men in the regiment, Young continued to micromanage affairs on his farm in western Glocester. He was aghast that Edgar had to travel the four miles to Chepachet each day for schooling. Since the Dorr Rebellion, the village remained a "devlish place," while a recruiting office continued to be opened throughout the war, forwarding recruits to the army. Each time Edgar Young went to school, the recruiter encouraged him to enlist, promising a large bounty for his services. His father fired back in a letter to Martha Young. "Tell Edgar the next man that asks him to enlist to ask him if he has a father in the army. Tell him that I do not want him to come into the army at any cost." Ever dutiful to his family, Private Young mailed home sixty dollars. As the presidential election loomed near, the men received news that those above the age of twenty-one would be able to participate. Because of the suffrage movement during the Dorr Rebellion, the Irish and French-Canadians serving in the Seventh were able to vote as well. Due to its reduced size, and large percentage of underage men, only 148 votes were cast. The Seventh Rhode Island cast 120 ballots for Lincoln and only twenty-eight for McClellan. One soldier wrote about why he voted for Lincoln. "I am willing to have Old Abe for the President for I think that he has done his duty in every respect for the benefit of the country and I think he will do more toward bringing the war to a close than either army that could be done for the rebs know that they have no friend of peice unless they lay down there arms and come back."

Private Horace Slocum served in Company A. Courtesy of Kris VanDenBossche.

On November 12, the Army of the Potomac received the welcome news that Lincoln was reelected to his second term. Private William O. Harrington wrote, "You could hear them cheering for two miles. Our lines are clost to the Rebels so that they could hear plain."[15]

The Seventh continued with their tasks on the picket line, while completing a significant fortification named Fort Fisher. Because the men were constantly engaged in guard duty, they became quite friendly with the Confederates in front of them. One day Captain George Wilbur was conversing with a Confederate officer about the Battle of Poplar Spring Church. The officer told Wilbur that his men could not advance and finish off the Ninth Corps because "a little god damned regiment stopped them." With a smile Wilbur replied that it was the Seventh Rhode Island that stopped the assault. Even more shocking to the Confederate officer was when Colonel Daniels appeared. The officer told the colonel that his men had shot down an officer from his horse, and presumed they killed the man. It turned out that Daniels only received a shock after his horse was killed from under him.[16]

With Fort Fisher completed, the men sat down to a day of rest and prayer on November 24 in celebration of

Thanksgiving. Each man received three-fourths pound of turkey provided by Rhode Island to celebrate the holiday. Since Sergeant Simpson was killed at the North Anna River, Sergeant John B. Stoothoff carried the U.S. flag throughout the campaign. Now he found that the banner was deteriorating and tried to repair it. The colors, although riddled with bullet holes and the blood of the Color Guard from Spotsylvania, "still shone bright." It carried battle honors from two states and nine battles. It was a proud symbol for the Seventh to carry. Unfortunately, Stoothoff could not find any material so he tried to patch the flag as best he could. When Company D was disbanded to allow for a company of the Fourth to replace it in the regimental line, the men were distributed to all of the companies. They still remembered the small flag they purchased on their way to Washington in September 1862. The colors were carried through Fredericksburg and then served as the headquarters flag for the Seventh. Due to its deteriorating condition, Colonel Daniels allowed each member of Company D to cut a piece of the banner and keep it. Each survivor of Company D proudly received his piece and kept it as a memento of the battle they had gone through. First Lieutenant Henry Young, now serving in Company H, mailed his piece home with a small note telling of the flag's service. In a grim reminder of the Seventh's losses, Young's small piece of flag was still stained with the blood of Corporal Joseph Marcoux, who was shot through the neck at Marye's Heights.[17]

In addition to performing picket duty, the Seventh had the unfortunate opportunity to witness what no soldier ever wanted to see. Because desertion was occurring so often, Grant ordered that those caught be given a public execution before a firing squad. The affair was thought to prevent further desertion, since the men would know the punishment. The offender was a soldier from the Second Maryland. He was brought out to a field where the Second Division of the Ninth Corps formed a hollow square around a freshly dug grave, as the prisoner sat on his coffin. After a short prayer, a dozen men from the Second Maryland stepped forward and fired the coup de grace. The deserter fell into the casket, and he was thrown into the hole.[18]

As the Rhode Islanders completed the tasks around Poplar Spring Church and the Hatcher's Run line in late November 1864, they again received marching orders. The Christmas before they had marched to an isolated post on the Cumberland River. Now Grant was ordering the Ninth Corps back to its original lines. For the Seventh Rhode Island, it was going to be a journey to hell.

12

Fort Hell

The cannons could be herd verry plain.
— *Private Emor Young, January 6, 1865*

After leaving the relative safety and quietness of the lines near Poplar Spring Church, the Ninth Corps marched back to its original line of entrenchments to the right of the Federal line. They occupied the first positions that the corps had captured in June. The men were moving to a relatively dangerous position, as the lines near the Appomattox River were less than one mile apart. At some locations, the picket lines were only fifty yards apart, creating a hazardous position. With the move, the Ninth Corps again was reorganized. The Third Division was removed and sent to the newly formed Twenty-Fifth Corps, composed entirely of U.S. Colored Regiments. They were replaced with a new division of one-year Pennsylvania regiments. The parting of the black soldiers had at least one benefit; the Confederates would not bombard the lines constantly in an attempt to get rid of them. General Potter's Second Division was placed in the middle of the other two divisions. In effect, Colonel John Curtin's First Brigade was assigned to the two fortifications closest to Petersburg. Curtin assigned the Forty-Eighth Pennsylvania and Seventh Rhode Island to a large earthen fortification named Fort Sedgwick.[1]

The position was named after Union Major General John Sedgwick, who was killed at Spotsylvania. It was the closest fortification to the Confederate defenses, with Fort Mahone scarcely a half mile away; one private wrote, "we can hear the church belles ring in the city." Due to its exposed position, death was a constant threat, leading the men to live underground in the bombproofs. The soldiers, and indeed the army staff soon came to call it Fort Hell. Across the way was Confederate Fort Mahone, which garnered the name Fort Damnation. The Rhode Islanders moved into a fortification which had been erected during the summer months at night while the men were under fire. It was a strong position, which could not be carried by a direct Confederate assault. The fort mounted several cannon and was garrisoned by 1,000 men. As he was the senior officer present, Colonel Daniels commanded the post. He assigned the Forty-Eighth to the east bastion, although the Thirty-Sixth Massachusetts and Forty-Fifth Pennsylvania also took their turn of duty at the location. The Seventh was assigned to garrison the western portion of the fort. In yet another show of power against the veterans

12. Fort Hell

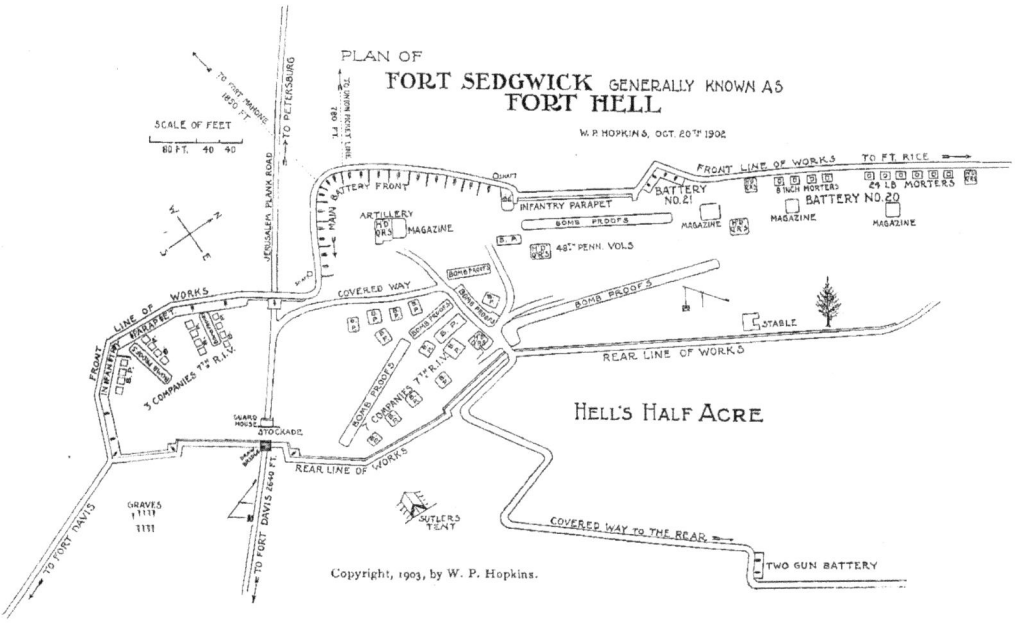

Drummer William P. Hopkins sketched this small map of Fort Hell.

Lieutenant Edwin Allen was the last Company A commander.

of the Fourth, Daniels assigned them to the most exposed position nearest to Fort Mahone and gave them to constant picket duty.[2]

While the Ninth Corps was receiving a facelift, so too was the Seventh Rhode Island. Sergeants who had been commanding companies since the summer finally received their commissions to take their places in the company lines. Many were promoted directly to first lieutenant and continued commanding the company. With Brevet Major Peleg Peckham still on detached duty to brigade headquarters, First Sergeant William H. Barstow had been commanding Company A since Petersburg. Now Sergeant Major Edwin R. Allen, the brother of Captain Edward T. Allen, was promoted to command of Company A. Barstow became the acting sergeant major. Two days before joining the Seventh, Cap-

Due to the constant threat of death from Fort Mahone, the Seventh lived underground during their stay at Fort Hell. Courtesy of Kris VanDenBossche.

This large bombproof served as regimental headquarters at Fort Sedgwick. The men in the image are from the Seventh Rhode Island. Courtesy of the Library of Congress.

tain George Wilbur was admitted to the Rhode Island Bar. Now he used his skills as a lawyer to serve as the judge advocate for the Second Division. Because the casualties among the officers in the division had been so heavy, Wilbur found himself as the senior captain in the Second Division in addition to commanding Company K, acting as a field officer, and commanding the picket line.[3]

As the men settled down into their new quarters, they quickly became adept at dodging the constant fire that was becoming almost unbearable outside. The deep bombproofs that were left to the men became a safe refuge as they remained in them nearly all day, only venturing outside to perform vital duties and to cook rations. Inside the cavernous holes, the only light came from candles or "slush lamps," made from filling a sardine can with oil. They built bunks to keep off of the damp Virginia soil, trying to pass the time. As the men adjusted to living in Fort Hell, William O. Harrington received the worst news of his life. His brother Josiah had been deathly ill since he left the army. Returning home to Foster, Lieutenant Harrington failed to recover and died on December 1 at William's farm. Unable to secure a furlough to attend his brother's funeral, Harrington could only wait to return home to console his grieving family. William had last seen his brother when the Seventh passed through Baltimore in September 1862 and he only remained in contact through their letters. One day Sergeant George Potter received a copy of the *Providence Journal* carrying Josiah's obituary. After reading it, Private Harrington wrote to his wife, "It does me a Greate deal of good to hear him spoken of so well of and to think that he merited the good name that he fetched home."[4]

Because the work was not yet complete, the men performed constant fatigue duty to finish the bastion. The roads were corduroyed while the breastworks were strengthened and artillery emplacements completed. The bombproofs became a refuge for the soldiers to spend idle moments in, reading letters from home, playing games, and planning what they would do after leaving the service. Relief came on December 11, when the Ninth Corps marched forty miles in twenty-eight hours in support of Second Corps, still attempting to close the remaining sectors of the Weldon Railroad near the North Carolina border. After marching the distance, one soldier wrote, "The Seventh is a regiment of cripples." Emor Young was tired of the cold winters and poor soil of Glocester. He heard rumors that the soldiers were to be given land grants in the West. He wrote, "My notion is to go where there will be shorter winters." He had in mind Indiana or Kentucky, both places he had visited two years earlier. The men had not been supplied since the start of the Overland Campaign. Many of the men were wearing rags while their shoes disintegrated in the Virginia mud. The bombproofs became flooded with each passing rainstorm, which necessitated that the men bail them out. The paymaster had not visited the regiment in six months and so the soldiers could not purchase warm clothing. On December 14, Colonel Daniels wrote to the ladies of Providence asking them to knit mittens for the Seventh: "While you are preparing for the Christmas holidays please remember us who certainly have never disgraced our State, and think we have gained her an honorable name." The situation was remedied on December 20, when the men received a supply of bootees, trousers, and blouses. The ordnance stores that were issued in Providence, including the ever-present Enfields, remained. Christmas of 1864 offered an opportunity to reflect on the year, while planning for 1865. It rained all day, as the men huddled into their bombproofs to enjoy a cup of coffee and some hardtack. The Federal artillery celebrated the capture of Savannah, Georgia, by firing 100 cannons into Petersburg.[5]

New Year's Day was spent eating hardtack, beans, and coffee. For the New Year, General Grant instituted an attempt to gain the hearts and minds of the Confederate soldiers in the trenches. After closing the Weldon Railroad and after the March to the Sea, the Union high command knew the Confederate supply situation was dire. Now Grant instructed that broadsides be printed up and handed to the pickets, who threw them to the Confederates near their lines. The leaflets told the Confederates that if they deserted to the Union lines, they would be paid a fair wage, given food and clothing, and would be transported to any destination that was held by the Union. As an added bonus, they would be given three dollars if they brought their musket and equipment. The Confederate government was aghast that the Union forces went to such an extent to end the war. They firmly believed that none of their men would respond. Unfortunately, the politicians keeping warm in Richmond failed to grasp the situation in the trenches. Hundreds of Confederate soldiers deserted when they received the news, not wanting to experience another spring campaign in Virginia. The men in the Seventh were often swamped by their southern brethren; one night 200 men came over. The pickets provided cover as the Rebels ran the half mile from Fort Damnation into Fort Hell. Many of the men chose to travel to New York City, where some even joined the Federal army.[6]

By January, the soldiers had become almost accustomed to the dangers outside. Even with the constant explosions and debris flying around, the men could still sleep comfortably, leading one private to write, "I can lay down on some boards and sleepe sound and easy as on a feather bead and if the bullets fly and canon roar." Every four days the companies were rotated on the picket line while the rest of the time was spent strengthening the works. During some nights, the men loaded their pockets and haversacks with ammunition and fired all night at Fort Mahone. The next morning they were surprised to find the Confederates scurrying outside of the fort to collect the lead, which was then melted down and fired at the Seventh. The Seventh gathered the bullets that the Confederates shot into their position. The sailors in Company I, long used to idle moments on board ships, would carve the bullets and engrave them into chess pieces and other items to pass the time. Some of the officers mailed home the trinkets to Governor Smith. The mittens finally arrived, nearly 650 of them made by the women of Rhode Island for the Seventh. It had been a year since Corporal Charles P. Nye wrote to his friend Benjamin Pendleton in Richmond; Nye himself was wounded at Petersburg. Now a noncommissioned officer, he supervised Company K in building abatis and other defensive structures. The strangest of these included gabions, baskets filled with dirt to build up the ramparts and protect the artillery emplacements. The corporal described the gabions thus: "it is made like a basket only there is no Bottom. They are three feet high and eighteen inches wide." In addition, Nye was pleased with one prospect of his service, "I have got about eight more months to serve for Uncle Sam."[7]

With the downfall of the Confederacy apparent, the South's diplomatic corps attempted one last try to win independence. During one attempt to negotiate a peace with the United States, Vice President Alexander Stephens appeared on the parapet of Fort Mahone. Under a flag of truce, Colonel Daniels took the Southerners onto the Jerusalem Plank Road and escorted them to City Point to meet with U.S. diplomats. Lincoln remained adamant in all of these negotiations. He affirmed that there would be no peace until the United States was restored, with no distinction between North and South. As the two sides argued over political ideals, Emor Young faced a problem of his own in Glocester. His teenage son Edgar had taken up smoking, while he continued to press his mother for permission to enlist. Emor wrote, "I dont want him to form any habit for it." As the war moved into a stalemate in the East, William T. Sherman was steadily advancing through the Carolinas, where the port of Wilmington, North Carolina, was shut down. These two events severely cut Confederate supplies to Petersburg, leading the men in gray to eat almost anything.[8]

For all the hatred and animosity between the Federal and Confederate soldiers, one indisputable fact remained — they were both Americans who had been killing and maiming each other for nearly four years. With the closeness of the lines, the men exchanged pleasantries daily and also the plans for the day's engagement. When the Confederates would open fire, the pickets yelled out, "Billy, look out now we uns got to shoot." At the signal, the Rhode Islanders ducked into the bombproofs until the engagement was over. Ever observant of the Confederates, Corporal Nye wrote, "Our boys are on the very good terms with the Rebs here you can hear them talking to gather near half of the time." Because Fort Hell was situated on the Jerusalem Plank Road, near City Point, which was army headquarters, the fort often received visitors. The men saw more women then they ever had before during their term of service. During a visit to the fort, Lieutenant Colonel Elisha Hunt Rhodes, commanding the Second Rhode Island Volunteers, peered over the parapet at the Confederates in Fort Damnation. Because the men were under orders not to speak this day, Rhodes found it interesting that the two sides could remain so civilized, despite being so close. The colonel said, "It seemed queer to visit." When the Confederates fired their artillery, it was largely eight-inch mortars that were terribly inaccurate, but they served as a shock weapon to stun the men. The picket firing often did not occur, and indeed, on some nights, Colonel Daniels forbade the men to open up because a local truce was declared. Even when engaged on the picket line, the men tried to remain civil. They exchanged hardtack for tobacco. The Confederates often sent over samples of their rations for the Rhode Islanders to try. One day, Drummer William P. Hopkins traded some hardtack for Confederate bacon. The young musician was unable to swallow the mixture, which contained tar after being shipped from the Bahamas. Hopkins referred to the substance as "nausea bacon."[9]

When a truce was not held along the lines, the Confederates in Fort Damnation bombarded the Rhode Islanders constantly. They were lucky that the fire was not very accurate, and that only two officers were injured during their time at Fort Hell. During one bombardment in January, the Seventh was holding dress parade. Rather than abandon the ceremonies, Adjutant Henry J. Spooner calmly walked up and down the line instructing the men in the manual of arms while the mortar shells burst around them. When the parade was dismissed, the men promptly returned to their shelters. By February, Lieutenant Spooner found himself without a job. Colonel Daniels received word that a prisoner exchange was about to take place, and that Adjutant John Sullivan would finally be released from prison. As such, Spooner was discharged from the service. He returned home to Providence to take the bar exam and become a successful lawyer. No prisoner exchange occurred, and again the adjutant's position was filled by a string of company lieutenants detailed for the task daily. Although the bombproofs became the men's homes, few outfilled them to the personal standards of the small cottages that had been built at Falmouth and Point Burnside. Grant had the men remain in constant preparedness to march, but no orders ever came, allowing the Rhode Islanders to remain at Fort Hell.[10]

In February the Seventh finally received the recruits they had been waiting nearly two years to receive. On December 19, 1864, President Lincoln issued his final call for 300,000 men to serve for one to three years in the service. Rhode Island again scoured its manpower and managed to find 1,563 men. After completing setup of the Second regiment and the First Light Artillery batteries, the Seventh was fortunate to receive twenty-five men. With these men, and the return of soldiers from the hospital, the Seventh continued to maintain a strength of 500 officers and men present for duty; the largest number since 12:19 P.M. on December 13, 1862. On paper, the regiment had 709 officers and men, but half of the number were in the hospitals, in prison, or were still being discharged from the service for illness or battle wounds suffered the previous summer. Since 1863, the Union high command had learned a valuable lesson: Rather than sending men straight to the front without any training, these men received several weeks of basic training at a recruit camp near New Haven, Connecticut. Several of the sergeants were relieved of duty in the Seventh and were sent to the camp to drill and acclimate the men to army life. These recruits arrived in the field with a working knowledge of the manual of arms and battalion drill. All of the recruits were from Providence. One of them, David G. Sherman was somewhat bewildered to become part of the Seventh. Wanting to enlist in the Veterans Reserve Corps, Sherman was sent to Company B of the regiment. Unlike the deserters and shirkers so prevalent at this time in the war, none of the twenty-five recruits left the regiment. They were distributed two or three to a company, where they were closely supervised and drilled by the company sergeants.[11]

The winter of 1865 was a surprising one for the men in the Seventh. It was cold one day and warm the next. Some weeks, the snow and sleet pelted the position, while other times the weather was pleasant and warm. When the ice formed on the earthworks, the Confederate shells and bullets would hit the parapet and slide down into the fort. Occasionally a shell would land in a bombproof, causing the structure to explode but without injuring any of the inhabitants. The Seventh was fortunate during their time at Fort Hell. The regiments garrisoning the east bastion were not as fortunate, and they often suffered heavy casualties during a bombardment. Because the men were often tasked with picket duty and digging in the fort, Colonel Daniels discontinued the daily dress parades and inspections, allowing the men to concentrate on their deadly work. When the Seventh was not on duty, the men retreated into the bombproofs to pass the time. Private Peleg Jones continued to complete complicated mathematical problems in his diary, in addition to maintaining an account of all his income and expenditures. In Company K, William O. Harrington was relieved as the company cook and returned to the firing line. He was replaced by Private James Gavitt. The switch left something to be desired, as the men from Foster and Scituate were not pleased with the food Gavitt cooked. In February, the Seventh Maine Battery moved into position near the Seventh Rhode Island's bastion, and began throwing shot and shell into Fort Damnation. The Confederates were surprised when the artillerymen appeared with the number "7" on their hat, when they thought it was the Rhode Islanders. The Confederates thought it was one regiment, with different caliber guns.[12]

With the arrival of March, the weather grew better as the Confederates increased the daily bombardment of Fort Sedgwick. They positioned extra men on the picket line to stop the desertions, and frequently fired into their men as they ran for safety. On March 13, the Confederates in Fort Damnation opened up with a "violent mortar attack." Indeed it was the heaviest bombardment the men had seen in three months. The Rhode Islanders loaded their Enfields and prepared for what many thought would be a large-scale Confederate assault. In Company A, Private Aldrich C. Kenyon observed: "For about an hour the rebels had as many as from 15 to 20 shells bursting in and over our fort at a time I am happy to say that no one was injured in our Reg." After an hour, the shelling stopped, as the men wondered what had just occurred. The damage was frightful; all of the bombproofs were destroyed while the men were somewhat shell shocked from the experience. All along the line, the Federal soldiers prepared for an attack, getting ready to move at ten minutes' notice. The mortars in Fort Damnation again visited the Seventh on March 20. Lieutenant George B. Costello was reading a copy of the *New York Herald* when the paper was ripped from his hand. The shot also wounded his arm. Major Jenks was struck in the shoulder by a small shell fragment. These were the only two injuries that the Seventh would suffer during their four months at Fort Hell. Major Jenks's injury was only minor, and the piece of shell was dug out by Colonel Daniels. The Confederates directed their firing at the Avery House, which was the headquarters of the Ninth Corps.[13]

12. Fort Hell

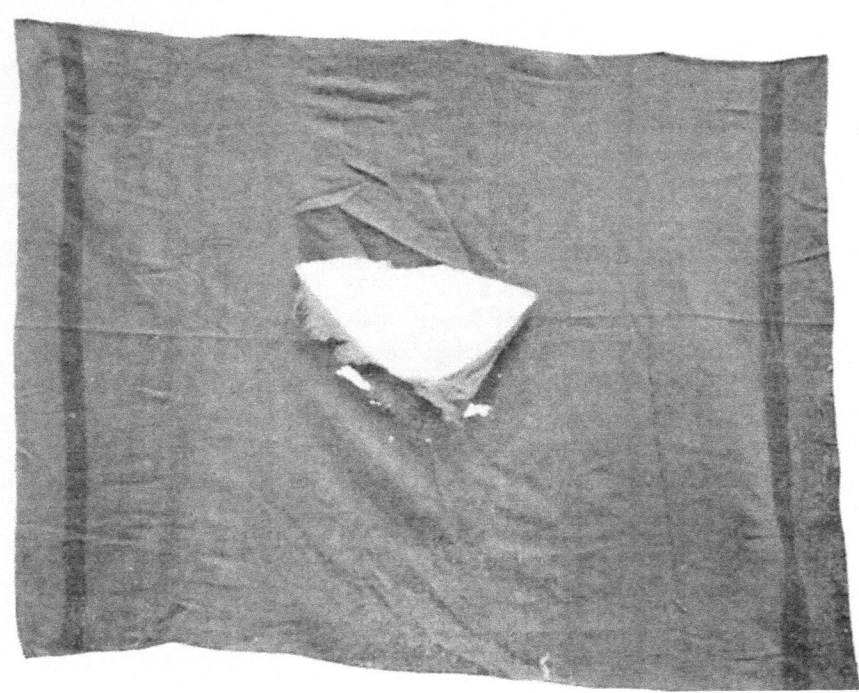

First Lieutenant James F. Merrill served in a variety of staff positions. His blanket was shredded when a mortar shell destroyed his bombproof at Fort Hell.

As the end of March 1865 approached, the Rhode Islanders knew that the war was becoming one Union victory after another. To the south, Sherman had marched through the Carolinas and was poised to finish off the Army of Tennessee, while Sheridan had thrashed all Confederate forces in the Shenandoah. On the Petersburg line, the bombardments grew heavier each day as the southern forces tried to buy time for their failing cause. Sergeant William Bisbee recalled, "At the present time the situation is looking rather gloomy for Johnny Reb, and very bright for the Union army. All signs indicate a very speedy overturn of this rebellion." Each night, more and more deserters crossed the lines into Fort Hell. They brought news that the Confederate forces were about to launch a major assault. As such,

Colonel Daniels strengthened his picket lines from five posts to twelve, all the while, the Confederate mortars continued to rain fire down upon the Rhode Islanders in Fort Sedgwick.[14]

On March 25, 1865, Confederate general John B. Gordon launched a predawn raid upon Fort Steadman, located a half mile to the right of Fort Hell. Using the guise of having his men approach the Union forces to desert, the Confederates quickly swamped the Union picket line. At daylight the Southerners overwhelmed the New Yorkers defending the fort. Watching on at Fort Hell, the Rhode Islanders thought that the Confederates exploited their success to capture the entire line. Fortunately Gordon did not have enough men to maintain the assault. In a fierce counterattack, John Hartranft, commanding the Third Division of the Ninth Corps, sent the Confederates reeling in retreat. Gordon lost 3,500 irreplaceable men. Corporal George Allen was pleased that the Rebels were defeated; he considered it revenge for the Crater. In Company A, Private John Barber thought that something was occurring at army headquarters and soon the Seventh commenced another campaign. "We have been quit busy in the fort tho it looks like a strong eartywrk I suppose likely tho peck was all sent away yesterday the letters and all surplus bagg is ordered to City point we are still n the fort but for long we shall stay I cant say." As April 1865 appeared on the horizon, the veterans of the Seventh Rhode Island saw that the end of the war was near.[15]

13

The Final Charge

Our troops charged the whole rebel line.
— Private Peleg Jones, April 2, 1865

    Lieutenant General Ulysses S. Grant pondered the situation in late March 1865. For nine months the Army of the Potomac had been besieging Richmond and Petersburg. Lee's lines were stretched to the breaking point; his 45,000 men were stationed along a forty-mile front. In effect they were surrounded by the Federal forces. For the Seventh, the time at Fort Hell had bolstered the ranks of the regiment while only two men were injured. There was the constant threat of death from Fort Mahone, but the bombproofs and entrenchments were sound. With deserters pouring in each day, Grant knew that Lee's lines were stretched to the breaking point; he now planned to launch the assault to finally capture Richmond and end the Civil War.
    The plan was set in motion on March 30 when the Cavalry and Fifth Corps marched to the left. On April 1 they attacked and captured the strategic cross roads at Five Forks. The Confederate commander here was enjoying a fish bake, rather than attending to his men. Now one of Lee's lines of retreat was cut off. Unable to flank the lines, Grant would have to order a direct frontal assault on Petersburg itself. In the Seventh, the men wrote letters home, knowing that this last charge could be their final one as well. In Company C, Emor Young cautiously mailed eighty dollars home, instructing his wife Martha to deposit it in a Chepachet bank. He wrote, "We shall not move unless compelled." The only chance that the attack would succeed, many believed, lay in the hope that the Confederates were spread out in the trenches, so the Union forces could successfully carry the works. Grant decided to attack the Petersburg defenses at 4:30 on the morning of April 2, 1865.[1]
    The Seventh received their orders to follow the Second Division into Petersburg. The night before the battle, the men cleared out their personal possessions from the bombproofs and packed them in the knapsacks. The noncommissioned officers checked to make sure each man had rations and ammunition. Instead of placing the rounds in the cartridge box, they were deposited in pockets, making them easier to handle in the heat of combat. Whatever occurred, the Army of the Potomac would not be returning to the trenches; Richmond was going to fall, no matter what the cost. The colors were uncased as the men loaded their

Enfields in the predawn hours of April 2. It was the last time the bloodstained and shot torn U.S. and Rhode Island flags would fly above the battlefield. The men nervously waited for the shot to be fired that would order them forward.[2]

On the extreme left of the Federal line, Battery E, First Rhode Island Light Artillery, fired the first shot; the result was every cannon firing simultaneously into Petersburg. On the left, near the Sixth Corps line, the Second Rhode Island successfully charged the works, planting the first U.S. flag on the Confederate works. Battery G, First Rhode Island Light Artillery, also charged, capturing some cannon and turning them on the fleeing Confederates, earning seven Medals of Honor. The mission was successful; the guns were captured.[3]

At 4:40 in the morning at Fort Hell, Colonel Daniels gave the command the Seventh had been waiting to hear for nine long months. The men silently exited the fort from the rear and formed "en masse" on the left. All along the line the officers yelled out "forward" as the Rhode Islanders surged out of Fort Sedgwick into the no-man's-land that separated the two bastions. The Confederates knew an attack was coming, and they were prepared. First Lieutenant Albert A. Bolles received a mortal wound to the throat while Captain Edwin L. Hunt went down with a slight wound, but could not be helped as the men surged forward. Corporal George H. Allen rushed onward, all the while starring down the barrel of a Confederate cannon. One private wrote, "I tell you it was rather a dark look to face the rebel cannons that was not more than eight hundred yards off." Private Young received two slight wounds to the hand and the knee. Soon, the men were "jumping into the rebel rifle pits in our front, with a cheer, they charged home." Company B, rushed forward with shovels and piled up the dirt as the men clambered into the fort, fighting hand to hand with the Confederates for its possession. Jared J. Potter claimed, "The Reb works were strong, but not sufficient to stop our brave men." For Potter's Company G, it was the only engagement in which they did not suffer any loss. Private Peleg Jones called it "a terrible fight." Sergeant John Stoothoff mounted the parapet with the U.S. colors. With this act, the men knew that finally Fort Damnation was in their possession. After the last Confederates were repulsed, Colonel Curtin dispatched the Seventh back to Fort Hell to carry ammunition up to the Union soldiers in Fort Mahone, as they waited for the expected counterattack.[4]

That morning as the Seventh set out, the musicians were again ordered to remain behind to carry in the wounded. Drummer William P. Hopkins recalled seeing his friend Richard Edwin Taylor rushing forward with a

An egotistic carpenter from Charlestown, Rhode Island, Peleg Peckham complained constantly about army life.

13. The Final Charge

Surgeon William Blackwood (center) was awarded the Medal of Honor for his efforts to rescue Major Peleg Peckham. Courtesy of the Library of Congress.

gun crew, carrying some ammunition. Fifteen minutes later, Hopkins saw Taylor stumbling back from Fort Mahone, clutching his face, his jacket covered in blood. Taylor "no longer possessed a face." The unfortunate private was carried by his friend to the field hospital, upon being examined by the surgeons, Taylor "howled," every time the wound was examined. Hopkins remained by his side until Taylor was transported to Lincoln General Hospital in Washington. William Hopkins never forgot the sight as he said good-bye to his friend. He remembered him as "a model comrade and a staunch friend." Taylor remained in agony until he died on April 16, at age nineteen. The body of the young man was returned to Scituate, where he was buried near his family. His epitaph eventually served as the memorial for all of the Scituate soldiers to be lost in the war. "Rest soldier in thine honored grave. Thy duty nobly done." Private Richard Taylor had the unfortunate distinction of being the last soldier from the Seventh Rhode Island to lose his life in combat.[5]

At 12:00, the Confederates counterattacked in force, and attempted to push back the Rhode Islanders. Colonel Curtin brought up two fresh regiments, and the Rebels were repulsed, but not before one last tragedy for the Seventh. Still assigned to staff duty at First Brigade headquarters, Major Peleg Peckham sat down to eat lunch. During the Confederate charge, he was struck behind the right ear by a minié ball, tearing the eye from its socket. Caught under a heavy fire, the major lay stricken as Surgeon William R. D. Blackwood of the Forty-Eighth Pennsylvania rushed forward in the midst of the Confederate counterattack and dragged Peckham to his tent near Fort Hell. He attempted to do everything he could to save the major, but the wound was mortal. Peckham was spitting out blood and was "partially insane." Blackwood's actions earned him the Medal of Honor for the heroism he showed in trying to save Peckham. After regaining his thoughts for a few moments, the major only said, "Tell my wife." Three hours later, Major Peleg E. Peckham, who won his lieutenant's straps for heroism at Fredericksburg, survived the elements in the West, and earned a much coveted promotion for gallantry at Spotsylvania, died. For all of his complaints and bitterness toward the army and the cause which he was fighting for, Peckham proved himself on the field, earning the respect of the men under his command. After resigning due to accidentally shooting himself in the foot at Petersburg, Captain Edward T. Allen returned to Rhode Island and moved to Pawtucket. Peckham and Allen's brother Edwin took over the command of Company A. In a letter of condolence to Peckham's widow, Allen wrote. "The whole regiment will feel to mourn your loss and theirs in the death of so good and valuable an officer as Maj. Peckham was. I have been very intimately and happily acquainted with your husband and have shared with him the privation as well as the glory of the battlefield." Major Peckham's remains were returned to Westerly where he was interred overlooking the Pawcatuck River.[6]

Private William O. Harrington quickly scribbled a letter to his wife about the battle, "we routed the rebs out of Petersburg yesterday." Following the capture of Fort Mahone and the entire Confederate line, Grant ordered the men to wait as he plotted the next move. This distressed the men, for they could have marched into Petersburg and cut off Lee's line of retreat. The next morning, Petersburg was finally captured and Richmond was evacuated. Grant then dispatched the Army of the Potomac west in the greatest pursuit of the war — trying to finally capture the Army of Northern Virginia. The Seventh marched into the city, and saw President Lincoln for the last time as he toured Richmond. The men cheered as Grant rode past them; although he was known as the "butcher" for his actions the previous summer, the war finally appeared as if it would end. At the field hospitals, the Seventh again took stock of its losses: sixteen men were wounded, four of them mortally. In Glocester, Martha Young received news from Emor that he was wounded. She pleaded with him to come home on furlough; ever stoic in his sense of duty, he refused. The wounds were not troubling and he was back on duty two weeks later. The prospect of the end was near, Emor wrote; "I have seen enough blood shed and the possibility is that the thing is about plaid out."[7]

Lee and the Army of Northern Virginia fled west, closely followed by Federal cavalry and infantry. The Seventh turned west from Petersburg and began to pursue Lee. At 10:00 on the night of April 3, the men went into camp and welcomed the return of a long forgotten sight. After being taken prisoner at Jackson, Adjutant John Sullivan was taken to Richmond where he was imprisoned for nearly two years. After the Union forces liberated the city, he was finally freed and, along with several men from the Fourth Rhode Island who were captured at the Crater, finally returned to his regiment. The soldiers rejoined the Seventh as they continued westward. At every bridge and river crossing, the Confederates fought bitterly for their survival, but they could not stop the Federal pursuit. On April 6, a third of Lee's forces were captured at Sailor's Creek while the Second Rhode Island lost heavily. Because the men had not been resupplied with rations since leaving Petersburg, they now foraged through the countryside looking for food. Major Jenks led four companies out to search for provisions, and they were rewarded with a large amount of food caches. While the Confederate army starved in the trenches around Petersburg, these wealthy plantation owners had stockpiled tons of meat, which the Rhode Islanders liberally took. In Company G, Private Potter found a turkey, duck, and two hams, in addition to some molasses. The men filled their haversacks and moved on. Colonel Daniels spent sixty dollars on a horse, and later shipped it home to Rhode Island. They continued to march to Farmville until they received the greatest news of their life on April 9, 1865.[8]

That night a staff officer came galloping up to Daniels and handed him a message. It had been two years and seven months since the men left Rhode Island. Now they received the news that they had been waiting for all that time — Lee surrendered the Army of Northern Virginia at Appomattox Court House. Immediately, the men began yelling like a band of Narragansett warriors while they built a large bonfire to dance around. They threw their caps and shoes into the air and hugged each other, many weeping. They sacrificed so much of their lives for this moment, and now it appeared as though the war was finally over. Corporal Allen recalled, "Words cannot describe the feeling of surprise and joy with which we listened to this most welcome dispatch, that we waited, fought, and struggled four long years to hear." The artillery of the Ninth Corps began to fire in celebration. Private Potter, a keen diarist who always kept his entries to the brief, wrote. "We got news in evening that Lee had surrendered + such cheering never was hurd in the 7th R.I. Vols." With the thrill of victory still resounding through the Union camps, a vital task needed to be accomplished. Nearly 25,000 Confederate prisoners needed to be paroled and sent home. Colonel Daniels dispatched Major Jenks with four companies to Appomattox itself to assist, while the rest of the battalion returned to High Bridge, near Farmville.[9]

With Major Jenks occupied with provost duties, the remaining men set up an encampment and began to visit the sights of the last battles of the war. The relative quietness suddenly dawned upon them; the Seventh had been under fire constantly for a year. In a letter home to Moosup Valley, Private William O. Harrington wrote, "We have not seene any fighting since Apr 2nd from May the 12th to Apr 2d 1865 there was not two weeks put together that we want under fire but since then we have not sene an armed rebel." With the surrender of the Army of Tennessee in late April, the Civil War in the East was effectively over. Due to the relative isolation of their post, the men were still short on rations. Some ate tree bark and mule grain in an attempt not to starve. Still relishing their victory, the Army of the Potomac was devastated to hear the news on April 15 that President Lincoln was assassinated. One private wrote, "it has cast a sad shade on all our late victoreys there is not a man living that was more esteemed than was Father Abraham."[10]

After remaining at High Bridge until April 21, the Seventh moved back toward Petersburg, where they were rejoined by Major Jenks. They marched by Fort Hell for the last time and boarded a transport for Washington. On April 29, the men went into camp near Arlington Heights; the same location they had camped at when they first arrived in the South. Camp life brought the monotony of guard duty and dress parade every night, which fatigued the men; it was a way to keep them occupied while the Federal high command made plans for a review of all of the Union forces. The army that William Tecumseh Sherman led on the March to the Sea arrived in Washington and encamped near the Army of the Potomac. Many of the men in the eastern Federal forces had never seen these men; however, they were quite familiar to the Seventh, having served alongside each other in Mississippi. On the night of May 12, the Seventh decided to celebrate the one-year anniversary of Spotsylvania. That night, the men lit candles on their tent poles while several in the Seventh placed a candle in the muzzle of their Enfields and began to parade while performing the manual of arms. Soon the rest of the regiment, and then the entire Second and Third Divisions of the Ninth Corps — nearly 20,000 men — were marching past General Potter's headquarters in review, all while the burning candles illuminated their movements on Arlington Heights. Corporal Charles P. Nye wrote, "it was one of the finest sights that I ever saw it all started from our Regiment." The following day, the men heard that Confederate president Jefferson Davis was captured. They began singing, "We'll hang Jeff Davis to the sour apple tree." With the city nearby, Colonel Daniels allowed the men passes to visit the different sights, while some in the regiment went to view Mount Vernon, the home of George Washington. Private Potter called it "splendid." Peleg Jones viewed the key to the Bastille, presented to Washington by Lafayette. After enjoying the city, and the food that came with it, the men again settled into camp and waited. The next days were spent drilling the recruits and the veterans as they prepared for what was being dubbed the Grand Review.[11]

The review was set to take place on two days: the Army of the Potomac would march on May 23, while the Army of Georgia paraded on May 24. The men repaired their clothing and cleaned their Enfields to a gleaming white. Although this was a formal review, gone were the fancy trims and gleaming trappings unnecessary for soldiering. The men would appear as they did in the field. One Federal commander wrote concerning the appearance of the soldiers. "The men brought themselves up to regulation field inspection; themselves their dress and accoutrements clean and bright, but all of the every-day identity. And for officers no useless trappings; service uniform-shoulder-straps, belts, scabbards, boots, and spurs of the plainest." Some men in the Seventh were not pleased at the ideas of the review. Corporal Nye wrote, "I shall be glad when it all comes off for we will stand some sight to get home I hate a review worse then any thing in soldiering." The men were awake at 3:00 in the morning of May 23, 1865, as they prepared for their last official duties in the Army of the Potomac. In the line of review that day, the cavalry paraded first, followed by the infantry. The first command in line was the Ninth Corps. Riding at the head of 20,000 veterans and recruits was Major General John G. Parke. Of the two million men who had served in the Federal army, these men had traveled farther and fought in a wider variety of engagements then any other group of Federal soldiers. The soldiers of the Ninth Corps fought battles in ten states

The Ninth Corps leads the Grand Review on May 23, 1865.

and left their dead behind in fourteen. Now the veterans of the Burnside Expedition, Second Bull Run, South Mountain, Antietam, Fredericksburg, Vicksburg, Jackson, Knoxville, the Wilderness, Spotsylvania, Cold Harbor, Petersburg, and Poplar Spring Church marched in review before President Andrew Johnson. Colonel Daniels and Major Jenks rode in front of the combined remnants of the Fourth and Seventh Rhode Island. For the final time the blue banner with the fouled anchor flew above the men from Rhode Island who had witnessed the very worst of war. Sergeant Stoothoff still carried the battle-shot and bloodstained U.S. flag as the men from the smallest state in the Union proudly paraded by their commanders before returning to camp.[12]

Following the review, the officers prepared the forms necessary to let the Seventh leave the service; every soldier had to be accounted for and the amount of money each man was to receive upon discharge. As the men waited in camp, they pondered what would happen once they became civilians again. Sergeant Charles F. Colvin worried that his wife would divorce him after being away for almost three years. More alarmingly, Maria Colvin had "sold my things, if so I am in a bout the same fix the rebs." Colvin returned safely to Scituate and his family. Fellow Company K soldier William O. Harrington, always a faithful correspondent, mailed home his last letter from Virginia. The survivors of Company A welcomed the end of the war. John N. Barber mailed some extra clothing home to Richmond while he continued to attend prayer meetings nightly. Barber weighed 160 pounds, and he feared his family would not remember him. Wanting to see his wife, Barber wrote, "I hope soon you will have the privalage of holding you all in my arms." Another Company A soldier, George Henry Lewis, feared that upon his return to Richmond, he could not find any women to marry. The wait would not be much longer.[13]

The staff officers of the Seventh completed the paperwork while the captains dipped their pens into ink to sign the discharges of the men under their command. Only five of the Seventh's original officers remained, the rest were promoted from the ranks. Private Harrington was pleased for the men to receive orders, writing, "our Colonel have had orders to have the papers made out to discharge us immediately." On June 6, the First Brigade, Second Division, Ninth Corps, ceased to exist as several regiments left the service. That day, the Seventh held one final parade and inspection before Brigadier General Curtin. Returning the compliment of the review, Curtin said, "In the Carolinas, in Maryland, in Kentucky, in Mississippi, in Tennessee, and in Virginia, your valor and heroic endurance have won for you an imperishable name." On June 8, all of the men who had been detached to staff duty, and to Battery D, First Rhode Island Light Artillery, returned to the regiment. On Friday, June 9, 1865, the Seventh Rhode Island Volunteers was mustered out of United States service and the veterans finally prepared to return home.[14]

14

Afterwards

Abraham Lincoln never called truer men to defend our flag than those who have fought under the colors of the Seventh Rhode Island Volunteers.
— *Colonel Percy Daniels, June 21, 1865*

  The soldiers of the Seventh Rhode Island awoke early on the morning of June 10, 1865, to receive their orders. After spending two years and nine months in the South, the Rhode Islanders were going home. Packing their tattered blankets and small battlefield relics in the well-worn knapsacks, the regiment marched to the Potomac docks. The three companies comprising the recruits and veterans of the Fourth Rhode Island were to remain behind. After crossing the river, the men marched into Washington. Turning around for one last look at where so many Rhode Islanders had given the "last full measure of devotion," Benjamin Joslin yelled out: "The Lord help old Virginia." In company with the Thirty-Fifth Massachusetts, by whose side the Rhode Islanders had fought and died since Sulphur Springs, the two regiments boarded a train to Baltimore. They followed the same path they took three years earlier. Arriving in Philadelphia, where only a short time earlier they were warmly welcomed and given a bountiful meal, they now marched through the city silently to the depot for a train to take the regiment to New York. Upon arrival in the city, the two regiments boarded the steamer *Oceanus* and began the journey home.
  The date June 13, 1865, was the day that many of the men had been waiting for since leaving Rhode Island. Sailing up Narragansett Bay, the Seventh broke out in cheers as they first saw Providence at six in the morning. The Providence Marine Corps of Artillery, comprised of veterans from the First Rhode Island Light Artillery, began firing their cannons to notify the state that the Seventh was finally home. Docking at Fox Point, the regiment was greeted by the Brigade of Rhode Island Militia and a band. The crisp, dark blue uniforms of the militia stood in sharp contrast to the faded, weather-worn blouses and trousers of the Seventh. The Enfields were still present; the muskets, issued to the regiment at Providence in September 1862, had never been replaced. The rifling was nearly gone, but the barrels and bayonets still shone brightly in the morning sunshine. Marching up Benefit Street, the men walked in front of Ambrose Burnside's house and cheered the beloved Ninth Corps commander one last time. After parading through the narrow streets of the city, before "multitudes," the

After leading the musicians of the Seventh, James Carpenter (front, center) continued to lead bands in Wakefield after the war. Photo courtesy of the Pettaquamscutt Historical Society, Kingston, R.I.

Seventh finally came to rest in Exchange Place. Here Colonel Percy Daniels issued a welcome order to the regiment to "stack arms." Abraham Payne, a member of the Rhode Island General Assembly, then stepped forward to address the men before him. "The names which you have permitted to inscribe upon your banner render all account of your exploits unnecessary." After this, the Rhode Islanders were treated to an "abundant" breakfast, to which the Thirty-Fifth Massachusetts was invited. Following the meal, Daniels dismissed the regiment until June 21.[1]

At 10:00 in the morning on Saturday, June 21, 1865, the Seventh Rhode Island Volunteers met for the last time as a regimental organization. Of the 960 officers and men who left Providence in September 1862, only 325 were left. Seated behind a large table, Colonel Daniels called each man forward to receive his discharge and the bounty that each man had rightly earned. Nearly all of the men paid the six dollar fee to the United States, which allowed them to take their Enfields and "traps" home. After all of the men were paid, the line officers formed the men up for the last time to listen to their commander, as the final command was given: "Battalion, order arms, Parade rest." The men were pleased to finally say good-bye to Percy Daniels. He had badly bungled the Seventh's desperate bayonet charge at Spotsylvania, while his performance in the subsequent battles and treatment of the men had never shown his ability as a leader. Daniels did not have reciprocal feelings for the men under his command; his farewell message, like all of his writings, praised the Seventh Rhode Island. The men had entered the service in the "dark days of 62," as the last of the true volunteers who were willing to go and defend the flag. Fighting in engagements from Virginia to Mississippi, the Seventh had proved itself as a regiment whose discipline and battlefield exploits were equal to those of the United States Regulars. This was because of the strict training and discipline instilled into the officers and enlisted men by Colonel Zenas R. Bliss. In four months he created a force that had almost reached the stone wall at Fredericksburg, survived the elements at Falmouth, fought for forty-eight hours at Jackson, battled disease in the West, and had given its all in the forty days of combat during the Overland Campaign. Of the 1,145 men who served in the Seventh, few survived unscathed through the struggle. A total of 24,000 Rhode Islanders served in the rebellion: 2,000 died. The largest number of these came from the Seventh Rhode Island Volunteers: 101 officers and men perished in combat, while 126 died from illness and other causes. The Seventh sustained an 80 percent casualty rate. As the men left that summer day in June 1865, many never to see each other ever again, Colonel Daniels said to them: "Abraham

General Zenas R. Bliss, United States Army. Courtesy of Bliss Camp 12, Sons of Union Veterans.

14. Afterwards

Left: "The toll of battle:" Private Alfred Sheldon Knight of Scituate was one of 227 men to perish in the Seventh Rhode Island. *Right:* Although severely wounded at Fredericksburg, William Rathbun maintained an active life. Courtesy of David Rathbun.

Lincoln never called truer men to defend our flag than those who have fought under the colors of the Seventh Rhode Island Volunteers."[2]

The homecoming of the Seventh was finally complete on July 13, when the remaining three companies of the regiment were mustered out and returned home. The detachment was composed of the reenlisted veterans of the Fourth Rhode Island, and the few recruits the regiment had finally received. Numbering 177 officers and men, these were the men who had fought in the North Carolina Campaign, the hell that was Otto's Cornfield at Antietam, and the unspeakable scenes of the Crater. Before leaving the men symbolically buried a hatchet in the "sacred soil" of Virginia. Unable to parade because of a rainstorm, the remnant of the Fourth Rhode Island quietly received their discharges and returned home.[3]

After all of the men were dismissed, Colonel Daniels took the blood-stained and bullet-riddled U.S. and Rhode Island colors to the State House on Benefit Street. Here he presented them to Governor Smith. Upon the red and white stripes of the U.S. flag were painted the official battle honors awarded to the Seventh by Lieutenant General Grant: Fredericksburg, Vicksburg, Jackson, Spotsylvania, North Anna, Cold Harbor, Petersburg, Weldon Railroad, Poplar Spring Church, and Hatcher's Run.[4]

After leaving their regiment for the final time, the veterans of the Seventh Rhode Island stepped out into a world that had changed dramatically in four years of war. Slaves were now free, the United States was finally reunited, and over 625,000 young men were dead in a struggle fought over ideals. In the Seventh, 1,145 Rhode Island men went off to fight in the Great

Rebellion, 227 had died in places that seemed so foreign, but whose names now became a part of the Rhode Island lexicon. Gone were so many men who were irreplaceable to their communities. In South Kingstown, the students at Tower Hill were never to be taught again by John K. Hull. In Exeter, the Brown family mourned the loss of two sons who died in the Seventh's campaigns. Even the egocentric and always complaining Major Peleg Peckham was missed in Shannock; he never saw his only son become a successful doctor. The war had its greatest impact in the cities and towns of Rhode Island. No community lost more men than South Kingstown. On June 2, 1865, the First Baptist Church in Wakefield held a memorial service in honor of the young men who died. Of the ninety-three who banded together to form Company G of the Seventh, thirty-seven were killed or died of disease, a 40 percent mortality rate. On Memorial Day in 1888 the town unveiled a beautiful monument in Riverside Cemetery in Wakefield near the graves of those who had fallen in the war, among the names inscribed upon the monument were the eight men who died in that sanguinary charge up Marye's Heights. In 1913 two veterans of the regiment presented the town with a memorial listing all those who fought and died from Company G. The war was finally over, but the scars would never fade.[5]

The survivors returned to their families and friends, while the families of the dead continued to mourn. For those mangled for life, the tasks that had come so easy, such as picking apples or weaving thread at a mill, were now impossible. Rheumatism, arthritis, and dysentery turned boys into old men. When John F. Austin, badly wounded at Fredericksburg, returned to his western Scituate home, many of his neighbors were gone. Resuming work at the Ashland Manufacturing Company after the war, something was different. Many of the young men from the local villages never returned from the South. Down the road in the Clayville village cemetery lay the remains of five Seventh Rhode Island soldiers; four of whom died during the war. Taking off the battered wool uniforms and hanging the Enfield musket over the mantel, they put the war away for a later day to tell their children and grandchildren about what they had seen and done. Although the overwhelming majority of the veterans returned to their previous occupations, some rose to great prominence because of their actions during the war.

Colonel Zenas R. Bliss was mustered out of the volunteer service on June 9, 1865. Instead of returning to Rhode Island, he decided to remain in the U.S. Army, reverting to his regular rank of captain. Leaving his family in Providence, Bliss supervised recruiting efforts for the army in New York, Pennsylvania, and South Carolina, including a tour in the Freedmen's Bureau helping with the relief of the newly freed slaves. In 1867, he was promoted to major and returned to take command of Reconstruction efforts in Texas. By 1875, he commanded Fort Bliss, the post from where the Eighth United States had left on their disastrous march in 1861. Promotion to lieutenant colonel came in 1879. Instead of entering the army, his only son Zenas W. Bliss became a lawyer and later lieutenant governor of Rhode Island. Lieutenant Colonel Bliss again received his eagles with a promotion to colonel of the Twenty-Fourth infantry in 1886; all of these regiments were composed of black soldiers. Colonel Bliss again sought the one thing he was unable to achieve during the Civil War, the star of a general. On April 25, 1895, he finally became a brigadier general and assumed command of United States forces in Texas, where he had spent so much of his life. In 1897 Bliss was awarded the two stars of a major general, but one week later he retired from the U.S. Army after serving for forty-seven years. In 1898 he was presented the Medal of Honor for his actions in leading the Seventh at Fredericksburg. He also became involved in writing the regimental history of the Seventh, but his days were fading. Major General Zenas Randall Bliss died on January 1, 1900, in Washington, D.C. Governor Sprague, who had issued him the commission to take command of Rhode Island's seventh regiment, wrote a letter of condolence to Mrs. Bliss. In it the governor said, "He distinguished himself and his command on many fields." General Bliss was buried at Arlington National Cemetery near the location where he created the Seventh Rhode Island Volunteers.[6]

Lieutenant Colonel Percy Daniels moved to Kansas where he became active in politics and commanded the state national guard. In 1892 he became the lieutenant governor of the state. General Daniels took command of the guard in 1895 and helped to suppress a mining strike in southern Kansas. Daniels moved to Oklahoma in 1900, opening up a large cattle farm, where he died in 1916. His antagonist, Major Ethan Amos Jenks, became a lawyer after the war and served as the president of the Seventh Rhode Island Veterans Association. In January 1901 he and William P. Hopkins traveled to Vicksburg to find a location for the regimental monument. Five months later he was dead at age seventy-four from a heart attack. His funeral was well attended by the members of his regiment while the pallbearers were former Seventh officers. One of his soldiers eulogized him: "Unflinching devotion to duty was his prominent characteristic, and yet he was careful and considerate of others and of the sensibilities of those under his command."[7]

Colonel Daniels never forgave Hospital Steward Stephen F. Peckham for the letter he wrote to the *Providence Journal* about Major Jenks. After the war, Peckham traveled around the country prospecting in oil and teaching chemistry. Adjutant Henry Joshua Spooner became a successful lawyer and was elected to the U.S. House of Representatives for five terms.[8]

In Hopkinton, Tryphena Cundall welcomed the return of her son Isaac. Despite suffering from typhoid and Yazoo fever, he was never wounded in action. The men who left Ashaway and Rockville to join Company A were less fortunate. Thirty-three men served, while thirteen died in the service. Tryphena continued writing in her diary until her death in 1889. Emor Young returned to his wife Martha in Glocester, but suffering from the illness he contracted in the army, he died in 1868.[9]

The Civil War helped shape the lives of the two Allen brothers from South Kingstown. After surviving his Petersburg wound, Captain Edward T. Allen moved to San Francisco where he opened a successful grocery firm. His brother, First Lieutenant Edwin R. Allen, returned to Hopkinton where he became town clerk. He was later elected to the General Assembly and for three terms as lieutenant governor. Lieutenant Allen became a trustee in the Washington Trust Company and rose to prominence in the Connecticut department of the Grand Army of the Republic.[10]

William O. Harrington returned to a drastically changed Foster. Of the twenty-four men who had joined Company K and the Seventh Rhode Island, ten died in the service. Harrington was finally able to see his three-year-old son for the first time. He remained a dairy farmer, while his family cherished the 100 letters he wrote to his wife, Eunice. His homecoming also brought sadness, as he visited the grave of his brother Josiah. Harrington helped to maintain the graves of the men of Moosup Valley who fought in the war. When he died in 1904, his headstone, like many of the veterans of the regiment, was marked for eternity to show what unit he served in. "A member of Co. K 7th R.I. Vols."[11]

While the majority of the veterans of the regiment returned to Rhode Island, some moved west into new lands to lead new lives. Alonzo Jenks recovered after losing a hand at Fredericksburg to become the orderly sergeant of Company C. After being mustered out with the regiment, he became a bookkeeper in Pawtucket. In the early 1870s Jenks became caught up in "Western fever." Moving to Los Angeles, he lost his wife and daughter to an epidemic. After his loss, Jenks became a seller for a whip manufacturing company and moved to Butte, Montana, where he was never heard from again.[12]

William P. Hopkins and Nathan B. Lewis became two of the Seventh Rhode Island veterans who sought to remember the deeds of the regiment for posterity. Hopkins had served as a drummer in Company D while Lewis was a corporal in Company F and commanded the company for a time after Bethesda Church. Lewis became one of the most successful veterans of the regiment, serving as a school superintendent, postmaster, judge, and representative from Exeter. Hopkins moved to Massachusetts and supervised the machinery in a Lawrence mill. He later returned to Coventry while still practicing the music that had carried him through the war.[13]

In 1906, the veterans of the Seventh Rhode Island finally received something they had been lacking. In 1886, every Rhode Island regiment that had fought at Gettysburg and

Edwin R. Allen served three terms as Rhode Island's lieutenant governor. Courtesy of Katie and Luane McDonald.

William O. Harrington (second seated from left) is joined by other Foster veterans in 1890. Courtesy of the Town of Foster.

14. Afterwards

The Seventh's monument at Vicksburg. Courtesy of Katie and Luane McDonald.

North Carolina was awarded with a monument to signify its deeds on the field. The veterans of the Seventh petitioned the General Assembly and in 1906 were awarded $4,500 to build the monument. The veterans then met to vote on what the monument should depict. Some members wanted it to be a memorial to Colonel Bliss, but the majority voted to have the monument portray a private soldier. It was to be placed at Vicksburg, Mississippi, where the Seventh was the only Rhode Island unit present, and where the men had suffered perhaps the greatest. The monument was designed and composed entirely of Rhode Island components, including a Westerly granite base and a Gorham cast bronze statue. The figure depicted a soldier, carrying a musket and the American flag. The monument was dedicated on November 11, 1908, by a large delegation from Rhode Island, which traveled to the battlefield. Corporal Lewis wrote, "It presupposes in the heat of action, the color bearer having been shot down, the flag itself rent and torn by shot and shell, the staff broken, the flag is caught up by a private soldier and carried forward." During the presentation, Charles W. Hopkins, the brother of William P. Hopkins, stepped forward to read a brief poem he composed about the Seventh.

> Our "Seventh Rhode Island" banner, How proudly it did wave.
> O'er boys in blue, with hearts so true, Who fought our land to save.
> How bright was all its gleaming, In those eventful days.
> Mid battle's stroke, where clouds of smoke, Obscured the sun's bright rays.
> From Spottsylvania's meadows, To distant Vicksburg shore.
> Its stars shone bright in many a fight, Till ceased the battle's roar.
> And now its tattered form repeats, In faded red and blue.
> The story old, of soldier's bold, Whose hearts were brave and true.

Under a clear sky, veterans from Rhode Island and Mississippi met where forty-five years earlier they had engaged in deadly combat in the swamps and fields of Vicksburg and Jackson.[14]

The veterans of the Seventh met twice each year to remember their comrades and the accomplishments of the regiment. The winter meeting was held on December 13 at night. Here the survivors could recall the horrible scenes of that day, in addition to the glory gained by the regiment as they attempted to reach that stonewall. Hardly any business was undertaken by the organization, other then serving as a social gathering. Colonel Bliss attended the 1878 reunion and the men were very pleased to see their former commander, as the colonel had not been seen since 1865. In the 1890s Colonel Bliss, Corporal Lewis, and Drummer Hopkins began to write a history of the Seventh Regiment. With the colonel's death, Lewis and Hopkins continued to write the massive narrative. Published in 1903, the volume amounted to a 544-page tome that utilized a diary format to narrate the path of the Seventh. The book included 250 images of the soldiers in addition to a complete roster and biographical references. The book, in conjunction with the Vicksburg monument, was designed to be permanent monuments to the deeds of the Seventh Rhode Island Volunteers.[15]

The memory of the Civil War did not fade from Rhode Island for eighty years. In 1866, the veterans formed an organization called the Grand Army of the Republic. Forming posts around the world, the organization stood to remember the sacrifices of the Union veterans and to fight for the rights of the veterans in such actions as pension reform. In 1886, the veterans of Scituate and Foster formed the James C. Nichols Post 19 in western Scituate. Meeting monthly, the over 100 men on the rolls were largely drawn from the many mills around the area. William O. Harrington and the men of the Seventh comprised nearly a third of the post. Each Memorial Day the veterans traveled to the graves of their fallen comrades to decorate them "with the choicest flowers of spring." Buried one mile from the Nichols Post in Rockland was the grave of Private Alfred Sheldon Knight, who perished from pneumonia caused by the rain during the Mud March. In 1890, the veterans placed an iron marker on each grave. In the shape of a star, the inscribed flag holders told all who read it that the man buried underneath it was a "Veteran of 1861–1865." By 1913, only twenty of the aged old men were left to attend a dedication of a monument in Scituate. The memorial depicted an artilleryman, with the names of the fifty-five Scituate men who died during the war carved onto its base. Of the sixty Scituate men who joined the Seventh, twelve perished.

14. Afterwards

The veterans of the Seventh Rhode Island met each year after the war. Courtesy of Bliss Camp 12, Sons of Union Veterans.

One veteran said, "The toll of sacrifice was a costly one, but the results were well worth the cost."[16]

As the years passed, so too did the veterans of the Seventh Rhode Island Volunteers. With their deaths went the story of the regiment that they fought with. Many left their letters and journals to family members, only to have them lost or destroyed in more turbulent times. The fortunate few were left to the local historical societies to be placed in cardboard boxes, waiting to be discovered. By 1930, only ten men in the regiment were left. In 1938, there were only two. Elisha R. Watson was one of them. Described as a "short, rosy-cheeked man," Watson lived in Coventry and had joined the Fourth Rhode Island in August 1862. One month later, he fought at South Mountain and Antietam, where his company lost half its strength. In 1864, he was captured at the Crater and sent to Libby Prison. Upon his exchange in April 1865, he joined Company G, Seventh Rhode Island. After the war, Watson returned to Coventry

Elisha Watson survived Otto's Cornfield, the Crater, and prison to become the last surviving member of the Seventh Rhode Island. Courtesy of Katie and Luane McDonald.

and helped to found the McGregor Post of the Grand Army of the Republic, rising to the rank of post commander. Each Memorial Day, he traveled fifty miles through West Greenwich, Scituate, Coventry, and Foster placing flags and flowers on the graves of 500 of his comrades, many of whom fought in the Seventh. Meticulous in his recordkeeping, Watson kept specific details on the exact location where each comrade was buried. He operated a packing business and spent many hours traveling to schools talking about the Civil War, including educating children in the responsibilities of American citizenship. Watson made his last trip to the cemeteries in 1938 as his advanced age began to take its toll. His health continued to decline until April 20, 1939. On this day, Private Elisha R. Watson, age ninety-six years and the last surviving veteran of the Seventh Rhode Island, passed into Valhalla. His body was brought to the Gorton Funeral Home where a three-day vigil was held. On the morning of April 22, 1939, his flag-draped casket was brought out and placed upon an artillery caisson. Under escort of the members of the Sons of Union Veterans, the procession slowly marched the half-mile to the Knotty Oak Baptist Church, where the services of so many Seventh soldiers were held during the war and after. Following the simple Baptist ceremony, the procession entered Knotty Oak Cemetery. The column marched past the grave of Corporal Oliver J. Phillips, killed at Bethesda Church. Buried across from him was William P. Hopkins, who devoted his life to retelling the Seventh's story. Farther up the narrow lane was a memorial stone to Christopher Pierce; his remains were still interred at Vicksburg. Buried nearby was First Sergeant George W. Bennett, who lost a foot at Fredericksburg. Finally they stopped at the Watson family tomb. With tender care, the descendents of the soldiers of the Union placed Private Watson into the enclosure with his family, as the flag was removed and presented to his son. Three volleys of rifle fire rippled through the morning sky, followed by the calming, soothing notes of taps that had sounded the men to sleep all those years earlier. The Seventh Rhode Island Volunteers were finally at rest.[17]

Appendix I: Casualties of the Seventh Rhode Island

Battle	Killed/mortally wounded	Wounded	Missing	Total
Fredericksburg December 13, 1862	44	136	40	220
Vicksburg June–July, 1863	0	0	0	0
Jackson July 13, 1863	4	8	2	14
Wilderness May 5–9, 1864	0	2	0	2
Spotsylvania May 12, 1864	6	24	0	30
Spotsylvania May 13–17, 1864	5	8	0	13
Spotsylvania, May 18, 1864	10	30	0	40
North Anna River May 25, 1864	2	2	0	4
Interlude, May 26–June 1, 1864	0	2	0	2
Mechanicsville, June 2, 1864	1	1	0	2
Bethesda Church June 3, 1864	15	35	0	50
Cold Harbor June 4–14, 1864	2	5	0	6
Petersburg June 15–September 29, 1864 [Includes Crater]	4	47	0	51
Poplar Spring Church September 30, 1864	4	8	0	2
Fort Hell November, 1864–April 1, 1865	0	2	0	2
Storming of Petersburg April 2–3, 1865	4	12	0	16
Total	101	322	42	464

Appendix I

Captured in action	10
Discharged for disability	155
Resigned Commission	35
Veterans Reserve Corps	62
Deserted	66
Died of illness	126
Total Loss	917

Deaths by Company — The casualties for the veterans of the Fourth are included in B, D, G Companies

Company	*Killed in action/mortally wounded*	*Death by other causes*
Field and Staff	3	1
Company A	9	16
Company B	7	11
Company C	9	14
Company D	4	10
Company E	8	7
Company F	13	9
Company G	16	24
Company H	13	9
Company I	9	7
Company K	10	18
Total	101	126

Appendix II: Roll of Honor

During their term of service, the Seventh Rhode Island lost more men killed than any other Rhode Island regiment. It is only fitting that this list be reproduced on the following pages. The names are gathered from William Hopkins's *Roster*, the *Revised Register of Rhode Island Volunteers*, *The Monument in Memory of the R.I. Soldiers and Sailors who fell Victims to the Rebellion*, and cemetery visits by the author.

For the sake of brevity, the following abbreviations are given to denote rank.

Pvt: Private, Corp: Corporal, Sgt: Sgt, 1Sgt: First Sergeant, Mus: Musician, Wag: Wagoner, 2Lt: Second Lieutenant, 1Lt: First Lieutenant, Ajt: Adjutant, Bvt: Brevet rank, Capt: Captain, Maj: Major, LtCol: Lieutenant Colonel

Field and Staff

Name	Rank	Residence	Date of Death	Battle/Illness	Place
Arnold, Job	LtCol	Providence	Dec. 28, 1869	Disease	Providence
Babbitt, Jacob	Maj	Bristol	Dec. 23, 1862	Fredericksburg	Washington
Cole, Darius	Ajt	Providence	May 13, 1864	Spotsylvania	
Sayles, Welcome B.	LtCol	Providence	Dec. 13, 1862	Fredericksburg	

Company A

Name	Rank	Residence	Date of Death	Battle/Illness	Place
Austin, Benjamin K.	Pvt	Hopkinton	May 12, 1864	Spotsylvania	
Bentley, William	Pvt	Hopkinton	June 6, 1863	Boiler explosion	Nicholasville, KY
Burdick, Weeden	Pvt	Hopkinton	July 19, 1863	Yazoo Fever	Milldale, MS
Clark, John B.	Pvt	Richmond	May 10, 1863	Dysentery	Baltimore, MD
Collins, Gideon F.	Pvt	Hopkinton	Oct. 17, 1862	Pneumonia	Pleasant Valley, MD
Colwell, William	Wag	Providence	Jan. 14, 1863	Typhoid	Falmouth, VA
Flaherty, Michael	Sgt	Providence	June 3, 1864	Bethesda Church	
Gardner, George W.	Pvt	Hopkinton	Oct. 18, 1862	Typhoid	Pleasant Valley, MD
Godfrey, Henry H.	Pvt	Hopkinton	Sept. 7, 1863	Yazoo fever	Hopkinton
Gorton, Joel B.	Pvt	West Greenwich	Sept. 11, 1864	Yazoo fever	Nicholasville, KY
Greene, Charles B.	Pvt	Hopkinton	Oct. 5, 1862	Typhoid	Frederick, MD
Greene, Jedidiah	Pvt	Hopkinton	Dec. 13, 1862	Fredericksburg	

(Company A)

Name	Rank	Residence	Date of Death	Battle/Illness	Place
Greene, William H.	Mus	Providence	April 21, 1863	Typhoid	Baltimore, MD
Hughes, James	Pvt	Providence	Feb. 9, 1863	Drowned	Potomac River
Kenyon, James G.	Pvt	Charlestown	June 19, 1864	Petersburg	
Kenyon, Joseph J.	Pvt	Hopkinton	Nov. 24, 1862	Typhoid	Falmouth, VA
Kenyon, Thomas R.	Pvt	Hopkinton	Aug. 9, 1863	Yazoo fever	*David Tatum*
Lewis, John D.	Pvt	Hopkinton	Dec. 25, 1862	Typhoid	Falmouth, VA
Lillibridge, Amos A.	Sgt	Richmond	May 18, 1864	Spotsylvania	
Marcoux, Joseph A.	Corp	Providence	Jan. 10, 1863	Fredericksburg	Washington
Peckham, Peleg	Bvt. Maj	Charlestown	April 2. 1865	Petersburg	
Phillips, Oliver J.	Corp	Coventry	July 20, 1864	Bethesda Church	Washington
Saunders, Isaac	Pvt	Hopkinton	May 12, 1864	Spotsylvania	
Thomas, George A.	Pvt	Hopkinton,	April 14, 1863	Typhoid	Baltimore, MD
Worden, Charles H.	Pvt	Hopkinton	Jan. 15, 1863	Typhoid	Washington

Company B

Name	Rank	Residence	Date of Death	Battle/Illness	Place
Arnold, Benjamin F.	Pvt	Coventry	July 15, 1865	Drowned	New York Harbor
Ballou, George E.	Pvt	Uxbridge, MA	Jan. 15, 1863	Disease	Washington
Bishop, Charles H.	Corp	Providence	Dec. 13, 1862	Fredericksburg	
Brickley, James	Pvt	Woonsocket	Dec. 13, 1862	Fredericksburg	
Bridgehouse, Timothy	Corp	Providence	Sept. 14, 1863	Typhoid	Camp Denison, OH
Caswell, Alfred A.	Pvt	Scituate	Sept. 22, 1863	Dysentery	Lexington, KY
Cox, William	Pvt	Providence	Dec. 13, 1862	Fredericksburg	
Crane, Thomas	Pvt	Woonsocket	Nov. 7, 1863	Yazoo fever	Lexington, KY
Ferry, James	Pvt	Woonsocket	March 22, 1863	Typhoid	Hampton, VA
Kay, James	Pvt	Providence	Sept. 28, 1864	Disease	Washington
Lynch, John	Pvt	Providence	Dec. 25, 1862	Fredericksburg	Washington
Mulvey, Thomas	Pvt	Providence	Sept. 30, 1864	Poplar Spring Church	
Robley, George W.	Pvt	Providence	June 19, 1863	Typhoid	Providence
Rowan, Thomas	Pvt	Providence	Aug. 13, 1863	Dysentery	Covington, KY
Spencer, William	Pvt	Providence	Aug. 11, 1863	Yazoo fever	*David Tatum*
Steere, John F.	Pvt	Smithfield	Oct. 1, 1863	Yazoo fever	Lexington, KY
Whitcomb, Lyman	Corp	Worcester, MA	May 17, 1864	Spotsylvania	
Wright, Harris C.	Pvt	Burrillville	Dec. 13, 1863	Fredericksburg	

Company C

Name	Rank	Residence	Date of Death	Battle/Illness	Place
Adams, Sabine G.	Pvt	Bellingham, MA	Jan. 20, 1863	Typhoid	Baltimore, MD
Aldrich, Moses H.	Corp	Blackstone, MA	Dec. 17, 1865	Disease	Burrillville
Budlong, Benjamin	Pvt	Warwick	Jan. 12, 1863	Fredericksburg	Washington
Burgess, Benjamin W.	Pvt	Glocester	Dec. 13, 1862	Fredericksburg	
Colvin, Nathan D.	Pvt	Coventry	Sept. 26, 1864	Disease	New York City
Coman, William	Wag	Glocester	Dec. 13, 1863	Fredericksburg	
Converse, William J.	Pvt	Exeter	1864	Yazoo fever	Exeter
Dorrance, John	Pvt	Foster	Jan. 26, 1863	Typhoid	Falmouth, VA

(Company C)

Name	Rank	Residence	Date of Death	Battle/Illness	Place
Durfee, Gilbert	Pvt	Glocester	Sept. 30, 1864	Poplar Spring Church	
Eddy, John H.	Pvt	Glocester	1865	Disease	Glocester
Hadfield, Richard	Pvt	Glocester	Nov. 19, 1862	Typhoid	Washington
Harrah, Matthew	Pvt	Providence	1865	Disease	Providence
Howarth, Abraham H.	Corp	Providence	Dec. 19, 1862	Fredericksburg	Falmouth, VA
Knight, Alfred S.	Pvt	Scituate	Jan. 31, 1863	Pneumonia	Falmouth, VA
Lawton, Joseph	Pvt	Glocester	April 13, 1865	Petersburg	
Morse, Henry L.	Sgt	Coventry	April 12, 1864	Dysentery	Annapolis, MD
Potter, Francis W.	Corp	Cranston	May 20, 1864	Spotsylvania	Field Hospital
Potter, James	Capt	Providence	Nov. 29, 1868	Disease	Providence
Ratcliffe, Richard	Pvt	Providence	Dec. 13, 1862	Fredericksburg	
Robbins, Nathan N.	Pvt	South Dennis, MA	July 22, 1863	Dysentery	Milldale, MS
Sweetland, Job R.	Pvt	Pawtucket	Feb. 27, 1863	Fredericksburg	Washington
Westcott, David B.	Sgt	Medford, MA	Oct. 26, 1863	Dysentery	Lexington, KY
Young, Emor	Pvt	Glocester	Nov. 20, 1868	Disease	Glocester

Company D

Name	Rank	Residence	Date of Death	Battle/Illness	Place
Congdon, George W.	1Sgt	Pawtucket	June 3, 1864	Bethesda Church	
Donnelly, Patrick	Pvt	Providence	June 30, 1863	Disease	Lexington, KY
Harrington, William	Sgt	Scituate	Aug. 31, 1863	Dysentery	Nicholasville, KY
Kettle, Charles A.	Pvt	Coventry	March 19, 1865	Disease	Annapolis, MD
McKenna, Owen	Pvt	Cumberland	May 18, 1864	Spotsylvania	
McQueeny, Barnard	Pvt	Boston, MA	Aug. 6, 1865	Yellow Fever	Dry Toturgas, FL
Pierce, Christopher	Pvt	Coventry	July 9, 1863	Dysentery	Milldale, MS
Sherman, Daniel B.	Corp	East Greenwich	May 18, 1864	Spotsylvania	
Smith, Albert L.	1Lt	Pawtucket	Aug. 31, 1863	Yazoo fever	Nicholasville, KY
Smith, Thomas E.	Pvt	Newburyport, MA	Jan. 29, 1865	Disease	Danville, VA
Steere, Benoni	Pvt	Burrillville	Dec. 23, 1862	Typhoid	Falmouth, VA
Taylor, Richard E.	Pvt	Scituate	April 16, 1865	Petersburg	Washington
Whipple, Olney	Pvt	Burrillville	Sept. 19, 1863	Yazoo fever	Nicholasville, KY
Whitman, Reuben A.	Pvt	Warwick	March 20, 1865	Dysentery	Fort Hell, VA

Company E

Name	Rank	Residence	Date of Death	Battle/Illness	Place
Alexander, Hartford	Pvt	Woonsocket	June 3, 1864	Bethesda Church	
Boyle, Charles	Pvt	Johnston	Feb. 1, 1863	Fredericksburg	Washington
Calhoun, Sylvester	Pvt	Exeter	Nov. 8, 1862	Typhoid	Pleasant Valley, MD
Dempster, John	Pvt	Providence	Dec. 13, 1862	Fredericksburg	
Essex, Richard	Pvt	West Greenwich	Sept. 23, 1863	Dysentery	Lexington, KY
Grant, Ira W.	Pvt	Cumberland	June 3, 1864	Bethesda Church	
Holbrook, Joseph H.	Pvt	Glocester	July 21, 1863	Exhaustion	Jackson, MS
Kelley, Patrick	Pvt	Blackstone, MA	Dec. 13, 1862	Fredericksburg	
Malone, John	Pvt	Cumberland	Feb. 4, 1863	Typhoid	Falmouth, VA
Maloy, Thomas	Pvt	Fall River, MA	Dec. 13, 1862	Fredericksburg	

(Company E)

Name	Rank	Residence	Date of Death	Battle/Illness	Place
McCasline, Thomas	Pvt	Pawtucket	Feb. 1, 1863	Typhoid	Falmouth, VA
Pelan, Robert T.	Pvt	Providence	Dec. 15, 1862	Fredericksburg	Falmouth, VA
Sisson, Benjamin F.	Pvt	West Greenwich	May 12, 1864	Spotsylvania	
Turner, Charles	Pvt	Cumberland	July 9, 1864	Dysentery	Andersonville, GA
Trainor, Michael	Pvt	Providence	July 7, 1865	Disease	Washington

Company F

Name	Rank	Residence	Date of Death	Battle/Illness	Place
Bolles, Albert A.	1Lt	Pawtucket	April 7, 1865	Petersburg	Petersburg, VA
Briggs, Rowland B.	Corp	Exeter	Nov. 29, 1862	Typhoid	Washington
Brown, Albert G.	Pvt	Exeter	Feb. 27, 1863	Pneumonia	Newport News, VA
Brown, John F.	Pvt	Exeter	Oct. 5, 1862	Typhoid	Frederick, MD
Carter, Joseph	Pvt	Exeter	Dec. 3, 1863	Typhoid	Falmouth, VA
Devitt, John M.	Corp	Boston, MA	July 3, 1864	Bethesda Church	Washington
Franklin, Chester L.	Pvt	Exeter	May 25, 1864	North Anna River	
Hunt, Benjamin	Pvt	North Kingstown	Dec. 13, 1862	Fredericksburg	
Kellen, Charles H.	2Lt	Willimantic, CT	Dec. 29, 1862	Fredericksburg	Washington
Kenyon, Albert D.	Pvt	South Kingstown	Feb. 27, 1863	Fredericksburg	Washington
Knight, Thomas	Pvt	Pawtucket	Dec. 15, 1862	Fredericksburg	Falmouth, VA
McDavitt, John	Pvt	Tiverton	July 8, 1864	Bethesda Church	Washington
Matthewson, Nicholas W.	Pvt	West Greenwich	Dec. 13, 1862	Fredericksburg	
Pate, William	Pvt	Mansfield, MA	June 3, 1864	Bethesda Church	
Perkins, Palmer G.	Pvt	Exeter	June 3, 1864	Bethesda Church	
Pierce, Horatio N.	Pvt	North Providence	Dec. 19, 1862	Typhoid	Falmouth, VA
Phillips, Ezekiel B.	Pvt	North Kingstown	Dec. 9, 1862	Typhoid	Falmouth, VA
Reed, Frank E.	Pvt	Attleboro, MA	July 30, 1863	Dysentery	Milldale, MS
Rose, George P.	Pvt	North Kingstown	Sept. 16, 1864	Disease	North Kingstown
Rhowerts, Charles	Pvt	Providence	May 18, 1864	Spotsylvania	
Spencer, John	Pvt	Exeter	Sept. 14, 1863	Dysentery	Camp Denison, OH
Straight, Potter P.	Pvt	Exeter	June 16, 1864	Bethesda Church	Washington

Company G

Name	Rank	Residence	Date of Death	Battle/Illness	Place
Austin, Manton G.	Pvt	South Kingstown	Aug. 10, 1863	Yazoo fever	*David Tatum*
Bacon, James H.	Pvt	South Kingstown	Jan. 24, 1864	Disease	Falmouth, VA
Barber, Jesse N.	Pvt	Hopkinton	Dec. 13, 1862	Fredericksburg	

(Company G)

Name	Rank	Residence	Date of Death	Battle/Illness	Place
Barber, Israel A.	Pvt	Hopkinton	Aug. 5, 1864	Yazoo fever	David Tatum
Baten, Nathan J.	Pvt	Coventry	Feb. 10, 1865	Disease	Coventry
Bollig, John N.	Pvt	Providence	1865	Disease	Providence
Borden, Thomas B.	Pvt	Hopkinton	Aug. 10, 1865	Disease	Hopkinton
Brayman, Henry	Pvt	South Kingstown	Sept. 14, 1863	Yazoo fever	Camp Nelson, KY
Browning, Orlando N.	Pvt	South Kingstown	Dec. 13, 1862	Fredericksburg	
Burdick, Welcome C.	Pvt	Hopkinton	Dec. 26, 1862	Fredericksburg	Washington
Cameron, Uz	Pvt	South Kingstown	June 9, 1863	Drowned	Mississippi River
Champlin, Charles E.	Pvt	South Kingstown	July 21, 1863	Disease	South Kingstown
Clarke, Jonathan R.	Pvt	South Kingstown	July 13, 1863	Jackson	
Eddy, John S.	Pvt	Cranston	June 9, 1864	Cold Harbor	
Finley, William	Pvt	South Kingstown	Aug. 15, 1863	Yazoo fever	Covington, KY
Gallagher, Owen	Pvt	South Kingstown	Dec. 13, 1862	Fredericksburg	
Gardiner, Charles W.	Pvt	South Kingstown	Aug. 24, 1863	Typhoid	Camp Denison, OH
Gilfoil, Patrick	Pvt	Providence	Mar. 3, 1865	Disease	Annapolis, MD
Greene, Robert B.	Pvt	South Kingstown	Dec. 13, 1862	Fredericksburg	
Healey, Horace D.	Pvt	South Kingstown	Aug. 2, 1863	Disease	Milldale, MS
Hull, John K.	1Sgt	South Kingstown	July 13, 1863	Jackson	
Jackson, Ambrose F.	Pvt	Providence	1865	Disease	Providence
Johnson, William H.	Pvt	South Kingstown	June 22, 1864	Petersburg	
Kenyon, John C.	Pvt	South Kingstown	Dec. 13, 1862	Fredericksburg	
Kenyon, Thomas G.	Pvt	South Kingstown	March 1, 1863	Disease	Washington
Knowles, Charles A.	Sgt	South Kingstown	Dec. 13, 1862	Fredericksburg	
May, Elisha	Pvt	South Kingstown	Aug. 29, 1863	Dysentery	Nicholasville, KY
O'Neil, James	Pvt	South Kingstown	Dec. 16, 1862	Fredericksburg	Falmouth, VA
Open, Manual	Corp	South Kingstown	May 18, 1864	Spotsylvania	
Pollock, William J.	Pvt	South Kingstown	Dec. 13, 1862	Fredericksburg	
Rose, Robert N.	Pvt	South Kingstown	Feb. 3, 1863	Disease	Falmouth, VA
Sisson, Randall	Pvt	Richmond	Aug. 28, 1863	Yazoo fever	Camp Denison, OH
Smith, Daniel	Pvt	Warwick	Dec. 13, 1862	Fredericksburg	
Smith, Roderick D.	Pvt	South Kingstown	May 18, 1864	Spotsylvania	
Snow, Samuel J.	Corp	Exeter	May 1, 1863	Disease	Lexington, KY

(Company G)

Name	Rank	Residence	Date of Death	Battle/Illness	Place
Sweat, Joseph S.	1Sgt	South Kingstown	Mar. 6, 1863	Typhoid	Boscowen, NH
Tourgee, William	Pvt	South Kingstown	Sept. 5, 1863	Dysentery	Nicholasville, KY
Trainor, Michael	Pvt	Providence	July 7, 1865	Disease	Washington
Underwood, Perry G.	Pvt	South Kingstown	Aug. 23, 1863	Dysentery	Camp Denison, OH
Willis, Jeremiah	Pvt	North Kingstown	1865	Disease	North Kingstown

Company H

Name	Rank	Residence	Date of Death	Battle/Illness	Place
Albro, Edmund B.	Pvt	East Greenwich	Dec. 30, 1862	Typhoid	Falmouth, VA
Arnold, Reuben	Pvt	East Greenwich	Dec. 13, 1862	Fredericksburg	
Briggs, Benjamin G.	Pvt	Newport	Nov. 4, 1862	Typhoid	Pleasant Valley, MD
Brown, Samuel G.	Corp	East Greenwich	Aug. 26, 1863	Dysentery	Camp Denison, OH
Burke, John	Pvt	Smithfield	July 12, 1863	Disease	Milldale, MS
Cornell, Martin H.	Pvt	Warwick	June 1, 1864	Spotsylvania	Washington
Follet, Samuel O.	Pvt	East Greenwich	June 16, 1864	Spotsylvania	Washington
Gorton, Richard	Pvt	North	May 18, 1864	Spotsylvania	
Gorton, Thomas	Pvt	East Greenwich	Dec. 13, 1862	Fredericksburg	
Hodson, James	Pvt	Warwick	June 6, 1864	Cold Harbor	
Hull, James S.	Pvt	Westerly	Aug. 13, 1864	Jackson	Camp Nelson, KY
Leary, Jerry	Pvt	Westerly	Dec. 13, 1862	Fredericksburg	
Leeden, Daniel	Pvt	North Providence	Dec. 13, 1862	Fredericksburg	
Olney, Zalmon A.	Pvt	Exeter	Dec. 13, 1862	Fredericksburg	
Place, Arnold J.	Pvt	East Greenwich	Feb. 26, 1864	Typhoid	Camp Nelson, KY
Rathbun, Nathan	Pvt	East Greenwich	Aug. 22, 1863	Jackson	Camp Nelson, KY
Rice, John E.	Pvt	Warwick	May 18, 1864	Spotsylvania	
Rice, Samuel E.	Sgt	East Greenwich	May 18, 1864	Spotsylvania	
Scott, Walter R.	Pvt	Coventry	Aug. 19, 1863	Dysentery	Camp Nelson, KY
Spencer, James B.	Sgt	Warwick	Mar. 6, 1864	Tuberculosis	Newport News, VA
Taylor, Stephen P.	Pvt	Warwick	April 13, 1864	Typhoid	Annapolis, MD
Wood, William T.	Sgt	Warwick	Sept. 10, 1863	Typhoid	Camp Nelson, KY

Company I

Name	Rank	Residence	Date of Death	Battle/Illness	Place
Collins, William	Pvt	Bristol	May 1, 1864	Disease	Knoxville, TN

(Company I)

Name	Rank	Residence	Date of Death	Battle/Illness	Place
Franklin, Josephus	Pvt	Bristol	Nov. 29, 1862	Typhoid	Falmouth, VA
Gladding, James H.	Pvt	Bristol	July 3, 1864	Spotsylvania	Washington
Gardner, Francis W.	Pvt	Smithfield	Aug. 28, 1863	Disease	Camp Nelson, KY
Hathaway, Alvin P.	Pvt	Fall River, MA	June 24, 1864	Petersburg	Washington
Kilroy, John	Pvt	Newport	June 30, 1864	Petersburg	
Manchester, Alexander	Pvt	Bristol	June 15, 1864	Bethesda Church	Washington
Manchester, Isaac	Pvt	Bristol	Dec. 1, 1862	Shock/Disease	Bristol
McIlroy, Samuel	1Lt	Pawtucket	Oct. 25, 1864	Poplar Spring Church	Field Hospital
Niles, Nelson	Pvt	Smithfield	Aug. 19, 1864	Disease	Camp Nelson, KY
Peckham, Benjamin	Pvt	Bristol	Aug. 11, 1863	Yazoo fever	*David Tatum*
Pierce, Allen	Pvt	Bristol	June 14, 1864	Bethesda Church	Field Hospital
Simpson, Samuel F.	Sgt	Newport	May 25, 1864	North Anna River	
Whitman, Olney A.	Corp	New Bedford, MA	Mar. 30, 1863	Disease	Baltimore, MD
Willis, Abel	Pvt	Bristol	Dec. 28, 1862	Fredericksburg	Washington
Winsemann, Henry	Pvt	Bristol	June 3, 1864	Bethesda Church	

Company K

Name	Rank	Residence	Date of Death	Battle/Illness	Place
Ashworth, William	Pvt	Barrington	Jan. 30, 1864	Disease	Lexington, KY
Battey, Hiram	Pvt	Johnston	Aug. 16, 1863	Dysentery	Camp Denison, OH
Bateman, George	Pvt	Providence	Aug. 20, 1863	Yazoo fever	Covington, KY
Clarke, Stephen A.	Pvt	Hopkinton	Sept. 30, 1864	Poplar Spring Church	
Cole, Henry S.	Pvt	Foster	Dec. 13, 1862	Fredericksburg	
Cole, John H.	Pvt	Scituate	Sept. 26, 1865	Disease	Scituate
Corbin, Amasa N.	Pvt	Scituate	Dec. 23, 1862	Typhoid	Falmouth, VA
Corey, Charles H.	Pvt	Foster	Sept. 15, 1863	Yazoo fever	Camp Denison, OH
Farnum, Samuel	Sgt	Uxbridge	Oct. 15, 1865	Drowned	
Farrow, Enos	Pvt	Foster	Dec. 3, 1862	Typhoid	Washington
Field, George A.	Pvt	Scituate	April 5, 1864	Dysentery	Lexington, KY
Holloway, Thomas T.	Pvt	Foster	Aug. 23, 1863	Disease	Memphis, TN
Hopkins, Asel A.	Pvt	Foster	April 11, 1864	Disease	Nashville, TN
Hopkins, Darius A.	Pvt	Scituate	Sept. 29, 1863	Yazoo fever	Camp Denison, OH
Hopkins, John	Pvt	Foster	Mar. 1, 1863	Typhoid	Newport News, VA
Hopkins, John E.	Pvt	Foster	Aug. 17, 1863	Disease	Memphis, TN
Hopkins, William D.	Sgt	Providence	Oct. 4, 1863	Disease	Providence

Appendix II

(Company K)

Name	Rank	Residence	Date of Death	Battle/Illness	Place
Maxon, Joel C.	Pvt	Hopkinton	Sept. 24, 1863	Yazoo fever	Hopkinton
Nye, Isaac	Corp	Coventry	May 30, 1864	Spotsylvania	Washington
Potter, Roswell H.	Corp	Providence	July 22, 1863	Dysentery	Milldale, MS
Reynolds, Edward S.	Corp	Scituate	June 2, 1864	Mechanicsville	
Salisbury, Alpheus	Pvt	Scituate	July 4, 1863	Fredericksburg	Providence
Simmons, George	Pvt	Foster	May 12, 1864	Spotsylvania	
Smith, George H.	Corp	Scituate	Jan. 3, 1863	Typhoid	Falmouth, VA
Taylor, James J.	Pvt	Smithfield	July 6, 1864	Bethesda Church	Washington
Williams, Olney D.	Pvt	North Providence	Dec. 13, 1862	Fredericksburg	
Winsor, Albert A.	Pvt	Foster	Dec. 13, 1862	Fredericksburg	
Wood, Oliver	Pvt	Foster	June 15, 1864	Bethesda Church	Washington

Appendix III: Enlistments by Town

The following is a listing of the communities that the men in the Seventh Rhode Island enlisted from. The numbers are garnered from the muster rolls and bounty receipts housed at the Rhode Island State Archives. Oftentimes a soldier traveled to a neighboring town to gain the larger bonus being offered by that town, even though their residence was elsewhere. For example, Scituate gave a bounty of 400 dollars and raised sixty men, although only thirty-five natives of the town served. The residence is given according to that on the enlistment papers.

Town	Number	Town	Number
Barrington	2	Newport	78
Bristol	37	New Shoreham	1
Burrillville	31	North Kingstown	36
Charlestown	6	North Providence	37
Coventry	36	Portsmouth	11
Cranston	28	Providence	317
Cumberland	42	Richmond	34
Exeter	23	Scituate	35
East Providence	3	Smithfield	41
East Greenwich	26	South Kingstown	65
Foster	24	Tiverton	5
Glocester	32	Warren	1
Jamestown	1	Warwick	59
Johnston	22	West Greenwich	12
Hopkinton	51	Westerly	15
Little Compton	4	Woonsocket	29
Middletown	1		

Notes

For brevity's sake, the following abbreviations are used in the notes and bibliography.

FPS: Foster Preservation Society.
FRSP: Fredericksburg and Spotsylvania National Military Park Library.
HL: Hay Library, Brown University.
LOC: Library of Congress
LPL: Langworthy Public Library.
NA: National Archives.
NHS: Newport Historical Society.
NSPL: North Scituate Public Library.
OR: Official Records of the War of the Rebellion.
PHS: Pettaquamscutt Historical Society.
PVHS: Pawtuxet Valley Historical Society.
RIHS: Rhode Island Historical Society.
RISA: Rhode Island State Archives.
RSG: Author's Collection.
USAMHI: United States Army Military Historical Institute.

Chapter 1

1. William P. Hopkins, *The Seventh Regiment Rhode Island Volunteers in the Civil War, 1862–1865.* [Providence: Snow and Farnum, 1903], 310–314.
2. *Revised Register of Rhode Island Volunteers.* [Providence: E.L. Freemanton, 1893] The *Revised Register* is composed of two volumes. Volume One is a listing of the men who served in the infantry, while Volume Two contends with men who fought in the cavalry, artillery, U.S. Army and the U.S. Navy. All references refer to Volume One.
3. Hopkins, viii–ix. *Pleas excuse all bad writing: A documentary history of Rhode Island during the Civil War era 1861–1865.* Edited by Kris VanDenBossche. [Peace Dale, R.I.: Rhode Island Historical Document Transcription Project, 1993]
4. *Providence Journal,* April 21, 1939.

Chapter 2

1. *Revised Register.* Augustus Woodbury, *A narrative of the Campaign of the First Rhode Island Regiment in the Spring and Summer of 1861.* [Providence: Sydney S. Rider, 1862], 225–231.
2. Hopkins, 1–3. *Providence Evening Press,* May 24, 1862.
3. Hopkins, 314–15. *Memoirs of Rhode Island Officers: Who were engaged in the service of their Country during the Great Rebellion with the South.* Edited by John R. Bartlett. [Providence: Sydney S. Rider & Brothers Press, 1867],430–32. Welcome B. Sayles to Thomas W. Dorr, July 1, 1845, HL.
4. William A. Spicer, *The History of the Ninth and Tenth Regiments of Rhode Island Volunteers and the Tenth Rhode Island Battery in the Union Army in 1862.* [Providence: Snow and Farnum, 1892], 121–130. *Write Soon and give me all the news.* Edited by Kris VanDenBossche. [Peace Dale, R.I.: Rhode Island Historical Document Transcription Project, 1993], 145–147.
5. *Memoirs of R.I.,* 1–93: 121–25: 147–50: 433–35. The assumption that Bliss was politically indifferent is the author's. After the war, nearly every Rhode Island officer ran for political office. Colonel Bliss did not, deciding to remain in the U.S. Army.
6. Zenas R. Bliss, *Memoirs,* USAMHI. Hopkins, 311–14. *Memoirs of R.I.,* 267–68.
7. Spicer, 138–200.
8. Julia Emily Babbitt, *Sketch of Major Jacob Babbitt: 7th Rhode Island Regiment.* [Bristol, R.I.: NP, 1890], 1–11. Hopkins, 325–26. *Memoirs of R.I.,* 264–66. Spicer, 194–95.
9. Hopkins, 332–37. Stephen F. Peckham, "Recollections of a Hospital Steward during the Civil War," NHS.
10. John K. Burlingame, *History of the Fifth Regiment, Rhode Island Heavy Artillery.* [Providence: Snow and Farnum, 1892], 299–327. Hopkins, 373–75. Augustus Woodbury, *The Uprising of 1861: The illustration of True Patriotism.* [Providence: Snow and Farnum, 1895], 17–19.

11. Hedley Smith, *History of Scituate, Rhode Island.* [C.T.: Racine Publishing, 1976], 157–163. Town of Scituate, *Tax Book.* [Phenix, R.I.: John H. Campbell Book and Job Printer, 1865], 11–13: 24–27.
12. Hopkins, 368–70. *Pleas excuse,* 59–60.
13. Samuel G. Arnold to *Providence Journal,* April 21, 1861, RIHS.
14. Hopkins, 2–6. Peckham, "Recollections." Elisha Hunt Rhodes, *All for the Union: The Civil War Diary and Letters of Elisha Hunt Rhodes.* Edited by Robert Hunt Rhodes. [New York: Random House, 1985], 6–11. Seventh Rhode Island Volunteers, Quartermaster Returns: 1862, RISA. Spicer, 272–276. The overwhelming majority of images of the Seventh Rhode Island were taken when the regiment was still in Providence.
15. *Providence Daily Journal,* August 27, 1862.
16. Babbitt, 11–13. Spicer, 279–84. *War of the Rebellion: A compilation of the Official Records of the Union and Confederate Armies: Series III: Volume 2.* [Washington D.C.: Government Printing Office, 1880–1890], 269–70. Afterwards cited as *OR.* All references are made to *Series I,* except when noted.
17. George H. Allen, *Forty-Six Months in the Fourth Rhode Island Volunteers.* [Providence: J.A. & R.A. Reid Printers, 1887], 136–142. Hopkins, 1–6: 411–12. *Pleas Excuse,* 62.
18. Company A, Seventh Rhode Island Volunteers, Descriptive Book, RISA. Hopkins, 433–39:527–28. *Pleas Excuse,* 59–62.
19. Company B, Seventh Rhode Island Volunteers, Descriptive Book, RISA. Hopkins, 366–67: 439–45.
20. Company C and Company D, Seventh Rhode Island Volunteers, Descriptive Books, RISA. Hopkins, 361: 453–61. Knight Genealogy, RSG. *Write Soon,* 57.
21. Company E, Seventh Rhode Island Volunteers, Descriptive Book, RISA. Hopkins, 393:474–80. Peckham, "Recollections." Thomas F. Tobey to John Hay, April 26, 1862, HL.
22. Company F and Company G, Seventh Rhode Island Volunteers, Descriptive Books, RISA. Hopkins, 340–343: 398–99:480–99. *Narragansett Times,* October 3, 1862. *Voices of the Civil War: Letters and Journal Excerpts of South Kingstown Men in the Union Army, 1861–63.* Edited by Shirley L. Barrett. [South Kingstown, R.I.: Pettequamscutt Historical Society, 1992], 16–18.
23. Thomas Allan, *The Kentish Guards: A History.* [East Greenwich, R.I.: NP, 1918.], 17–19. Company H and Company I, Seventh Rhode Island Volunteers, Descriptive Books, RISA. Hopkins, 501–17.
24. John F. Austin to Emily Austin, August 23, 1862, RIHS. Company K, Seventh Rhode Island Volunteers, Descriptive Book, RISA. William O. Harrington to Eunice Harrington, September 13, 1862, NSPL. Hopkins, 517–23. Squire Wood, *A History of Greene and vicinity: 1845–1929.* [Providence: NP, 1936], 38–41.
25. Edward T. Allen to John R. Stanhope, August 1, 1863, RSG. Hopkins, 1–6. Seventh Rhode Island Volunteers, Clothing Books, RISA. Seventh Rhode Island Volunteers, Ordnance Returns, RISA. All images of men in the Seventh clearly show the Enfield rifle-musket and the cartridge box worn on the belt.
26. Harrington, September 13, 1862. Hopkins, 4–11.

Chapter 3

1. John D. Billings, *Hardtack and Coffee: The unwritten story of Army Life.* [Lincoln: Nebraska University Press, 1993], 108–111. Hopkins, 10–11. *Write Soon,* 57–8.
2. Hopkins, 12–13. William O. Harrington to Eunice Harrington, September 13, 1862, NSPL. Peleg Jones to Mother, September 15, 1862, RIHS.
3. John F. Austin to Emily Austin, September 13, 1862, RIHS. Jones, September 15, 1861. Alfred S. Knight to William W. Knight, September 14, 1862, RSG.
4. Hopkins, 11–15.
5. Hopkins, 354. *Memoirs of R.I.,* 357–61.
6. John F. Austin to Emily Austin, September 18, 1862, RIHS. Silas Casey, *Infantry Tactics.* [Washington D.C.: N.P., 1862] *Memoirs of R.I.,* 97–103.
7. Hopkins, John Hull to Harriet Hull, September 21, 1862, PHS.
8. Peckham, "Recollections."
9. John F. Austin to Emily Austin, September 18, 1862, RIHS. William O. Harrington to Eunice Harrington, September 26, 1862, NSPL. Hull, September 21, 1862. *Pleas Excuse,* 63–65.
10. John F. Austin to Emily Austin, September 29, 1862, RIHS. Hopkins, 15–16. John Hull to Harriet Hull, October 8, 1862. Peckham, "Recollections."
11. John F. Austin to Emily Austin, October 2, 1862, RIHS. Hopkins, 17–20. Hull, October 8, 1862. Peckham, "Recollections." *Pleas Excuse,* 64–67.
12. *Memoirs of R.I.,* 9–25. Benjamin P. Poore, *The Life and Public Services of Ambrose E. Burnside.* [Providence: J.A. & R.A. Reid, 1882], 16–125.
13. *A History of the Ninth Regiment New Hampshire Volunteers in the War of the Rebellion.* Edited by Edward O. Lord. [Concord: Republican Press Association, 1895], 174–76. Lyman Jackman, *History of the Sixth New Hampshire Regiment in the War for the Union.* [Concord: Republican Press Association, 1891], 59–108.
14. John F. Austin to Emily Austin, October 19, 1862, RIHS. Hopkins, 21–23. William O. Harrington to Eunice Harrington, October 17, 1862, NSPL. John Hull to Harriet Hull, October 16, 1862, PHS. E. Rhodes, 14–15.
15. Austin, October 19, 1862. Billings, 61–72. Hopkins,
16. Charles F. Colvin to Brother, October 22, 1862, PVHS. Hopkins, 23. Charles P. Nye to Benjamin Pendleton, October 22, 1862, RIHS. *Pleas Excuse,* 65–67.
17. Billings, 114–42. Nye, October 22, 1862. James Remington to Sister, October 29, 1862, RIHS. Albert A. Winsor to Sister, October 18, 1862, FPS. Hugh McInnes, *Civil War Letters.* [Parsons, W.V.: McClain Publishing, 1981.], 7. Enos Farrow died of typhoid on December 3, 1862.
18. John F. Austin to Emily Austin, October 15, 1862, RIHS. John Hull to Harriet Hull, October 19, 1862, PHS. Winsor, October 18, 1862.
19. Allen, 15:130. Harrington, October 17, 1862. The Twenty-First Connecticut was recruited along the Rhode Island border, and included several Rhode Islanders in its ranks. In addition an entire brigade of Connecticut troops was in the Third Division of the Ninth Corps.
20. John F. Austin to Emily Austin, October 25, 1862, RIHS. Hopkins, 22–24.

Chapter 4

1. Scott Hartwig, "The Volunteers of '62 in the Maryland Campaign," *The Antietam Campaign.* Edited by Gary W. Gallagher. [Chapel Hill, N.C.: University of North Carolina Press, 1999], 143–68. Stephen W. Sears,

George B. McClellan: The Young Napoleon. [New York: Ticknor and Fields, 1988], 296–344.

2. Hopkins, 26–27. Jackman, 117–19. James Remington to Benjamin F. Remington, November 17, 1862, RIHS. *Revised Regulation for the Army of the United States.* [Philadelphia: G.L.B. Brown, 1861], 341–46.

3. John F. Austin to Emily Austin, November 1, 1862, RIHS. Zenas R. Bliss to Company Commanders, October 29, 1862, RIHS. Hopkins, 431–525. All casualty figures in this book are the author's own, based upon research conducted into a variety of sources, including the Regimental Books and Papers, William Hopkins, *Revised Register of Rhode Island Volunteers,* Soldier's correspondence, and visits to cemeteries across Rhode Island.

4. *Memoirs of R.I.,* 26–34. Poore, 176–81. Remington, November 17, 1862.

5. John F. Austin to Emily Austin, November 7, 1862, RIHS. Hopkins, 27–29.

6. Bliss, *Memoirs.* William O. Harrington to Eunice Harrington, November 3, 1862, NSPL. Hopkins, 28–30.

7. Phebe Briggs to James Remington, October 23, 1862, RIHS. Hopkins, 504. John Seamens to James Remington, November 16, 1862, RIHS. Captain Remington's writings at the Rhode Island Historical Society are full of documents and official papers in communication with the War Department.

8. James Harris, papers, RIHS. John Hull to Harriet Hull, November 4, 1862, PHS.

9. Hopkins, 28–34. Horace Greenman to Sister, November 13, 1862, RIHS. Nye, October 22, 1862. *Pleas Excuse,* 66–71. John D. Lewis of Company A, ill with the typhoid in October died on December 25, 1862.

10. John F. Austin to Emily Austin, November 25, 1862, RIHS. Hopkins, 30–32. John Hull to Harriet Hull, November 22, 1862, PHS. Remington, November 17, 1862.

11. Billings, 108–142. Hull, November 22, 1862. Remington, November 17, 1862.

12. John F. Austin to Emily Austin, November 24, 1862, RIHS. *Write Soon,* 57.

Chapter 5

1. William O. Harrington to Eunice Harrington, November 24, 1862, NSPL. Hopkins, 35–38. *Memoirs of R.I.,* 376. Peckham, "Recollections."

2. John F. Austin to Emily Austin, December 2, 1862, RIHS. William O. Harrington to Eunice Harrington, December 7, 1862, NSPL. Foster Town Records, Foster, Rhode Island.

3. Billings, 73–89. Hopkins, 37. James Remington to sister, December 8, 1862, RIHS. "Hospital Returns, fourth quarter, 1862," Harris MSS, RIHS.

4. Joseph H. Alexander, "Defending Marye's Heights" in *With my Face to the Enemy: Perspectives on the Civil War.* Edited by Robert Cowley. [New York: Putnam, 2001], 166–174. William O. Harrington to Eunice Harrington, December 16, 1862, NSPL. William Miller, "A hot day on Marye's Heights." in *Battles and Leaders of the Civil War: Volume III.* [New York: Century, 1885], 97–99.

5. Babbitt, 9. Hopkins, Alfred S. Knight to Horace Ralph, January 12, 1863, RSG.

6. *Memoirs of R.I.,* 41–43.

7. William McCarter Bliss, *My Life in the Irish Brigade.* Edited by Kevin E. O'Brien. [El Dorado Hills, C.A.: Savas Publishing, 1996], 80–84. Bliss, *Memoirs.* Peckham, "Recollections." This was the standard combat load of the Federal soldier. The cartridge box only held forty round, leaving the men to place the other twenty in their pockets.

8. George W. Dinman, *Autobiography and sketches of my Travels by Sea and Land.* [Bristol, R.I.: Bristol Press, 1896], 46–53. Frank J. Wilder to Abby Westcott, November 8, 1862, RSG.

9. Bliss, *Memoirs.* Harrington, December 16, 1862. Hopkins, 39–42. T.A. Manchester, "Experiences of Fredericksburg," FRSP.

10. Bliss, *Memoirs.* Hopkins, 39–42.

11. Bliss, Memoirs. OR, 21:319–20. Leander Cogswell, *A History of the Eleventh New Hampshire Regiment Volunteer Infantry in the Rebellion War: 1861–1865.* [Concord: Republican Press Association, 1891], 45–52.

12. Mike Pride and Mark Travis, *My Brave Boys: To War with Colonel Cross and the Fighting Fifth.* [Hanover N.H.: University Press of New England, 2001], 174–176.

13. Edward T. Allen, Service File, NA. Cogswell, 45–52. William O. Harrington to Josiah V. Harrington, December 17, 1862, NSPL. Hopkins, 39–43:338–39. OR, 21: 319–21.

14. Bliss, *Memoirs.* Hopkins, 42–42: 401–402. Hopkins claims 550 enlisted men in the ranks on the morning of the battle. Bliss claims a total of 590, including company officers in his memoirs. This writer has taken the average of 570, including company, field officers, and enlisted men in the companies. Based on the returns of the many men still ill with typhoid, the average company mustered around fifty riflemen and two officers.

15. John F. Austin to Emily Austin, December 17, 1862, RIHS. William Cottam, "Affidavit of Fredericksburg," FRSP.

16. Bliss, *Memoirs.* Cogswell, 45–52.

17. Bliss, *Memoirs. History of the Twelfth Regiment Rhode Island Volunteers in the Civil War: 1862–1863.* Compiled by Pardon E. Tillinghast. [Providence: Snow and Farnum, 1892], 37–42. Hopkins, 382. OR, 21:321–324.

18. Bliss, *Memoirs.* Hopkins, 44. *Pleas Excuse,* 70–73.

19. Bliss, *Memoirs. Memoirs of R.I.* 330–332. Hopkins, 43–45. Peleg Peckham to David R. Kenyon, January 2, 1863, LPL. Peckham, "Narrative." *Pleas Excuse,* 70–73.

20. Hopkins, 43–45:345.

21. John H. Rhodes, *History of Battery B, First Rhode Island Light Artillery.* [Providence: Snow and Farnum, 1894], 138–142.

22. Gideon A. Burgess. *The Owen Soldiers Monument, North Scituate Rhode Island.* [North Scituate, R.I.: E.F. Sibley and Co., 1913], 4–6. Hopkins, 44–45: 395.

23. James Remington to Harry, January 7, 1863, RIHS. *Pleas Excuse,* 70–73. Harrington, December 16, 1862.

24. Bliss, *Memoirs.* Alfred S. Knight to Horace Ralph, December 21, 1862, RSG. A small piece of the "Fredericksburg Flag" is now in the possession of the Rhode Island Sons of Union Veterans. It remains stained by Marcoux's blood.

25. Babbitt, 12–14. Bliss, *Memoirs.* Hopkins, 45.

26. Babbitt, 12–14. Bliss, *Memoirs. Memoirs of R.I.,* 265–266. Harrington, December 16, 1862. Based upon descriptions stated in the listed works, this writer has come to the conclusion the 127th Pennsylvania that fired at the Seventh. All of the works claim it was a ninth month regiment, as was the Pennsylvanians. In addition, they were the only regiment near the Seventh's position at sundown.

27. Allen, 168–175. Hopkins, 44–46. *Narragansett*

Times, December 26, 1862. Frank Rathbun to Author, November 28, 2006.
  28. Hopkins, 51. *Providence Evening Press,* December 15, 1862.
  29. Bliss, *Memoirs.* Hopkins, 51. Edwin W. Stone. *Rhode Island in the Rebellion.* [Providence: Knowles, Anthony, 1864], 303–313.
  30. Bliss, *Memoirs.* Alfred S. Knight, December 28, 1862. RSG.
  31. Bliss, *Memoirs.* Hopkins, 44–47. Alfred S. Knight to William W. Knight, December 28, 1862, RSG. *Memoirs of R.I.,* 267–272. OR, 21:323. *Pleas excuse,* 71–73. Over the years, there have been many conflicting casualty returns of the 7th Rhode Island at Fredericksburg. These range from 133 to 300. This writer has determined the number to be 220, which is drawn from a number of sources, including letters, cemetery visits, and the Regimental Books at the Rhode Island State Archives.
  32. John F. Austin to Emily Austin, January 22, 1863, RIHS. Bliss, *Memoirs.* Hopkins, 44–47. Nathan B. Lewis to Nellie, December 28, 1862, PHS. *Memoirs of R.I.,* 267–272. OR, 21:323. *Pleas excuse,* 71–73.
  33. Babbitt, 14–17. *Memoirs of R.I.,* 263–266; 430–433. Hopkins, 50–54; 401–402.
  34. Cogswell, 49. OR, 21:320–23. Augustus Woodbury, *Major General Ambrose E. Burnside and the Ninth Army Corps: A narrative of campaigns in North Carolina, Maryland, Virginia, Ohio, Kentucky, Mississippi in the war for the preservation of the Republic.* Providence: Sydney S. Rider, 1867], 224.
  35. Harrington, December 16, 1862. Hopkins, 44–47. *Pleas Excuse,* 70–73
  36. William O. Harrington to Eunice Harrington, December 21, 1862, NSPL. William O. Harrington to Josiah V. Harrington, December 28, 1862, NSPL. Hopkins, 44–47. Remington, January 7, 1862.

Chapter 6

  1. *Revised Register,* 696–704. Stone, 283–385.
  2. Hopkins, 315–19:326–28. *Narragansett Times,* January 23, 1863. Peleg Peckham to David R. Kenyon, January 12, 1863, LPL.
  3. Edward T. Allen to Benjamin Hull, July 16, 1863, PHS. Hopkins, 65. Peleg Peckham to David R. Kenyon, January 4, 1863, LPL.
  4. Hopkins, 50–53:312. *Pleas excuse,* 73.
  5. John Hull to Harriet Hull, January 4, 1863, PHS. Peckham, January 4, 1863. *Pleas excuse,* 59. *Providence Journal,* January 18, 1918.
  6. Hull, January 4, 1863. Hopkins, 53–55. Alfred S. Knight to Horace Ralph, December 21, 1862 and January 12, 1863, RSG.
  7. Hopkins, 54–55: 312: 338. *Narragansett Times,* February 6, 1863. Peckham, January 12, 1863.
  8. Hopkins, 55. The flag, as with all Rhode Island battle flags are now at the Rhode Island State House.
  9. William O. Harrington to Eunice Harrington, January 2 and January 11, 1863, NSPL. John Hull to Brother, January 22, 1863, PHS. *Write soon,* 57.
  10. Allen, 183–86. Charles F. Colvin to Brother, January 18, 1863, PVHS. Peckham, January 12, 1863.
  11. Allen, 190. Colvin, January 18, 1863. Harrington, January 11, 1863. *Pleas excuse,* 73. *Write Soon,* 57.
  12. William O. Harrington to Eunice Harrington, January 21, 1863. Hopkins, 54–56. Hull, January 4, 1863. *Pleas excuse,* 73.

  13. Allen, 165:187–189. Harrington, January 21, 1863. Hull, January 22, 1863.
  14. Hopkins, 55–58. Hull, January 22, 1863. *Pleas excuse,* 73. *Write soon,* 58.
  15. Alfred S. Knight, Service File, NA. Almon Knight, "Lines on the Death of Alfred S. Knight," RSG. William W. Knight to Alfred S. Knight, January 26, 1863, RSG. The amount of Scituate soldiers dying at Falmouth is taken from observations gathered in the cemeteries of that town.
  16. Hopkins, 59–61:482. John Hull to Harriet Hull, January 30, 1863, PHS. Charles P. Nye to Benjamin Pendleton, February 2, 1863, RIHS. Poore, 203–7.
  17. Colvin, January 18, 1863. Charles P. Nye to Benjamin Pendleton, March 7, 1863, RIHS. *Pleas excuse,* 75. Harrington's letters are filled with comments of his good health; indeed he was never admitted to the regimental hospital.
  18. William O. Harrington to Eunice Harrington, February 1, 1863, NSPL. Hopkins. 62.
  John Hull to Cousin, February 8, 1863, PHS. *Narragansett Times,* February 6, 1863.Poore, 203–07. Benjamin E. Wells to Benjamin Pendleton, March, 1863, RIHS.
  19. William O. Harrington to Eunice Harrington, February 13, 1863, NSPL. Peleg Peckham to David R. Kenyon, February 15, 1863, LPL. *Pleas excuse,* 74–75.
  20. William O. Harrington to Eunice Harrington, February 26, 1863, NSPL. Hopkins, 64–66. *Pleas excuse,* 74–76.
  21. Burlingame, 136–42. Hopkins, 65–66. *Pleas excuse,* 74–76. Charles Slocum to Sister, March 19, 1863, RIHS. *Write Soon,* 59.
  22. Hopkins, 65–66. *Pleas excuse,* 77–79. Poore, 203–07. Benjamin E. Wells to Benjamin Pendleton, March, 1863, RIHS.

Chapter 7

  1. Hopkins, 67. Peckham, "Narrative."
  2. Hopkins, 68–69. *Pleas excuse,* 77–78.
  3. Poore, 204–10.
  4. William Chenery, *The Fourteenth Regiment Rhode Island Heavy Artillery in the War to Preserve the Union.* [New York: Negro University Press, 1960] William O. Harrington to Eunice Harrington, April 1, 1863, NSPL. Hopkins, 69–70. Jackman, 135–35.
  5. Billings, 331–49. Hopkins, 71–72. John Hull to Harriet Hull, April 10, 1863.
  6. Hull, April 10, 1863. Jackman, 136.
  7. Burlingame, 136–42. Hopkins, 73.
  8. William O. Harrington to Eunice Harrington, April 19, 1863, NSPL. April 20, 1863, Morning Report, Seventh Rhode Island Volunteers, RIHS. Peleg Jones to Mother, April 19, 1863, RIHS. Peckham, "Recollections." Peleg Peckham to David R. Kenyon, April 14, 1863, LPL.
  9. Wilbur Hinman, *Corporal Si Klegg and his Pard.* [Cleveland: Williams Publishing, 1887], 307–11. John Hull to Cousin, April 30, 1863, PHS.
  10. Hopkins, 75–76. *Pleas excuse,* 78–79. Peleg Peckham to David R. Kenyon, May 15, 1863, LPL.
  11. Jackman, 148–50. Hopkins, 77–78.
  12. William O. Harrington to Eunice Harrington, May 24, 1863, NSPL. Hopkins, 78–79.
  13. Clothing Books, Seventh Rhode Island Volunteers, RIHS. Hopkins, 82–83. William O. Harrington to Eunice Harrington, June 3, 1862, NSPL. *Narragansett Times,* June 5, 1863.

14. John Hull to Harriet Hull, June 6, 1863, PHS. Albert Perry to David R. Kenyon, August 31, 1863, LPL. *Pleas excuse,* 82. Poore, 210–12. Frank J. Wilder to Abby Westcott, January 21, 1863, RSG.
15. Billings, 331–49. Samuel G. Brown, Service File, NA. Hopkins 85–87. Nathaniel Low to Jen Low, May 28, 1863 and June 2, 1863, RSG. June 9, 1863, Morning Report, Seventh Rhode Island Volunteers, RIHS. *Narragansett Times,* July 31, 1863. Hull's knapsack is still in the possession of his family and was carried in the campaign.
16. Daniel Brownell to James Remington, June 9, 1863, RIHS. Hopkins, 87–88. The companies were again designated by the date of their captain's commission. Captain Theodore Winn remained the one original captain.
17. Hopkins, 89–91. John Hull to Harriet Hull, June 12, 1863, PHS.
18. Hopkins, 94–96. John Hull to Harriet Hull, June 14, 1863, PHS. Jackman, 166–67.
19. William O. Harrington to Eunice Harrington, June 17, 1863, NSPL. John Hull to Harriet Hull, June 17, 1863, PHS. Jackman, 188–89. Stone, 332–33.
20. William O. Harrington to Eunice Harrington, July 2, 1863, NSPL. Nat Low to Jen Low, June 20, 1863, RSG.
21. Brownell, June 9, 1863. Hopkins, 101–02: 129–30. Ethan A. Jenks, Service File, NA. *Providence Journal,* July 17, 1863.
22. Hopkins, 102–06. Nat Low to Jen Low, July 5, 1863, RSG.
23. William O. Harrington to Eunice Harrington, July 14, 1863, NSPL. Jackman, 174–79. Peckham, "Narrative."
24. Edward T. Allen to Benjamin Hull, July 16, 1863, PHS. Hopkins, 110–14. *Narragansett Times,* July 31, 1863.
25. Harrington, July 14, 1863. Hopkins, 348. Hopkins, 110–14. Jackman, 183. Jared J. Potter, diary of July 15, 1863, USAMHI. *OR,* 24:50–72. Nathan Rathbun, Service File, NA.
26. Edward T. Allen to Benjamin Hull, August 27, 1863, PHS. *OR,* 24:50–72. John Webster to Harriet Hull, August 28, 1863, PHS. Hull's remains were never recovered. His letters and personal effects now reside in South Kingstown, while the location where he was buried is now lost.
27. *OR,* 24:50–72. Hopkins, 115–17. Stephen Peckham to *Providence Journal,* July 15, 1863, RIHS. Stone, 331–33.
28. Bliss, *Memoirs.* Hopkins, 312–13.
29. William O. Harrington to Eunice Harrington, July 28, 1863, NSPL. Hopkins, 104:119. Stone, 333.
30. Hopkins, 120. *Pleas excuse,* 84.
31. Hopkins, 122–24. Peleg Jones to Mother, August 14, 1863, RIHS. Peckham, "Recollections." Peleg Peckham to David R. Kenyon, August 12, 1863, LPL.
32. Peckham, August 12, 1863.
33. Winfield S. Chappell to Harrison Steadman, December 4, 1863, PHS. Hopkins, 430–524. Charles P. Nye to Benjamin Pendleton, August 25, 1863, RIHS.

Chapter 8

1. Peckham, "Recollections."
2. William O. Harrington to Eunice Harrington, September 18, 1863, NSPL. Elisha Palmer and Albert Perry to David R. Kenyon, August 31, 1863, LPL.
3. *Pleas excuse,* 83. *Revised Register,* 221–304.
4. Palmer and Perry, August 31, 1863.
5. Hopkins, 124–30: 422–22. Peckham, "Recollections." Peleg Peckham to David R. Kenyon, September, 1863, LPL.
6. Chappell, December 4, 1863. Hopkins, 430–524. Morning Reports, RIHS. Charles P. Nye to Benjamin Pendleton, August 25, 1863, RIHS.
7. Poore, 213–15. Jackman, 197–99. Stone, 333.
8. William O. Harrington to Eunice Harrington, September 25, 1863, NSPL. Edwin S. Hunt to David R. Kenyon, September 13, 1863, LPL.
9. Hopkins, 131–34. Charles P. Nye to Benjamin Pendleton, September 21, 1863, RIHS.
10. P. Peckham, September, 1863. Stephen F. Peckham to *Providence Journal,* October 12, 1863, RIHS. *Pleas excuse,* 86–87.
11. William O. Harrington to Eunice Harrington, October 11, 1863, NSPL.
12. Hopkins, 135–38.
13. Billings, 217–23. Hopkins, 139–41. Peleg Peckham to David R. Kenyon, November 3, 1863, LPL. *Write Soon,* 60–61.
14. William O. Harrington to Eunice Harrington, December 28, 1863, NSPL. Hopkins, 141–46. William H. Jordan to Brother and Sister, January 11, 1864, RIHS.
15. Hopkins, 147–51. Peleg Peckham to David R. Kenyon, January 12, 1864, LPL. Potter, diary, January 5, 1864.
16. Hopkins, 151–52. Peleg Peckham to "York," January 25, 1864, RSG. *Write Soon,* 61.
17. Hopkins, 346–47, Peckham, "Narrative." *Pleas excuse,* 88–89.
18. Allen, 248–58. Potter, diary, February 27, 1864. *Write Soon,* 61–63.
19. Hopkins, 156–59. Potter, diary, April 2, 1864.
20. Hopkins, 160–61.

Chapter 9

1. Burlingame, 6–9. Woodbury, *Ninth Corps,* 364–67.
2. Billings, 260–61. Warren Wilkinson, *Mother, May you never see the sights I have seen: The Fifty-Seventh Massachusetts Veteran Volunteers in the Last Year of the Civil War.* [New York: Harper & Row, 1990], 39–43. Woodbury, *Ninth Corps.* The Ninth Corps badge is still used today as a symbol of the Rhode Island National Guard.
3. Peckham, "Recollections."
4. Hopkins, 161–62. Potter, diary, April 25, 1864. Thomas F. Tobey to John Hay, June 28, 1864, HL. *Write Soon,* 64.
5. Hopkins, 162–63. Peckham, "Recollections." *Write Soon,* 64–65.
6. William O. Harrington to Eunice Harrington, April 29, 1864, NSPL. *Memoirs of R.I.,* 268–69.
7. Poore, 231–35. Woodbury, *Ninth Corps,* 368–70.
8. Poore, 231–35. *Narragansett Times,* May 25, 1864. Woodbury, *Ninth Corps,* 371–381.
9. Hopkins, 165–67. *Memoirs of R.I.,* 268.
10. Hopkins, 165–67. Peckham, "Recollections."
11. Hopkins, 168–69. Peckham, "Recollections."
12. Bliss, "Memoirs." Hopkins, 169. *Memoirs of R.I.,* 268.
13. Jackman, 241–44. Hopkins, 169–172. Peleg Jones, diary, May 12, 1864, RIHS. J.H. Rhodes, 283–86.
14. Hopkins, 169–172: 394. Peckham, "Recollections." *Pleas excuse,* 89–91.

15. Hopkins, 169–172. *OR,* 42:927–32. *Revised Register,* 696–704.
16. Hopkins, 171–74. *Memoirs of R.I.,* 444.
17. Hopkins, 171–74. *OR,* 36:927–32
18. Hopkins, 174–75. Jackman, 250–52. Peckham, "Recollections."
19. Hopkins, 174–76:407–08. *Providence Daily Journal,* June 20, 1864. *Providence Evening Press,* June 13, 1864.
20. Hopkins, 291–94. *Providence Daily Journal,* June 20, 1864. *OR,* 36:927–32.
21. Hopkins, 174–76. *Ninth New Hampshire,* 364–66. Edward Stanton to Peleg Peckham, July 30, 1864, USAMHI.
22. Casey, 72–74. Hopkins, 175–76. Jones, diary, May 18, 1864. Peckham, "Recollections." *Revised Register,* 696–704.
23. William O. Harrington to Eunice Harrington, May 20, 1864, NSPL. Hopkins, 405. Jones, diary, May 18, 1864. Peckham, "Recollections." *Pleas excuse,* 90–91.
24. Stephen F. Peckham to *Providence Journal,* May 20, 1864, RIHS.
25. Hopkins, 177–79: 411–12. Poore, 235. *Providence Evening Press,* June 13, 1864.

Chapter 10

1. Hopkins, 367. *Narragansett Times,* August 8, 1864. *Pleas Excuse,* 89–91. *Revised Register,* 696–705.
2. Hopkins, 178–81. *OR,* 36:932. Potter, diary, May 27, 1864.
3. Hopkins, 180–81. *OR,* 36:585.
4. Hopkins, 182–84. William O. Harrington to Eunice Harrington, June 2, 1864, NSPL. *Ninth New Hampshire,* 425. Potter, diary, June 2, 1864. Woodbury, *Ninth,* 395–97.
5. William O. Harrington to Eunice Harrington, June 4, 1864, NSPL. Jackman, 277–78. Stephen F. Peckham to *Providence Journal,* June 1, 1864, RIHS. Woodbury, *Ninth,* 396–99.
6. Hopkins, 184–85. *Providence Daily Journal,* June 20, 1864.
7. Harrington, June 4, 1864. Hopkins, 398–99. *Providence Daily Journal,* June 20, 1864.
8. Harrington, June 4, 1864. Hopkins, 184–86. Jones, diary, June 3, 1864. *OR,* 36:933. Potter, diary, June 3, 1864.
9. Hopkins, 184–88. Potter, diary, June 3, 1864. *Providence Daily Journal,* June 20, 1864. *OR,* 36:933. *Revised Register,* 696–705.
10. William O. Harrington to Josiah Harrington, June 6, 1864, NSPL. Hopkins, 187–89. Peckham, "Recollections." *Providence Daily Journal,* June 20, 1864. *Providence Evening Press,* June 13, 1864.
11. Hopkins, 189–90. Jones, diary, June 15, 1864. Stephen Peckham to *Providence Journal,* June 17, 1864, RIHS. Woodbury, *Ninth Corps,* 405–06.
12. Allen, Service File. Jones, diary, June 18, 1864. *Narragansett Times,* September 30, 1864. Potter, diary, June 17, 1864. Woodbury, *Ninth Corps,* 409–11.
13. Ethan A. Jenks to Wife, June 27, 1864, RSG. Jenks, Service File.
14. *OR,* 40:565–66.
15. Charles F. Colvin to Brother, December 18, 1863, PVHS. June 20, 1864, Morning Report, RIHS. *OR,* 40:565–66.
16. William O. Harrington to Eunice Harrington, June 22, 1864, NSPL. *OR,* 40:565–66. Poore, 243. Woodbury, *Ninth Corps,* 413–14.
17. Henry Harkness, Service File, NA. Hopkins, 193–94. June 30, 1864, Morning Report, RIHS.
18. Billings, 217–19. Harrington, June 22, 1864. Hopkins, 322–25:346–347. *Memoirs of R.I.,* 161–63. Peckham, "Recollections." Woodbury, *Ninth Corps,* 519–20.
19. Allen, 273. Hopkins, 194–96. Jones, diary, July 4, 1864. Potter, diary, July 2, 1864.
20. Allen, 254–279. Jones, diary, June 30, 1864.
21. Allen, 281. Rhodes, 160–63. Peleg Jones diary is full of examples of passing time by completing math problems.
22. Woodbury, *Ninth Corps,* 421–24:581.
23. Woodbury, *Ninth Corps,* 425–33.
24. Allen, 280–82. Woodbury, *Ninth Corps,* 425–33.
25. Allen, 291–94. Hopkins, 198–201. Woodbury, *Ninth Corps,* 433–39.
26. Elisha R. Watson, "Memoirs," RSG.
27. Allen, 284–91. Jackman, 318–19. *OR,* 40:546–50. Woodbury, *Ninth Corps,* 439–43.
28. Allen, 284–91. *OR,* 40:546–50.
29. Allen, 284–91. Hopkins, 198–201. *OR,* 40:546–50. *Providence Journal,* February 11, 1938. Woodbury, *Ninth Corps,* 443–50.
30. Allen, 284–91. Hopkins, 198–201. *OR,* 40:546–50. *Providence Journal,* February 11, 1938. Woodbury, *Ninth Corps,* 443–50.
31. Jackman, 321–22. Woodbury, *Ninth Corps,* 449.
32. William O. Harrington to Eunice Harrington, July 31, 1864, NSPL. Stephen F. Peckham to Brother, July 31, 1864, RIHS. Potter, diary, July 30, 1864.
33. Allen, 294. *Memoirs of R.I.,* 199–206:227–240: 243–48:357–61. Buffum later joined the Regular Army and served with Bliss in Texas into the 1880's, when he committed suicide. Many believed the cause to be what is now termed post traumatic stress syndrome.
34. *Memoirs of R.I.,* 84–92. Woodbury, *Ninth Corps,* 451–62.
35. Hopkins, 202–09:313. Woodbury, *Ninth Corps,* 451–62.

Chapter 11

1. Woodbury, *Ninth Corps,* 466–68.
2. *Write Soon,* 65.
3. Allen, 295–96.
4. J. Rhodes, 325–29. William O. Harrington to Eunice Harrington, August 22, 1864, NSPL. Hopkins, 210–13: 417.
5. *Pleas excuse,* 90–93. All of the cemetery records are based on the author's visits to Hopkinton.
6. Allen, 295–308. Hopkins, 213. Emor Young to Martha Young, September 23, 1864, USAMHI. This is the only Emor Young letter at the USAMHI. All others are quoted from Kris VanDenBossche's *Write Soon and Give Me all the News.*
7. Allen, 308–15. *Revised Register,* 238.
8. William O. Harrington to Eunice Harrington, October 3, 1864, NSPL. Hopkins, 380. *OR,* 42:586–87.
9. Allen, 309–11.
10. Harrington, October 3, 1864. Hopkins, 215–17. *Memoirs of R.I.,* 223–24. Stephen F. Peckham to *Providence Journal,* November 2, 1864, RIHS. *OR,* 42:586–87. Potter, diary, Oct 1–3, 1864.
11. Allen, 309–10. Hopkins, 445–53: 466–73: 492–501.
12. Allen, 311–12.
13. E. Rhodes, 175–86. Jones, diary, October 20,

1864. During the war, Federal soldiers often gave "Three cheers and a tiger" when cheering. Rhode Islanders gave the three cheers, followed by a Narragansett Indian battle cry. Refer to Spicer, 318 and Jones' diary at the RIHS.
   14. Hopkins, 335–37. Stephen F. Peckham to Percy Daniels, November, ND, 1864, RIHS. Peckham, "Recollections." Peckham to *Providence Journal,* November 2, 1864. U.S. War Department to Stephen F. Peckham, May 25, 1865, RIHS. Unfortunately none of Daniels's writings survive, other than his reports in the *Official Records.* Daniels always praised the men under his command, but the evidence is overwhelming to support Stephen Peckham's claims that the colonel was "hated."
   15. William O. Harrington to Eunice Harrington, November 13, 1864, NSPL. Hopkins, 328–29. *Write Soon,* 65–66.
   16. Hopkins, 219–231.
   17. Hopkins, 219–231. Henry Young to Family, 1864, transcription in author's collection.
   18. Billings, 156–63.

Chapter 12

   1. Billings, 265–66. Potter, diary, November 29-December 4, 1864. Woodbury, *Ninth Corps,* 471–72.
   2. Potter, diary, December 4, 1864. Woodbury, *Ninth Corps,* 471–72.
   3. Hopkins, 358–59.
   4. Billings, 76–77. William O. Harrington to Eunice Harrington, December 15, 1864, NSPL.
   5. Hopkins, 235–237. Potter, diary, December 9–27, 1864. *Write Soon,* 66. Based upon two surviving 1853 Enfield rifle-muskets housed in private collections in Rhode Island, it is believed the Seventh's muskets were manufactured in 1862 by Tower and had "25–25" proof marks.
   6. Hopkins, 238–40. Potter, diary, January 1, 1865. *Write Soon,* 71.
   7. Allen 322–24. Harrington, December 15, 1864. Hopkins, 239–41. Charles P. Nye to Benjamin Pendleton, January 15, 1865, RIHS. Potter, diary, January 8–20, 1864.
   8. Woodbury, *Ninth Corps,* 472–73. *Write Soon,* 69–70.
   9. Hopkins, 232–33. Charles P. Nye to Benjamin Pendleton, February, 6, 1865, RIHS. Potter, diary, February 13, 1865. E. Rhodes, 212.
   10. Allen, 331–32. Hopkins, 232–33.
   11. E. Rhodes, 179–80:190:212. Hopkins, 241. *Revised Register,* 748–49. David G. Sherman to Jacob Dunnell, June 23, 1865, RIHS.
   12. William O. Harrington to Eunice Harrington, February 19, 1865, NSPL. Hopkins, 244–46: 289. Jones, diary, January-March, 1865.
   13. Hopkins, 246–47: 287–90. Aldrich C. Kenyon to Respected Friend, March 15, 1865, RIHS.
   14. Hopkins, 247–49.
   15. Allen, 343–344. John N. Barber to Clare Barber, March 15, 1865, RIHS. Potter, diary, March 24–30, 1865. Woodbury, *Ninth Corps,* 476–81.

Chapter 13

   1. Allen, 338. *Write Soon,* 74–74.
   2. Allen, 348.
   3. E. Rhodes, 216–19.

   4. Allen, 348–50. Jones, diary, April 2, 1865. Hopkins, 256–60. Potter, diary, April 2, 1865. *Write Soon,* 73.
   5. Hopkins, 416.
   6. William R.D. Blackwood to A.S. Burdick, February 6, 1907, USAMHI. *Memoirs of R.I.,* 362. *Write Soon,* 144–45.
   7. Allen, 352–53. William O. Harrington to Eunice Harrington, April 3, 1865, NSPL. *Write Soon,* 73–74.
   8. Hopkins, 263–64:327–28. Potter, diary, April 2–3:8, 1865. *Providence Journal,* February 11, 1938.
   9. Allen, 354–7. Potter, diary, April 9, 1865
   10. Allen, 358–60. William O. Harrington to Eunice Harrington, April 19, 1865, NSPL. *Write Soon,* 75.
   11. Allen, 361. Hopkins, 270–71. Jones, diary, May 31, 1865. Charles P. Nye to Benjamin Pendleton, May 18, 1865, RIHS. Potter, diary, May 15, 1865.
   12. Joshua L. Chamberlain, *The Passing of the Armies.* [New York: Bantam Books, 1993], 246–55. Jones, diary, May 23, 1865. Nye, May 18, 1865. Potter, diary, May 23–24, 1865.
   13. John N. Barber to Clare Barber, May 30, 1865, RIHS. Charles F. Colvin to Brother, June, 1865, PVHS. William O. Harrington to Eunice Harrington, May 21, 1865 NSPL. George H. Lewis to Benjamin Pendleton, May 11, 1865.
   14. Harrington, May 21, 1865. Hopkins, 296–98. J. Rhodes, 349. Potter, diary, June 6–9, 1865.

Chapter 14

   1. Hopkins, 298–301. Jones, diary, June 13, 1865.
   2. Jones, diary, June 21, 1865. June 8, 1865, Morning Report, RIHS. Seventh Rhode Island Volunteers, Regimental Books, RISA. These and all other casualty figures herein are based upon the author's research. Sources include the *Revised Register,* Hopkins' roster, and cemetery visits.
   3. Allen, 364–68.
   4. Hopkins, 293:304. The flags of the Seventh are now at the Rhode Island State House, being placed there in 1903. They have severely decomposed under less than ideal storage conditions. Unfortunately there is no money available to preserve these cherished banners.
   5. Hopkins, 394–95. *Narragansett Times,* September 12, 1862 and June 2, 1865. The memorial is now at the Narragansett Town Hall.
   6. Hopkins, 310–14. William Sprague to Martha Bliss, January 4, 1900, RIHS.
   7. Hopkins, 322–25:347.
   8. Hopkins, 335–37. Peckham, "Recollections."
   9. *Pleas excuse,* 95. *Write soon,* 76.
   10. Hopkins, 338–39: 358–359.
   11. Foster Town Records.
   12. Hopkins, 393.
   13. Hopkins, 391–92:398–99.
   14. State of Rhode Island, *Report of the Rhode Island-Vicksburg Monument Commission to the General Assembly.* [Providence: Snow & Farnham, 1909]
   15. Hopkins, 306–309:392. *Narragansett Times,* September 10, 1897.
   16. Burgess, *Scituate.* Nichols Post Records, Grand Army of the Republic Papers, RIHS.
   17. Jay S. Hoar, *New England's Last Civil War Veterans.* [Arlington T.X.: Seacliffe Press, 1976], 15–17. *Providence Journal,* April 21, 1939.

Bibliography

The following is the bibliography of works used in the research for this book, limited to those primary and secondary sources directly relating to the Seventh Rhode Island Volunteers and used in this project. The most important of these works are those manuscripts and printed primary sources written by the men who served in the ranks of the regiment and fought in the Civil War. Without these sources, this work would not have been possible. In addition, this author is indebted to the many authors who have contributed with their scholarly secondary sources to the understanding of the campaigns the Seventh Rhode Island was engaged in. These books are cited here, and in the bibliography rather than in the notes. The reason for this is to direct the reader to the primary sources, from which the history of the Seventh Rhode Island is best told.

Stephen Sears, *To the Gates of Richmond*, provided the necessary information for McClellan's Peninsula Campaign and to understand the general background into why the Seventh Rhode Island was activated.

William Marvel's *Burnside* gave invaluable material into the commander the Seventh served under and his plans for the Battle of Fredericksburg. In addition it gave an excellent overview into the origins of the Ninth Corps and its battles.

Francis O'Reilly's *The Fredericksburg Campaign: Winter War on the Rappahannock* is the best source for material pertaining to the 1862 Rappahannock Campaign. In addition, Joseph H. Alexander's essay on the defense of Marye's Heights provided insight into the Confederate view of the battle and the terrain and conditions the Seventh attacked.

The Final Fortress: The Siege and Campaign of Vicksburg, 1862–1863 by Samuel Carter III provided the best views into the origins, strategies, and ultimate victory in the Mississippi Campaign.

Of all of the books on the Overland Campaign, none were of more value to the understanding of the campaign than Gordon Rhea's four volume set. In these volumes, Rhea presents a balanced account of the forty days of continuous action between the Federal and Confederate forces.

The Petersburg Campaign is best understood in two parts. William Marvel's *The Horrid Pit* gives an excellent account of the beginning of the campaign to its climax at the Battle of the Crater. Richard J. Sommers' *Richmond Redeemed* provides vital information on Grant's assaults in September and October of 1864, including the Battles of Weldon Railroad, Poplar Spring Church, and Hatcher's Run.

The storming of Petersburg and subsequent retreat to Appomattox are understood through William Marvel's *Lee's Last Retreat*.

Three other volumes provide excellent background into the Seventh Rhode Island. Daniel P. Jones, *The Economic & Social Transformation of Rural Rhode Island, 1780–1850*, gives the necessary background into the communities that many of the men left behind, including religious and socio-economic affairs. Time Life Books, *Echoes of Glory*, provided illustrations and descriptions of the equipment used by both Confederate and Federal forces. In addition Gregory Coco's *The Civil War Infantryman: In camp, on the March, and in Battle* gives a good overview of the training, equipping and life of the Civil War infantryman.

Manuscripts and Unpublished Material

Allen, Edward T. Service File. NA.
Austin, John F. Letters. RIHS.
Barber, John N. Letters. RIHS.
Bliss, Zenas R. Memoirs. USAMHI.

Boss, W.A. "Lines on the Death of J. Weeden Burdick." LPL.
Brown, Samuel G. Service and Pension Files. NA.
Colvin, Charles F. Letters. PVHS.
Cottam, William. "Affidavit of Fredericksburg." FRSP.
Foster Town Records. Town Clerks Office. Foster, Rhode Island.
Fourth Rhode Island Volunteers. Regimental Books and Papers. RISA.
Grand Army of the Republic, Department of Rhode Island. Records. RIHS
Greenman, Horace. Letters. RIHS.
Harkness, Henry. Service File. NA.
Harris, James. Letters and Papers. RIHS.
Harrington, William O. Letters. NSPL.
Hopkinton Town Records. Town Clerks Office, Hopkinton, Rhode Island.
Kenyon, Aldrich C. Letters. RIHS.
Kenyon, David R. Letters. LPL.
Knight, Alfred S. Letters. RSG.
Knight, Alfred S. Service File. NA.
Knight, Almon. "Lines on the Death of Alfred S. Knight." RSG.
Knight Papers. RSG.
Jenks, Ethan A. Letters. RSG.
Jenks, Ethan A. Service File. NA.
Jones, Peleg G. Diary and Letters. RIHS and USAMHI.
Jordan, William. Letters. RIHS.
Lewis, George H. Letters. RIHS.
Lewis, Nathan B. Letters. PHS.
Low, Nathaniel. Letters. RSG.
Longstreet, Frank. Letters. HL and USAMHI.
Manchester, T.A. "Experiences of Fredericksburg." FRSP.
Nye, Charles P. Letters. RIHS.
Peckham, Peleg. Letters. LPL, RSG, and USAMHI.
Peckham, Stephen F. Letters and Remembrances. RIHS.
Peckham, Stephen F. "Recollections of a Hospital Steward during the Civil War." NHS.
Potter, Jared J. Diary. USAMHI.
Rathbun, Nathan. Service File. NA.
Remington, James. Letters and Papers. RIHS.
Sayles, Welcome B. Letters. HL.
Scituate Town Records. Town Clerks Office. Scituate, Rhode Island.
Seventh Rhode Island Volunteers. Regimental Books and Papers. RIHS.
Seventh Rhode Island Volunteers. Regimental Books and Papers. RISA.
Sherman, David G. Letters. RIHS.
Slocum, Charles. Letters. RIHS.
Soldiers and Sailors Historical Society. Papers. RIHS.
Spencer, George A. Letters. USAMHI and RSG.
Spooner, Henry J. Letters. RIHS.
Tobey, Thomas F. Letters. HL.
Twelfth Rhode Island Volunteers. Regimental Books and Papers. RIHS.
Twelfth Rhode Island Volunteers. Regimental Books and Papers. RISA.
Watson, Elisha. Letters and Memoirs. In private hands.
Wells, Benjamin. Letters. RIHS.
Wilder, Frank J. Letters. RSG.
Winsor, Albert A. Letters. FPS.
Young, Emor. Letters. USAMHI.

Printed Primary Sources

Allen, George H. *Forty-Six Months in the Fourth Rhode Island Volunteers.* Providence: J.A. & R.A. Reid Printers, 1887.
Babbitt, Julia Emily. *Sketch of Major Jacob Babbitt: 7th Rhode Island Regiment.* Bristol, R.I.: NP, 1890.
Billings, John D. *Hardtack and Coffee: The Unwritten Story of Army Life.* Lincoln: Nebraska University Press, 1993.
Bliss, William McCarter. *My Life in the Irish Brigade.* Edited by Kevin E. O'Brien. El Dorado Hills, C.A.: Savas Publishing, 1996
Burgess, Gideon A. *The Owen Soldiers Monument, North Scituate, Rhode Island.* North Scituate, R.I.: E.F. Sibley, 1913.
Burlingame, John K. *History of the Fifth Regiment, Rhode Island Heavy Artillery.* Providence: Snow & Farnum, 1892.
Carpenter, George B. "War and Other Remembrances." Edited by Kris VanDenBossche. in *Rhode Island History,* November, 1989.
Casey, Silas. *Infantry Tactics.* Washington D.C.: N.P., 1862.
Chamberlain, Joshua L. *The Passing of the Armies.* New York: Bantam Books, 1993.
Chenery, William. *The Fourteenth Regiment Rhode Island Heavy Artillery in the War to Preserve the Union.* New York: Negro University Press, 1960.
Cogswell, Leander. *A History of the Eleventh New Hampshire Regiment Volunteer Infantry in the Rebellion War: 1861–1865.* Concord: Republican Press Association, 1891.
Dinman, George W. *Autobiography and Sketches of My Travels by Sea and Land.* Bristol, R.I.: Bristol Press, 1896.
Grant, Joseph W. *The Flying Regiment: Journal of the Twelfth Regiment Rhode Island Volunteers.* Providence: S.S. Rider, 1865.
Hinman, Wilbur. *Corporal Si Klegg and His Pard.* Cleveland: Williams Publishing, 1887.
A History of the Ninth Regiment New Hampshire Volunteers in the War of the Rebellion. Edited by Edward O. Lord. Concord: Republican Press Association, 1895.
History of the Twelfth Regiment Rhode Island Volunteers in the Civil War: 1862–1863. Compiled by

Pardon E. Tillinghast. Providence: Snow & Farnum, 1892.
Hopkins, William P. *The Seventh Regiment Rhode Island Volunteers in the Civil War, 1862–1865.* Providence: Snow & Farnum, 1903.
Jackman, Lyman. *History of the Sixth New Hampshire Regiment in the War for the Union.* Concord: Republican Press Association, 1891.
Memoirs of Rhode Island Officers: Who were engaged in the service of their Country during the Great Rebellion with the South. Edited by John R. Bartlett. Providence: Rider, 1867.
McInnes, Hugh. *Civil War Letters.* Parsons, W.V.: McClain Publishing, 1981.
Miller, William. "A hot day on Marye's Heights." in *Battles and Leaders of the Civil War: Volume III.* New York: Century, 1885.
Morris, Curtis J., and State of Rhode Island. *The Monument in Memory of the Rhode Island Soldiers and Sailors Who Fell Victims to the Rebellion.* Providence: Urban League of R.I., 1971.
Pleas excuse all bad writing: A documentary history of Rhode Island during the Civil War era 1861–1865. Edited by Kris VanDenBossche. Peace Dale, R.I.: Rhode Island Historical Document Transcription Project, 1993.
Revised Register of Rhode Island Volunteers. Providence: E.L. Freemanton, 1893.
Revised Regulations for the Army of the United States. Philadelphia: G.L.B. Brown, 1861
Rhodes, Elisha Hunt. *All for the Union: The Civil War Diary and Letters of Elisha Hunt Rhodes.* Edited by Robert Hunt Rhodes. New York: Random House, 1985.
Rhodes, John H. *History of Battery B, First Rhode Island Light Artillery.* Providence: Snow & Farnum, 1894.
Seventh Rhode Island Volunteers. *Exhibition of the Vicksburg Statue.* Providence: N.P., 1908.
Spicer, William A. *The History of the Ninth and Tenth Regiments of Rhode Island Volunteers and the Tenth Rhode Island Battery in the Union Army in 1862.* Providence: Snow & Farnum, 1892.
Spooner, Henry J. *The Maryland Campaign with the Fourth Rhode Island.* Providence: Snow & Farnum, 1903.
State of Rhode Island. *Report of the Rhode Island-Vicksburg Monument Commission to the General Assembly.* Providence: Snow & Farnham, 1909.
Stone, Edwin W. *Rhode Island in the Rebellion.* Providence: Knowles, Anthony, 1864.
Sumner, George C. *History of Battery D, First Rhode Island Light Artillery in the Civil War: 1861–1865.* Providence: Snow & Farnum, 1897.
Town of Scituate. *Tax Book.* Phenix, R.I.: John H. Campbell Book and Job Printer, 1865.
Voices of the Civil War: Letters and Journal Excerpts of South Kingstown Men in the Union Army, 1861–63. Edited by Shirley L. Barrett. South Kingstown, R.I.: Pettequamscutt Historical Society, 1992.
War of the Rebellion: A Compilation of the Official Records of the Union and Confederate Armies. Washington D.C.: Government Printing Office, 1880–1901. 128 Volumes.
Wren, James. *Captain James Wren's Diary: From New Bern to Fredericksburg.* Edited by John Michael Priest. Shippensburg, P.A.: White Mane Books, 1990.
Write Soon and give me all the news. Edited by Kris VanDenBossche. Peace Dale, R.I.: Rhode Island Historical Document Transcription Project, 1993.
Woodbury, Augustus. *Major General Ambrose E. Burnside and the Ninth Army Corps: A narrative of campaigns in North Carolina, Maryland, Virginia, Ohio, Kentucky, Mississippi in the war for the preservation of the Republic.* Providence: Rider, 1867.
Woodbury, Augustus. *A Narrative of the Campaign of the First Rhode Island Regiment in the Spring and Summer of 1861.* Providence: Rider, 1862.
Woodbury, Augustus. *The Uprising of 1861: The Illustration of True Patriotism.* Providence: Snow & Farnum, 1895.

Secondary Sources

Allan, Thomas. *The Kentish Guards: A History.* East Greenwich, R.I.: NP, 1918.
Alexander, Joseph H. "Defending Marye's Heights" in *With my Face to the Enemy: Perspectives on the Civil War.* Edited by Robert Cowley. New York: Putnam, 2001.
Carter, Samuel III. *The Final Fortress: The Siege and Campaign of Vicksburg, 1862–1863.* Wilmington: Broadfoot Publishing, 1988.
Cavanaugh, Michael A. and William Marvel. *The Horrid Pit: The Battle of the Crater, June 25-August 6, 1864.* Lynchburg, V.A.: H.L. Howard, 1989.
Coco, Gregory A. *The Civil War Infantryman: In Camp, on the March, and in Battle.* Gettysburg, P.A.: Thomas Publications, 1996.
Hartwig, Scott. "The Volunteers of '62 in the Maryland Campaign," *The Antietam Campaign.* Edited by Gary W. Gallagher. Chapel Hill, N.C.: University of North Carolina Press, 1999.
Hoar, Jay S. *New England's Last Civil War Veterans.* Arlington T.X.: Seacliffe Press, 1976.
Jones, Daniel P. *The Economic & Social Transformation of Rural Rhode Island, 1780–1850.* Boston: Northeastern University Press, 1992.
Marvel, William. *Burnside.* Chapel Hill: The University of North Carolina Press, 1991.

Marvel, William. *Lee's Last Retreat: The Flight to Appomattox.* Chapel Hill: The University of North Carolina Press, 2006.

Marvel, William. *Race of the Soil: The Ninth New Hampshire Regiment in the Civil War.* Wilmington: Broadfoot Publishing, 1988.

Poore, Benjamin P. *The Life and Public Services of Ambrose E. Burnside.* Providence: J.A. & R.A. Reid, 1882.

Pride, Mike and Mark Travis. *My Brave Boys: To War with Colonel Cross and the Fighting Fifth.* Hanover N.H.: University Press of New England, 2001.

O' Reilly, Francis A. *The Fredericksburg Campaign: Winter War on the Rappahannock.* Baton Rouge: Louisiana State University Press, 2003.

Rhea, Gordon. *The Battle of the Wilderness: May 5–6, 1864.* Baton Rouge: Louisiana State University Press, 1994.

Rhea, Gordon. *The Battles for Spotsylvania Court House and the Road to Yellow Tavern: May 7–12, 1864.* Baton Rouge: Louisiana State University Press, 1997.

Rhea, Gordon. *Cold Harbor: Grant and Lee, May 26–June 3, 1864.* Baton Rouge: Louisiana State University Press, 2002.

Rhea, Gordon. *To the North Anna River: Grant and Lee, May 13–25, 1864.* Baton Rouge: Louisiana State University Press, 2000.

Sears, Stephen W. *George B. McClellan: The Young Napoleon.* New York: Ticknor and Fields, 1988.

Sears, Stephen W. *To the Gates of Richmond: The Peninsula Campaign.* New York: Ticknor and Fields, 1992.

Smith, Hedley. *History of Scituate, Rhode Island.* C.T.: Racine Publishing, 1976.

Sommers, Richard J. *Richmond Redeemed: The Siege of Petersburg.* New York: Doubleday, 1981.

Time Life Books. *Echoes of Glory: Arms and Equipment of the Union.* Edited by Henry A. Woodhead. Alexandria: Time Life Books, 1995.

Wilkinson, Warren. *Mother, May you never see the sights I have seen: The Fifty-Seventh Massachusetts Veteran Volunteers in the Last Year of the Civil War.* New York: Harper & Row, 1990.

Wood, Squire. *A History of Greene and Vicinity: 1845–1929.* Providence: NP, 1936.

Newspapers

Narragansett Times
Providence Daily Journal
Providence Journal
Providence Evening Press

Index

Numbers in ***bold italics*** indicate pages with photographs.

Alexander, Hartford 42, 92, 112
Allen, Edward T. 40, 54, 64, 74–75, 79, 83, 101, 107, 114, ***115***, 152, 161
Allen, Edwin R. 22–23, ***141***, 161–***162***
Allen, George H. 27, 57, 120, 122, 128–129, ***130***, 150
Antietam, Battle of 19, 24, 27, 120, 124, 132
Appomattox Court House 152–153
Arnold, Job 65, 83–84, 87–***88***
Ashaway, RI 6, 14, 30, 130
Ashland, RI ***12***, 26, 160
Austin, Benjamin R. 14, 97
Austin, John F. 16, 19, 22–23, 25–27, 29, 32–33, 40, 46–47, 54, 160

Babbitt, Jacob 9, ***10***, 13, 29, 38, 44, ***45***, 47
Ballou, Daniel 43
Barber, Jesse N. ***48***
Barber, John N. 148, 155
Barstow, William 11, 14, ***27***, 75, 111–112, 141
Battle Honors 159
Bennet, George 166
Bennett, Lyman 15, 50
Bentley, William 67
Bethesda Church, Battle of 111–114
Bisbee, William 147
Blackwood, William R.D. ***151***, 152
Bliss, Zenas R. 1, ***8***, 9, 13–15, 17, 20, 22–23, 28–29, 32, 34, 38, 40, 42–45, 48, 50, 54, 62, 66, 69, 74, 76, 78, 86, 92, 95, 114, 122, 125–127, ***158***, 160–161
Bolles, Albert A. 101
Bombproofs 129, 143
Bounties 12–13, 86–88
Boyden, Decatur M. 93
Bradbury, John 42
Briggs, George 30
Briggs, James A. 73–74
Briggs, Lemuel ***85***
Briggs, Richard 40

Bristol, RI 9, 47
Brown, Albert 59, 160
Brown, Joshua 59, 160
Brown, Samuel G. 68
Brown University 8, 16, 137
Browning, Charles O. 101
Buffum, Martin P. 122, 125, 126
Bull Run, First Battle of 8, 10, 15
Burdick, J. Weeden 14, 76, 97
Burke, Patrick 97
Burnside, Ambrose E. 8, 23–24, ***25***, 29, 32–33, 38, 45, 48, 58, 62, 67, 82, 88–92, 121–127, 156
Burrillville, RI 14–15

Cairo, IL 68, 78
Cameron, Uz 69
Camp Bliss 7, 13–14, 16–17
Camp Casey 20, 22
Camp Denison 82
Camp Mud 34, 38, 50, 54, 60
Camp Mud II 85
Carey, Ned 120
Carpenter, James ***157***
Carr, Jesse ***87***
Carr, Thomas 32, 50
Casey, Silas 19, ***20***
Casey's Tactics 20–***21***
Casualties 46, 76, 98, 103, 113, 117, 126, 133, 152, 158
Chappell, Winfield S. 79, 104
Chepachet, RI 137–138
Church, George E. 1, 19, 32, 36, ***37***, 50, 60, 62
Clarke, Jonathan 74
Clarke, Stephen A. 132
Clarke, William E. 130
Cold Harbor, VA 105, 109, 111, 113
Cole, Darius I. 14, 98, 104, 106
Cole, Henry S. 42
Colley, Thomas ***47***
Collins, Gideon F. 26
Colvin, Charles F. 26, 55, 59, 117, 155
Coman, William 36, 47
Companies 14, 69

Company A 14, ***15***, 26, 56, 60, 67, 73, 75, 100, 155, 161
Company B 14, 74, 112
Company C 14, 32
Company D 15, 32, 51, 75, 105, 112, 139
Company E 15, 23
Company F 15, 40, 112
Company G 15–16, 46, 74, 86
Company H 16, 30, 100, 117
Company I 16, 32, 144
Company K 14, 16, 23, 26, 59, 82, 109
Congdon, George W. 75, 112
Congdon, Oliver 75
Consolidation 134–135
Cooke's NC Brigade 42, 112
Corey, Charles G. 10, 81, 95, 115
Corps Badges 90
Costello, George B. 146
Coventry, RI 16, 104
Covill, George W. 117
Crandall, Davis 130
Crandall, Elisha K. ***57***
Crater, Battle of the 122–127
Crowley, Michael W. 98
Cumberland River Campaign
Cundall, Edward 14, 66, 80
Cundall, Isaac 14, 20, 48, 53, 56, 63, 66–67, 80, 104, 106, 161
Cundall, Tryphena 14, 26, 30, 48, 56–57, 60, 66, 86, 104, 106, 130, 161
Curtin, John I. 95, 109, 111, 120, 140, 150, 155
Curtis, Joseph B. 44–45, 126

Daniels, Percy 15, ***17***, 54, 71, 82, 90, 97, 100, ***101***, 102–104, 111, 112, 113, 117, 119, 125, 126, 132–135, 137–140, 143–144, 146, 150–156, 161
Desertion 14, 28–29, 143–144
Dingley, Fuller 75
Disease 30, 35, 71, 76–77, 82
Dorr, Thomas W. 7
Dorr Rebellion 7

Index

Dowd, Oliver 44, *46*
Draft 80–81, 145–146
Durfee, George N. 16
Durfee, Gilbert 16, 50
Dyer, Cyrus 41

East Greenwich, RI 16, 100, 117
Eighth US Infantry 9
Eleventh NH Infantry 22, 25, 89
Emancipation Proclamation 52–53
Enfield rifle-musket 16, 32
Entrenchments *109*, 117, 119–120
Exeter, RI 15, 112

Falmouth, VA 32
Farnum, Samuel *61*
Farrow, Enos 26
Ferrero, Edward 38, 40, 121, 127
Field, George W. 125
Fifth RI Infantry/Heavy Artillery 11, 65, 80
Fifty-First NY Infantry 40, 42, 44, 125
Fifty-Eighth MA Infantry 107, 124
First RI Artillery 22, 150, 155
First RI Infantry 7, 42, 57
Flags 18, 44, *51*, 53–54, 139, 159
Flaherty, Michael 112
Follansbee, Nathan G. 101
Fort Hell 140–152, *141–142*
Fort Mahone/Fort Damnation 140, 144–146, 150–151
Forty-Eighth PA Infantry 24, 82, 89, 121, 127, 140
Forty-Fifth PA Infantry 89
Foster, RI 12, 16, 42, 104, 112
Fourteenth RI Heavy Artillery 64–65
Fourth RI Infantry 26–27, 44, 55, 57, 88, 120, 122–126, 132–135 140–141, 159
Franklin, Chester L. 105
Franklin, William 33
Frederick, MD 22–23
Fredericksburg, Battle of 35–48
Fredericksburg, VA 33, 103

Gardiner, George W. 26, 130
Gavitt, Edwin D. 130
Gavitt, James W. 111, 146
Gaylord, William 10
Glocester, RI 14
Godfrey, Henry 34, 76, *77*, 130
Gonsolve, Franklin *53*
Grand Army of the Republic 164–166
Grand Review 154–155
Grant, Ira 112
Grant, Ulysses S. 63, 67, 69, 74, 76, 88–91, 104, 106, 115, 121, 132, 144, 149
Greene, Charles B. 22–23, *24*, 30, 130
Greene, Charles T. 42
Greene, Edwin 22
Greene, Jedidiah 47
Greene, Thomas 42, 52
Greene, RI 12
Greenman, Horace 32
Griffin, Simon G. 66, 76, 78, 89
Guerrillas 64, 69, 82

Halleck, Henry 56
Hancock, Winfield S. 127
Hanning, Robert 113
Harkness, Henry *118*
Harrington, Eunice and family 16, 25, 34, 48, 129–130, 143, 161
Harrington, Josiah V. 18, 49, 80, 113, 129–130, 143, 161
Harrington, William O. 16, 18, 25, 34, 43, 48–49, 54, 56, 59–60, 65–67, 72, 73, 77, 80, 82–83, 85–86, 92, 104, 106, 109, 111, 112, 113, 118, 126, 129–130, 133–134, 138, 143, 146, 152, 153, 155, 161–*162*
Harris, James 10, *11*, 35, 57, 95, 137
Harris House Hospital 95, 97, 103
Hartranft, John 76, 148
Hay, John 15, 90
Healey, Horace *71*
Hoard, James *135*
Hodson, James 113
Holbrook, Joseph H. 76
Hooker, Joseph 29, 33, 58–59
Hopkins, Charles 15, *58*
Hopkins, Darius 82
Hopkins, William P. 15, 29, 57, 65–66, 77–78, 81, *84*, 85, 93, 107, 113, 119, 125, 145, 150–151, 161–162
Hopkins Hollow, RI 16
Hopkinton Academy 12
Hopkinton, RI 12, 30, 34, 77, 151
Hospitals 34–35, 81–82
Howard, Harris 10, 26, 45, 65, 69, 79
Hull, John K. 15, 22–23, 26, 33, 51, 56, 60, 63–64, 67–69, 71, 74–*75*, 160
Hunt, Edwin L. 113, 150
Huts 34–35, 54–*55*

Inman, George B. 15, 45, *58*

Jackman, Lyman 71, 100–101, 122, 126
Jackson, Thomas J. "Stonewall" 7, 14, 35
Jackson, Battle of 74–78
James River 115
Jenks, Alonzo 43, *69*, 161
Jenks, Ethan 43, 73, 87, 97, *99*, 101, 107, 111, 113, 115–117, 119, 129, 133, 136, 146, 152–155, 161
Johnston, William *52*
Johnston, RI 9
Jones, John P. *53*
Jones, Peleg I. 16, 18–19, 78, 97, 104, 115, 120–121, 146, 150
Jordan, William H. 85
Joslin, Benjamin 156
Joyce, William 75
Joyeaux, Augustus 15, 97

Kellen, Charles H. 42, *44*
Kentucky Campaign 84–88
Kenyon, Abel B. 14, 42, 75–76
Kenyon, Aldrich C. 146
Kenyon, David R. 53, 65–67, 80, 83, 85–86, 101
Kenyon, James G. 115
Kenyon, Joseph J. 34, *35*, 130

Kenyon, Thomas R. 78
Kerr, Michael 41
Knight, Alfred S. 14–15, 18–19, 43, 46, 54, 57–58, *159*, 164
Knight, Jabez 16
Knowles, Charles K. 43

Lane, John P. *48*
Last veterans 165–166
Leavens, Lewis 14, 30, 38, 47, 50
Ledlie, James 121–122, 127
Lee, Robert E. 35, 92, 104, 106
Lewis, Edward S. 104
Lewis, George H. 155
Lewis, Nathan B. 15, 46, 112, *114*, 162, 164
Lexington, KY 64
Lillibridge, Amos 100
Lincoln, Abraham 11, 29, 83, 91, 120, 135–136, 138, 153
Linton, Jonathan 101
Low, Nathaniel 68, 73–74
Luther, John W. 97

Malone, John 52
Manchester, Isaac B. 17
Manchester, Joseph 42–*43*
Marcoux, Joseph 43
Marye's Heights, Defenses of 35–36
Matthewson, Calvin R. 40
Matthewson, Nicholas W. 40
Mauran, Edward C. 112
Maxon, Joel C. 76, 130
McClellan, George B. 19, 27–29, 135–136
McDonough, John 114
McIlroy, Samuel 112, 133–134
McInnes, Hugh 26
McKay, John *118*, 119
McKinley, William 1
McNaulty, Hugh 105
Meade, George G. 92, 122, 126
Medal of Honor 1, 42, 125, 150, 152, 160–161
Merrill, James F. *147*
Mitchell, Charlton 40, 44
Monument in MS 161–164, *163*
Moore, Winthrop A. *41*, 45, 52
Moosup Valley, RI 60
Morgan, John H. 64, 82
Morse, Henry 91
Morse, William 101
Morton, Joseph W. 12
Mud March 57–58
Murray, Adams 68
Muster in 16–17

Nagle, James 24, 40, 42, 47, 65–66, 127
Narragansett Guards 25
Narragansett Indians 153
Natick Guards 8
National Guard 8
Newport News, VA 60–61
Ninth Corps 23–24, 33, 38, 60, 63–64, 73, 74, 82, 88–90, 97, 107, 117–118, 121–128, 143, 148, 154–155
Ninth NH Infantry 24, 38, 40, 82, 89, 111

Index

Ninth RI Infantry 8, 13, 26
North Anna River, Battle of 103–105
North Kingstown, RI 15, 112
Northrup, William R. 38
Nye, Charles P. 26, 59, 82–83, 144, 153
Nye, Isaac 100, 104

One Hundred and Twenty-Seventh PA Infantry 44
Open, Manuel 75, 100

Page, Charles 9, 38, 43
Paint Lick, KY 65
Palmer, Elisha 80
Parke, John G. 66, *137*, 154
Paul, Gabriel 19
Pawtucket Light Infantry 8
Pay 28, 55, 62
Payne, Abraham 157
Peckham, Benjamin 78
Peckham, Peleg E. 14, 41, 53–54, 56, 62, 65, 78, 81–83, 85–86, 101, 104–105, 109, 111, 113, 119, 141, *150*, 151–152, 160
Peckham, Stephen F. 10, 13, 34, 38, 42, 63, 65, 74, 76, 80, 81, 87, 90, 95, 103–104, 111, 114, 119, 126, 133, *136*, 137
Perkins, Benjamin *121*
Perkins, Palmer G. 112
Perry, Albert 67, 78
Petersburg, storming of 149–152
Petersburg Campaign 115–121
Petersburg Mine 121–122
Phillips, Oliver J. 166
Picket Duty 29, 56, 130
Pleasant Valley, MD 24–27
Pleasants, Henry 121–122
Pollock, William J. 44
Poplar Spring Church, Battle of 131–133, *134*
Portsmouth Grove Hospital 10
Potter, Francis W. 98
Potter, George 16, 41, 54, 56, 118, 133, 143
Potter, James N. 54, 88
Potter, Jared J. 15, 75, 86, 89, 107, 113, 126, 150, 152–153
Potter, John 15
Potter, Robert B. 66–*67*, 101, 120, 121, 127
Potter, Roswell H. 76
Pray, Esais 97
Promotions 119
Providence Journal 100, 111, 136–137
Providence, RI 14

Rathbun, George *129*
Rathbun, Nathan 75, *78*
Rathbun, William 44, *46, 159*
Rations 22, 33, 61
Recruiting 12, 14–16
Reeve, Isaac 9
Regimental History 164

Remington, James 16, 26, 28–29, *30*, 33, 43, 49–50, 117
Return home 156–158
Reunions 164–166
Reynolds, Edward S. 111
Rhodes, Elisha H. 145
Rice, George E. 23
Rice, Samuel E. 100
Richmond, RI 15, 130
Richmond, VA 114
Roberts, Henry 23
Robinson, James 100
Rockville, RI 14, 76, 97
Rodman, Isaac P. 8, 19, 126
Rodman, Rowland G. 15, 19, 43, 50
Roemer's NY Battery (34th NY) 32, 84, 132–133
Rowley, John H. 107

Salisbury, Alpheus 76
Saunders, Isaac N. 14
Sayles, Welcome B. *6*, 7, 18–19, 38, 41, 44–45, 47
Scituate, RI 11–12, 16
Seamens, John 30
Second MD Infantry 24, 38, 139
Second RI Infantry 80, 106, 120
Seventh Day Baptists 12, 14, 26
Seventh ME Battery 146
Shelter Tents 25
Sherman, David G. 146
Sherman, William T. 144, 147, 153
Simmons, George 74, 97, 106
Simpson, Samuel F. 9, 100, *104*
Sisson, Benjamin T. 97
Sixth NH Infantry 24, 41, 73–74
Slaves 29, 65, 83
Slocum, Charles 61
Slocum, Horace *138*
Slocum, John S. 8, 47
Smith, Albert L. 81
Smith, Daniel B. 100
Smith, James Y. 80, 119, 144
South Kingstown, RI 15–16, 74, 106–107, 160
Spencer, James B. *62*
Spooner, Henry J. 137, 145
Spotsylvania, Battle of 94–104
Sprague, Albert G. 10, *93*, 95
Sprague, William 6, *7*, 8, 47
Stanhope, John R. 37, 54, 66
Steadman, Harrison 79
Steere, William H.P. 8, 126
Stevenson, Thomas G. 95
Stone, George N. 44, 82, 113, 136
Stoothoff, Samuel B. 100, 105, 139
Straight, Potter 112
Studley, John 16, 40
Sturgis, Samuel 24, 40
Sullivan, John 50, 75, 145, 152
Sumner, Edwin V. 33, 51

Taylor, Joseph 70–71, *128*, 129
Taylor, Richard E. 150–151
Tenth RI Infantry 8–9, 13, 15

Third RI Cavalry 80
Thirty-Fifth MA Infantry 25, 32, 74, 156
Thirty-Sixth MA Infantry 125, 127, 140
Tinsdale, Henry 74
Tobey, Thomas F. 15, 23, 50, 68, 79, 87, 90–*91*
Tompkins, Charles 37
Tourgee, William *81*
Tower, John K. 30
Turner, Chester T. 7
Twelfth NH Infantry 38
Twelfth RI Infantry 38, 40, 55, 67
Twiggs, Daniel 9

Uniforms 13, 16, 66
US Colored Troops 89–90, 122, 140

Veterans Reserve Corps 46, 90
Vicksburg Campaign 68–74
Vicksburg, MS 68

Warwick, RI 16, 82, 117
Watson, Elisha R. 124–125, *165*–166
Webster, John 75
Weigand, Frederic 20, 74, 97
Weldon, William 111
Weldon Railroad, Battle of 128–129
Wells, Benjamin E. 62
Wells, Horace 20
Welsh, James 125
Westerly Rifles 8, 14
Wheaton, Frank 8
Whitcomb, Lyman 99
White Sulphur Springs, Battle of 32–33
Wilbur, George 41, 66, 78, 83, 113, 132–*133*, 138, 145
Wilbur Hollow, RI 6
Wilderness, Battle of 92–93
Willcox, Orlando B. 82, 121
Williams, Olney D. 47
Wilson, Henry *53*
Winn, Theodore 77, 81, 90–91, 97, 100
Winsemann, Henry 53
Winsor, Albert A. 26, 47
Wood, George W. 82
Wood, Oliver 112
Wood, William T. 82
Woodbury, Augustus 11, 47, 115, 122, 128
Woonsocket, RI 6
Wright, Harris C. 42

Yazoo River 71
Young, Emor 14, 28, 33, 54, 57, 61, 84, 87–88, 91, 128, 137–138, 140, 143–144, 149, 152, 161
Young, Martha and family 57, 61, 87–88, 91, 137–138, 144, 152, 161

www.ingramcontent.com/pod-product-compliance
Ingram Content Group UK Ltd.
Pitfield, Milton Keynes, MK11 3LW, UK
UKHW050525150426
5217IPUK00026B/1797